THE ART OF feefal

3dtotal Publishing

Correspondence: publishing@3dtotal.com
Website: www.3dtotal.com

First published in the United Kingdom, 2022, by 3dtotal Publishing.

3dtotal.com Ltd, 29 Foregate Street, Worcester WR1 1DS, United Kingdom.

Hard cover ISBN: 978-1-912843-50-3
Printing and binding: Dongguan Everbright Printing Co., Ltd. (China)
www.everbrightprint.com

Visit www.3dtotalpublishing.com for a complete list of available book titles.

Managing Director: Tom Greenway
Studio Manager: Simon Morse
Lead Designer: Fiona Tarbet
Lead Editor: Jenny Fox-Proverbs
Editorial Project Manager: Sophie Symes

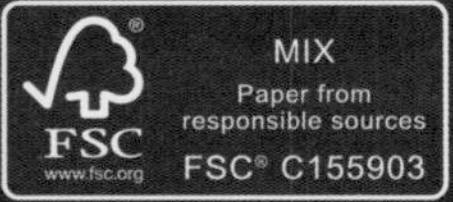

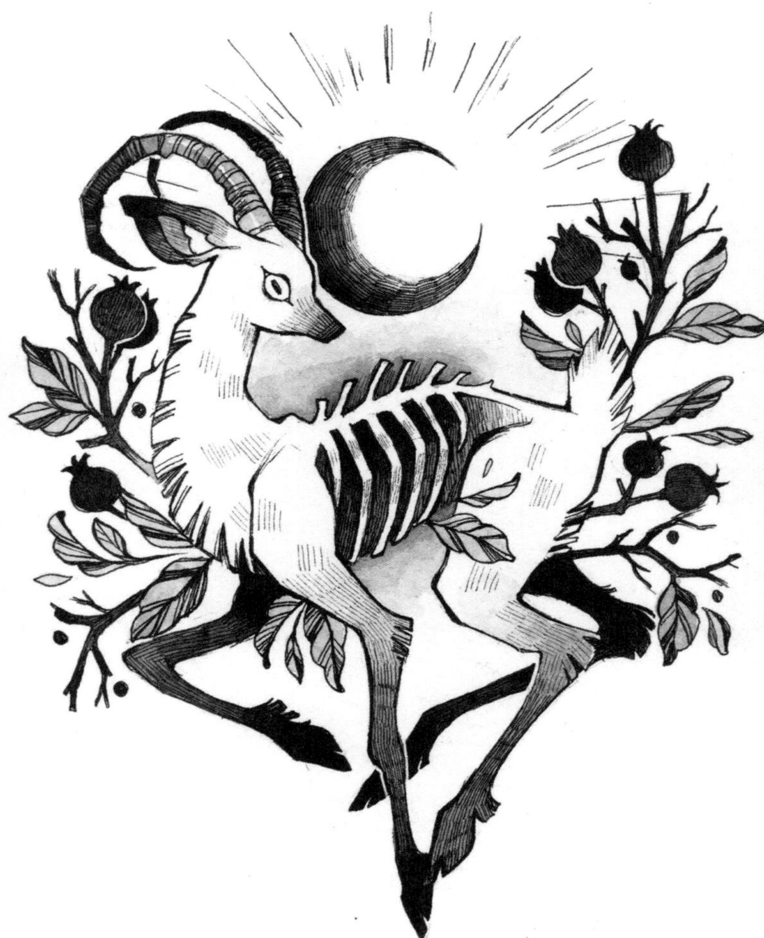

One tree planted for every book sold

OUR PLEDGE

3dtotal Publishing has committed to donate 50% of its net profits to a number of the most effective, high-impact charities, covering causes such as protecting existing rainforests, humanitarian work, and supporting animal welfare. As part of this, for every book sold, we donate to reforesting charities in our aim to be a carbon-neutral publisher with carbon-neutral products. Therefore, our customers can buy from 3dtotal Publishing in the knowledge that they are working with us to balance the environmental damage caused by the publishing, shipping, and retail industries as well as supporting many other causes. See 3dtotal.com/charity for full details.

Contents

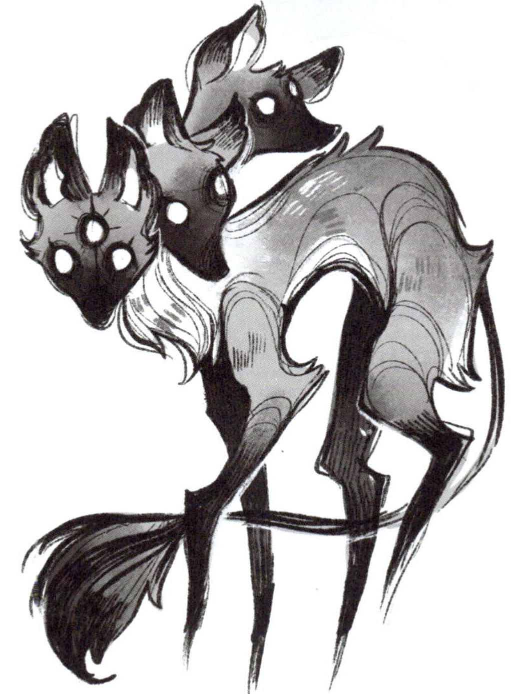

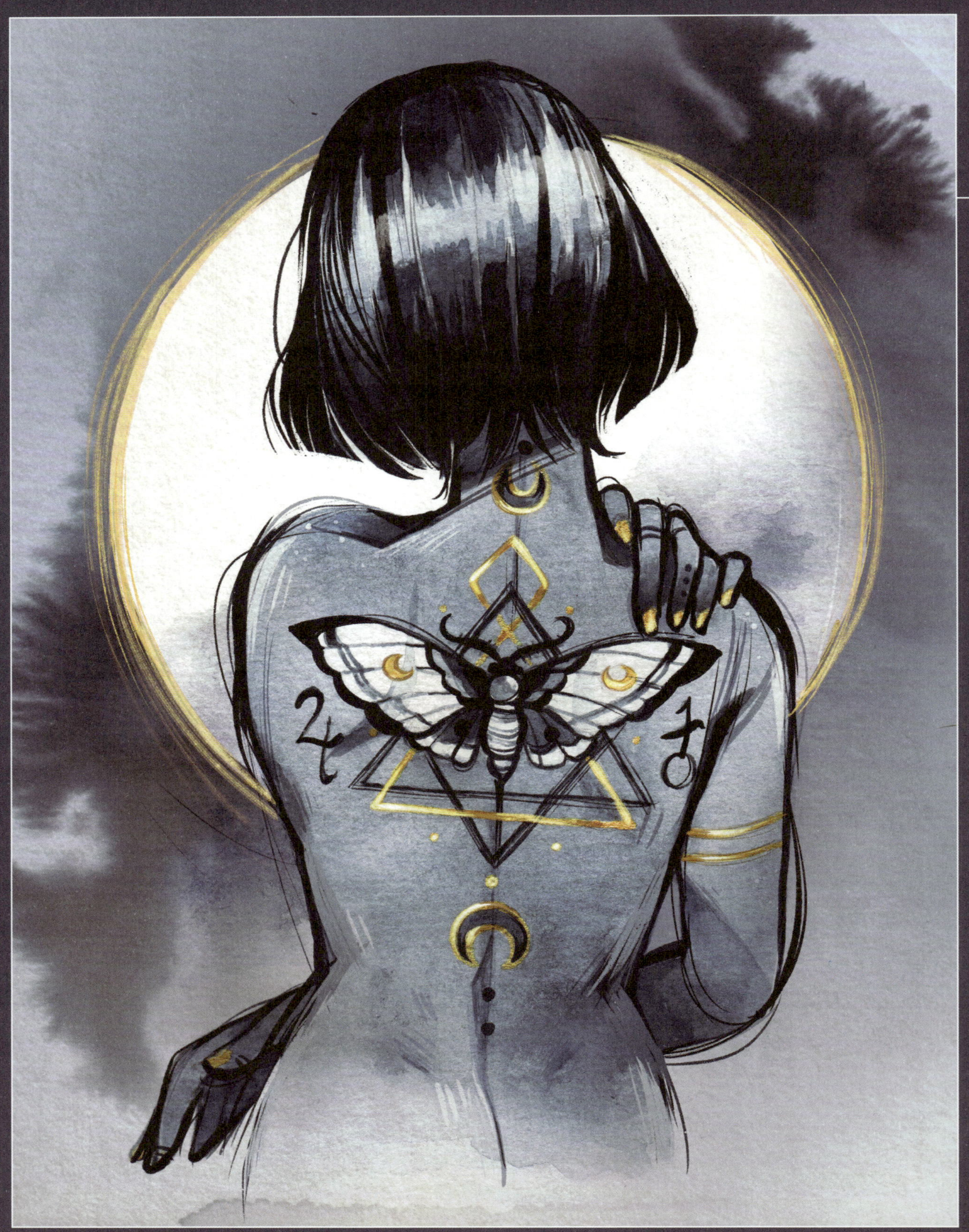

Introduction

Hi there!

My name is Linnea Kikuchi, although you might know me better by my internet name: Feefal.

You might be wondering how to correctly pronounce Feefal. I wish I could tell you, but I haven't really figured that out myself! It's just a strange name that I came up with on a whim when I was in desperate need of an Instagram handle, but I like that it sounds like a mixture between the words falafel and freefall.

Anyway, I really like drawing; I'm totally obsessed. I can't even explain why I love it so much, and I kind of wish I had some deeper, more insightful things to say on the topic, such as it's my way of communicating with the world – but I'm not sure if that's a genuine truth. I think it boils down to being the one thing in life that feels my own. Amidst the general stress that being alive brings, my love for creating has remained constant. I just have to do it – nothing else relaxes me or gives me such a sense of satisfaction. I still have much to learn when it comes to art, but nonetheless I'm really excited to share the bits of knowledge I've picked up on my journey so far with you all.

Publishing an art book has been a distant dream of mine since my early teens. Many times have I dreamily browsed through the art sections of bookstores imagining I would get to create one under my name one day. Well, the day has arrived my good folks! I always assumed that I would only get the chance to create my own book once I had decades of wisdom and experience under my belt – so to have my dream become a reality this soon came as a bit of a surprise I wasn't completely ready for! But then again, I often feel unprepared for what comes my way in life. I believe that's just the way the mind works, you always feel like you need more experience and talent in order to take the next leap forward, but in fact, the best way to gain and build those things is to just dive in head first and figure it out as you go.

I'm so honored that you looked at my work and thought it would be neat to own a whole collection of it – because that notion is what led me here! I hope you enjoy browsing my artwork while reading over my musings.

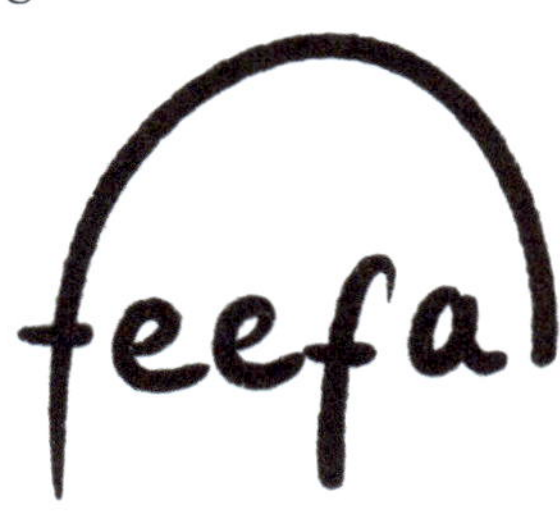

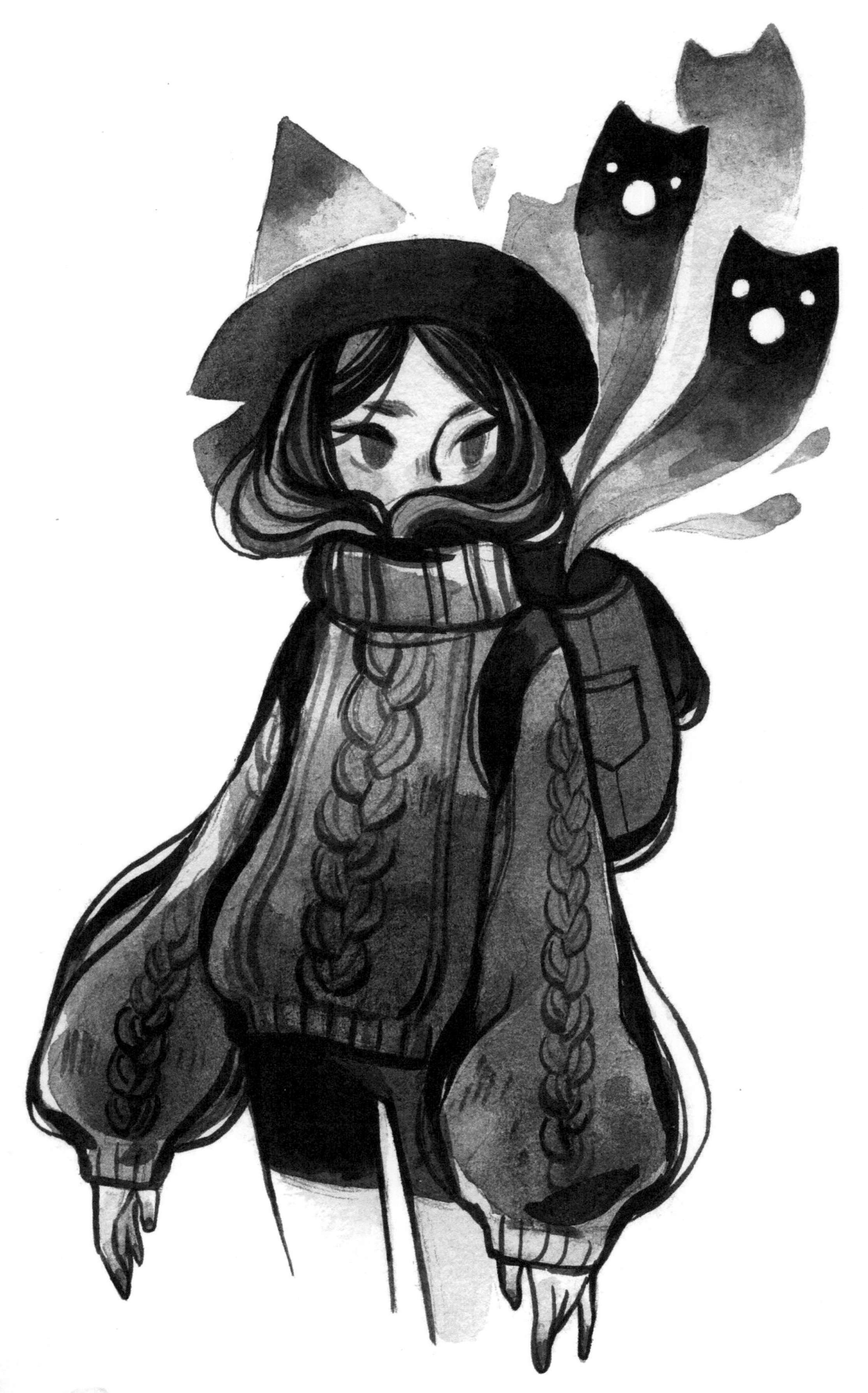

Artistic Journey

Early days

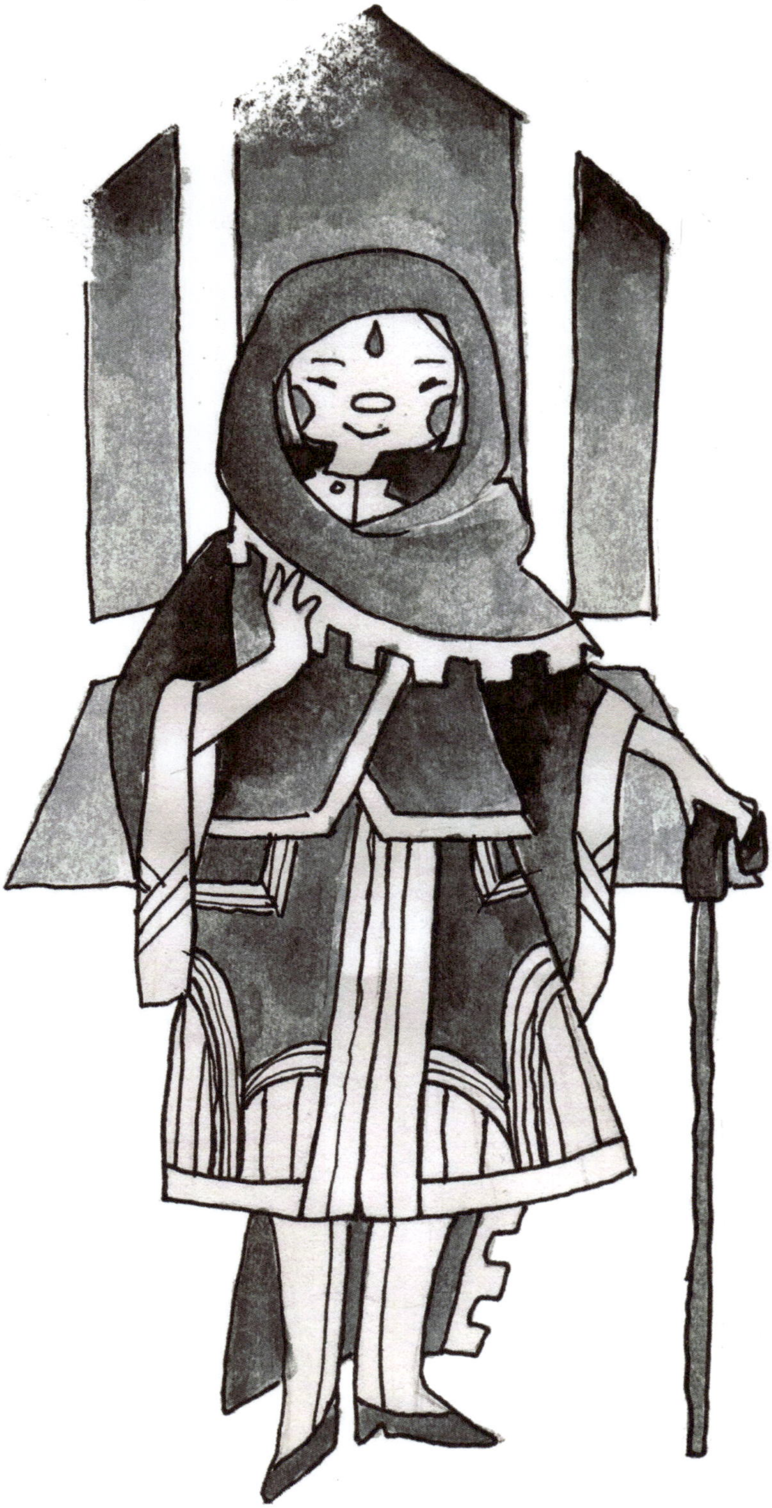

Drawing has been the focus of my life for as long as I can remember, pretty much since the moment I learned how to hold a pencil. I think it's common for children to have a love for drawing, since they seem to carry an inherent need to create and express themselves. What I think gave me an edge and motivated me to continue forward with my art was that I had an extremely supportive mom. I've heard many stories of people giving up art due to unsupportive comments from family members, which I think is just awful. So, I'm very grateful to have been raised in such an encouraging environment; I don't think I would have been able to take my art fixation this far if it wasn't for my amazing mom! It just goes to show that if you support the frivolous dreams of a child, they might just be foolish enough to try and make a living out of it!

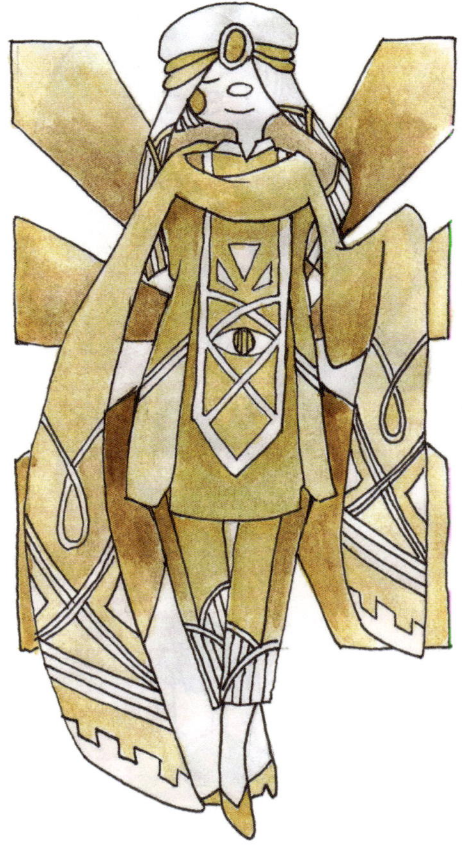

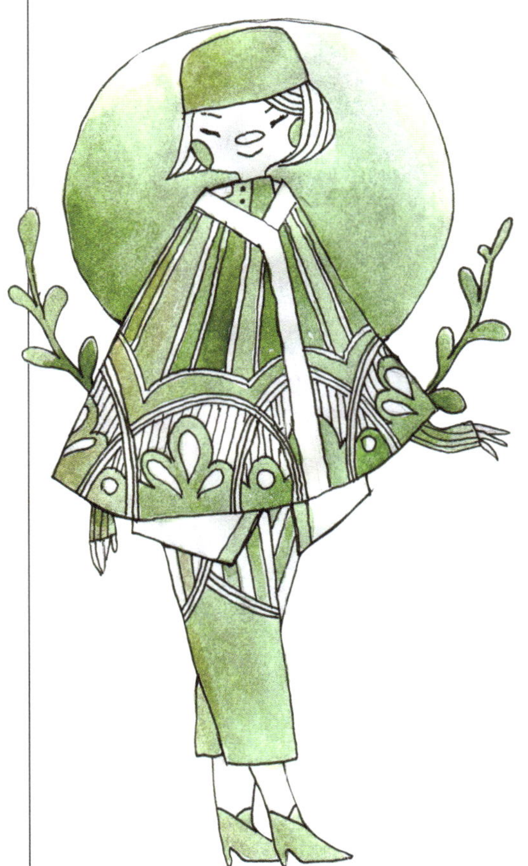

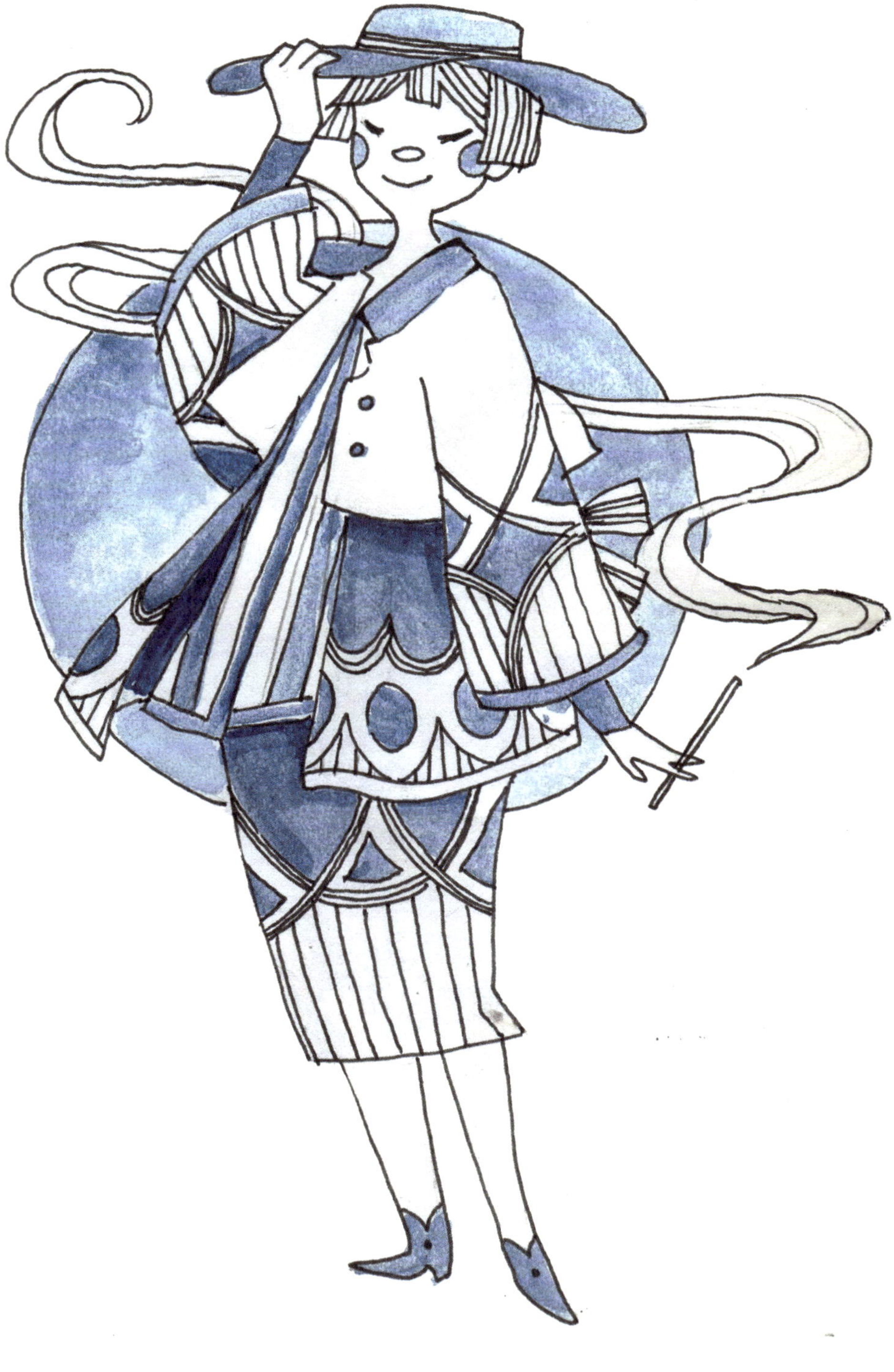

This is a little embarrassing, but as a child I really thought I was the Albert Einstein of drawing. I was a sheltered child that hadn't met anyone my age that was as good as me at my craft, but to be completely transparent with you all this was really only because I didn't have that many friends. Oh, and please note that this is not me feeling sorry for myself for not being popular as a child; I didn't really like playing with other children much when I was young because I preferred being indoors with my arts and crafts. I'm sure it also didn't help that I occasionally sneaked my pet rat into the sleeve of my hoodie during class! Safe to say I was pretty socially oblivious as a child. Good thing I outgrew that phase...

Looking back, I can't say I was even that good at drawing, I just had an inflated ego. I also had not yet discovered the wonders of the internet, which we all know is filled to the brim with people who are better at everything than you'll ever be.

Watercolor illustrations from 2014, age 19.

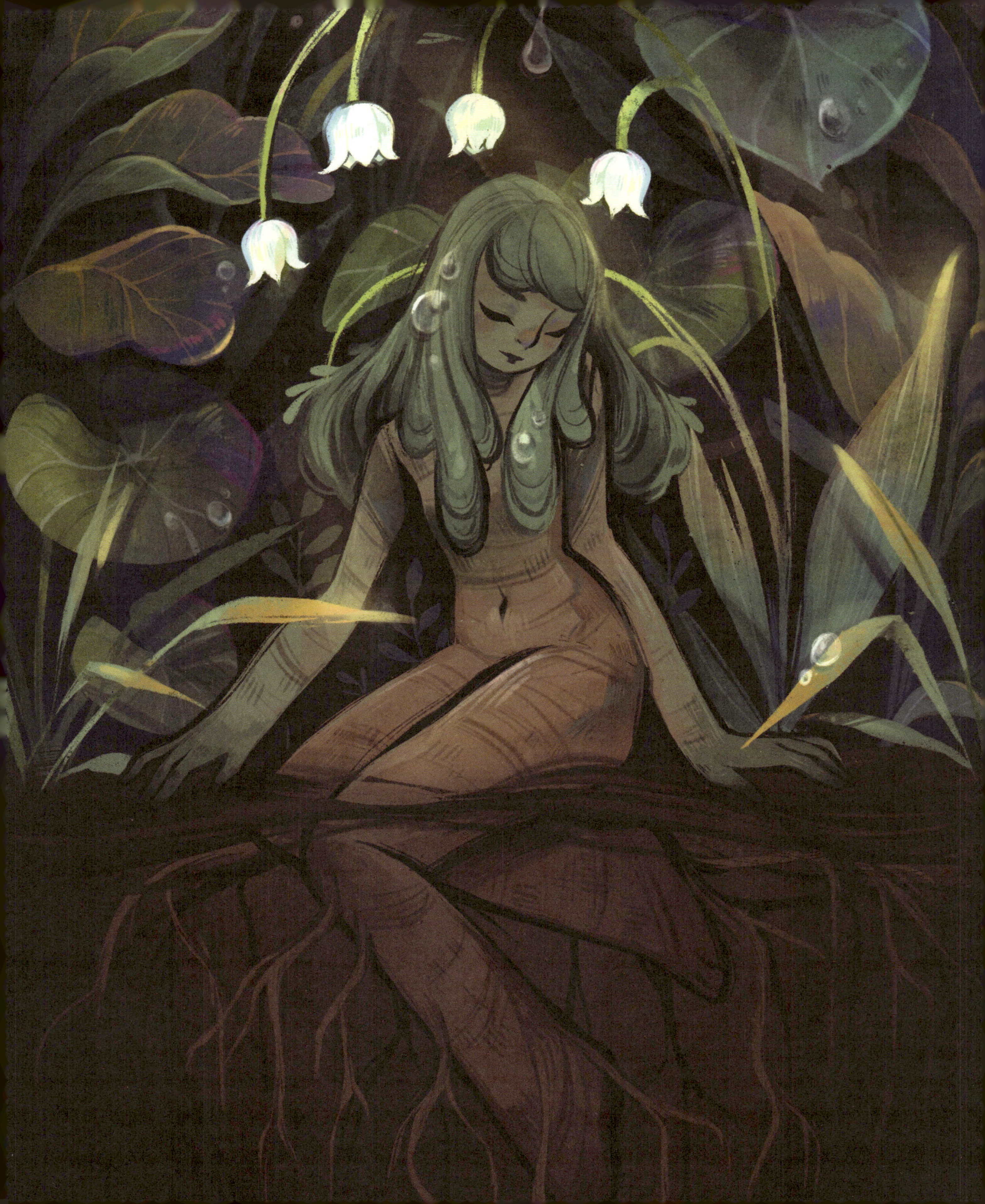

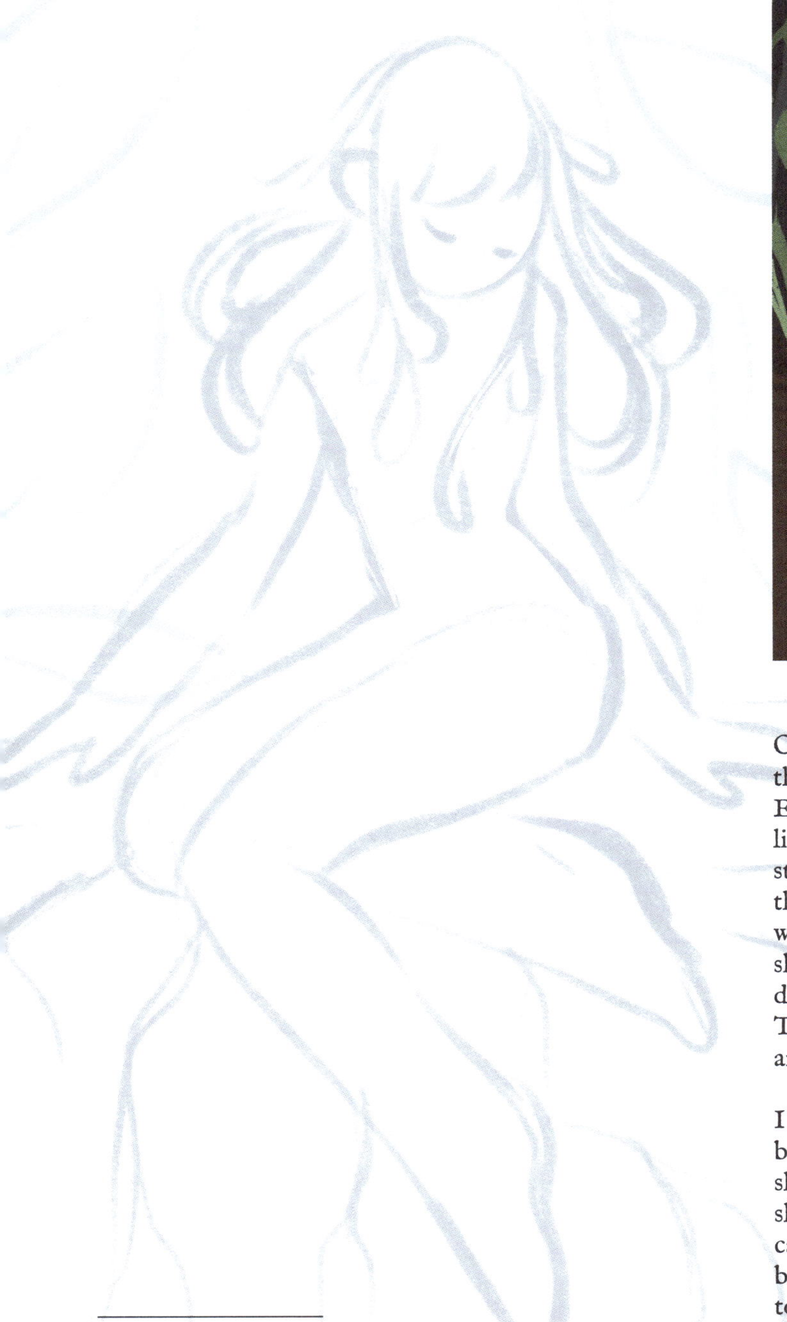

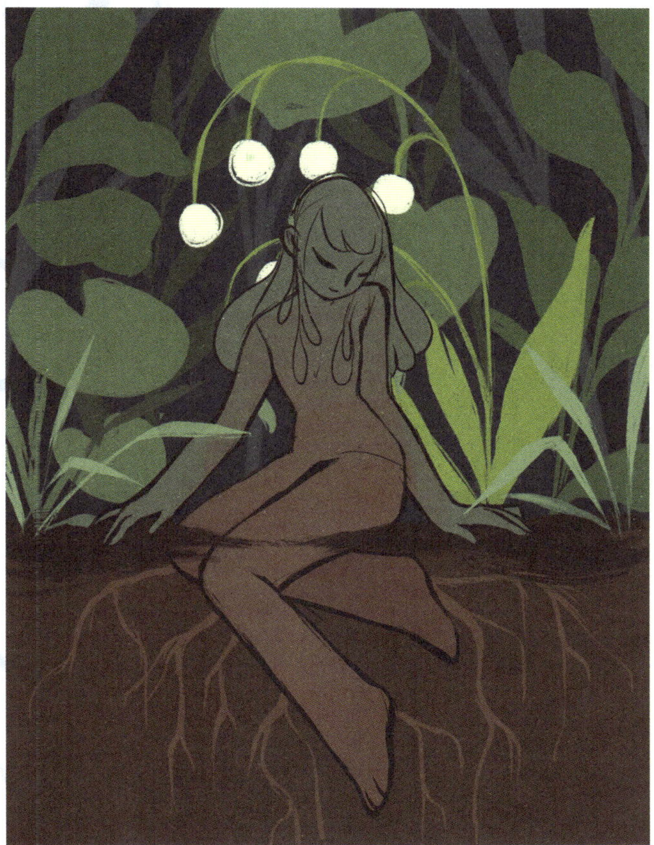

Once I entered middle school, I met a classmate who had the absolute audacity to be better than me at drawing. Enter Saliem, my childhood rival and eternal bestie. She lit a competitive fire within me, and thanks to her I really started to push myself in order to improve. One of the first things I said to her was to demand a draw-off to determine which one of us was the better artist, which is something she still makes fun of me for to this day. She had only been drawing for a couple of years and just saw it as a light hobby. That was the day I realized that I wasn't God's gift to the art world.

I cringe when I reflect back on how self-possessed I was, but at the same time I'm happy I got to experience that short period in my life of unfounded confidence. Children should think they're the best in the world and that they can accomplish anything, because they're too young to be burdened by the harsh reality. Life can be a difficult ordeal to go through, so to have those years where things were so straightforward was pretty darn neat. Being crippled by self-doubt is such a boring adult thing to experience, so why not postpone it for as long as possible?

Plantling
Progressive stages of a digital illustration.

Common symptoms of stomach butterflies

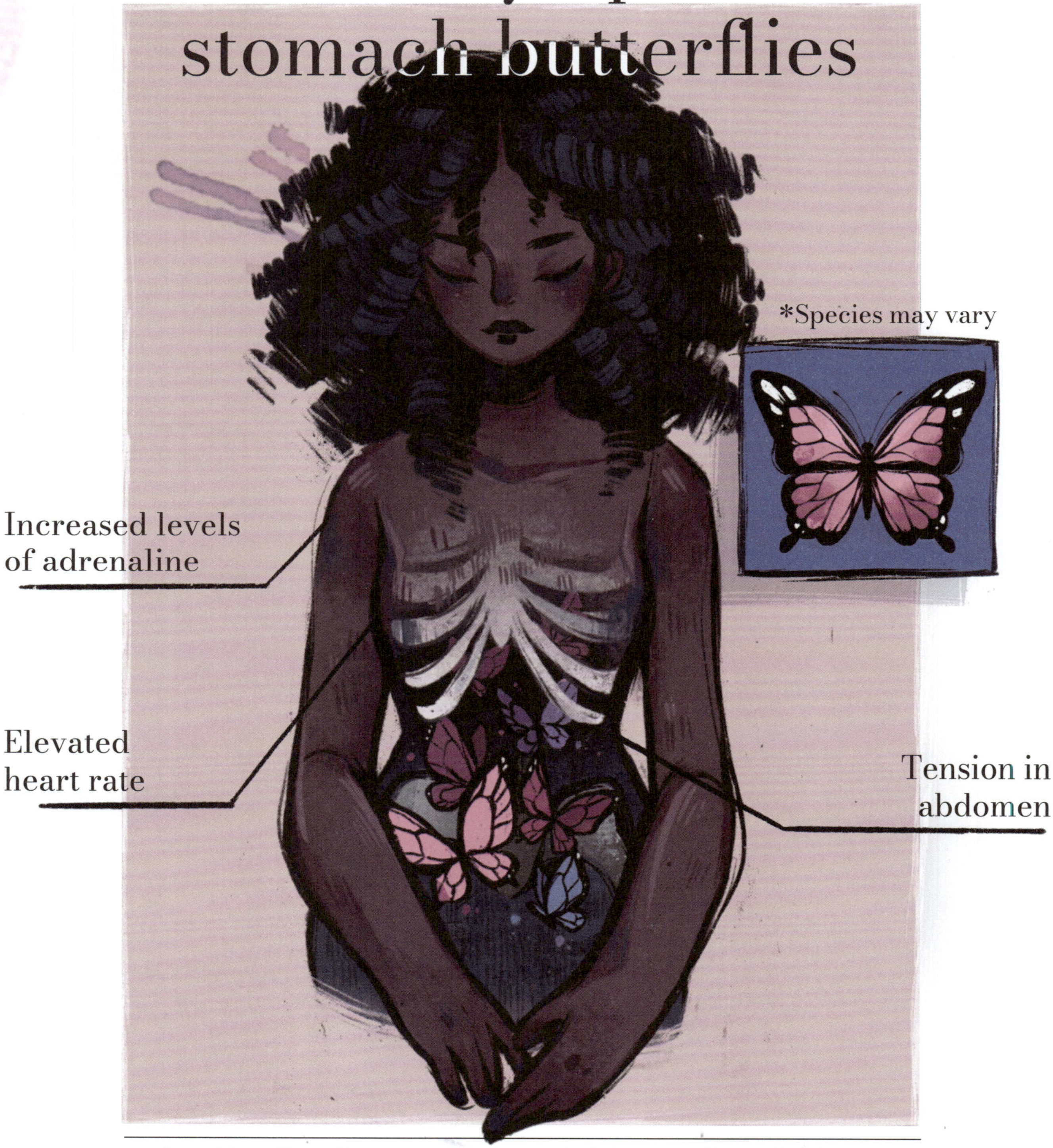

*Species may vary

Increased levels of adrenaline

Elevated heart rate

Tension in abdomen

Stomach butterflies are fluttering sensations in the abdominal area caused by a feeling of nervous anticipation. Common triggers are exams, heights and near proximity of an individual of romantic interest.

Deciding to pursue art

I decided very early on in my life that I wanted to pursue a career in art, and that I wouldn't want to work within any other field. Having a one-track mindset on an undeniably unstable career path sounds questionable, but it did benefit me – it allowed me to have a laser-focus on my hopes and dreams.

While at school, I had great difficulty concentrating during any classes that weren't art-related and would often zone out and start daydreaming. A lack of interest in other subjects fed into my powerful focus on developing my art career. My attention span has always been short, and maintaining focus can be challenging. The only way I was able to stop myself from fidgeting during class was to doodle in my notebooks the entire time, so while my drawing skills improved, I never paid much attention to the lessons being taught. The teachers occasionally scolded me for sketching instead of making notes, but I'd defend myself by claiming it was something I did to keep focused – which was partially true! Sketching kept my mind occupied during those tedious school hours.

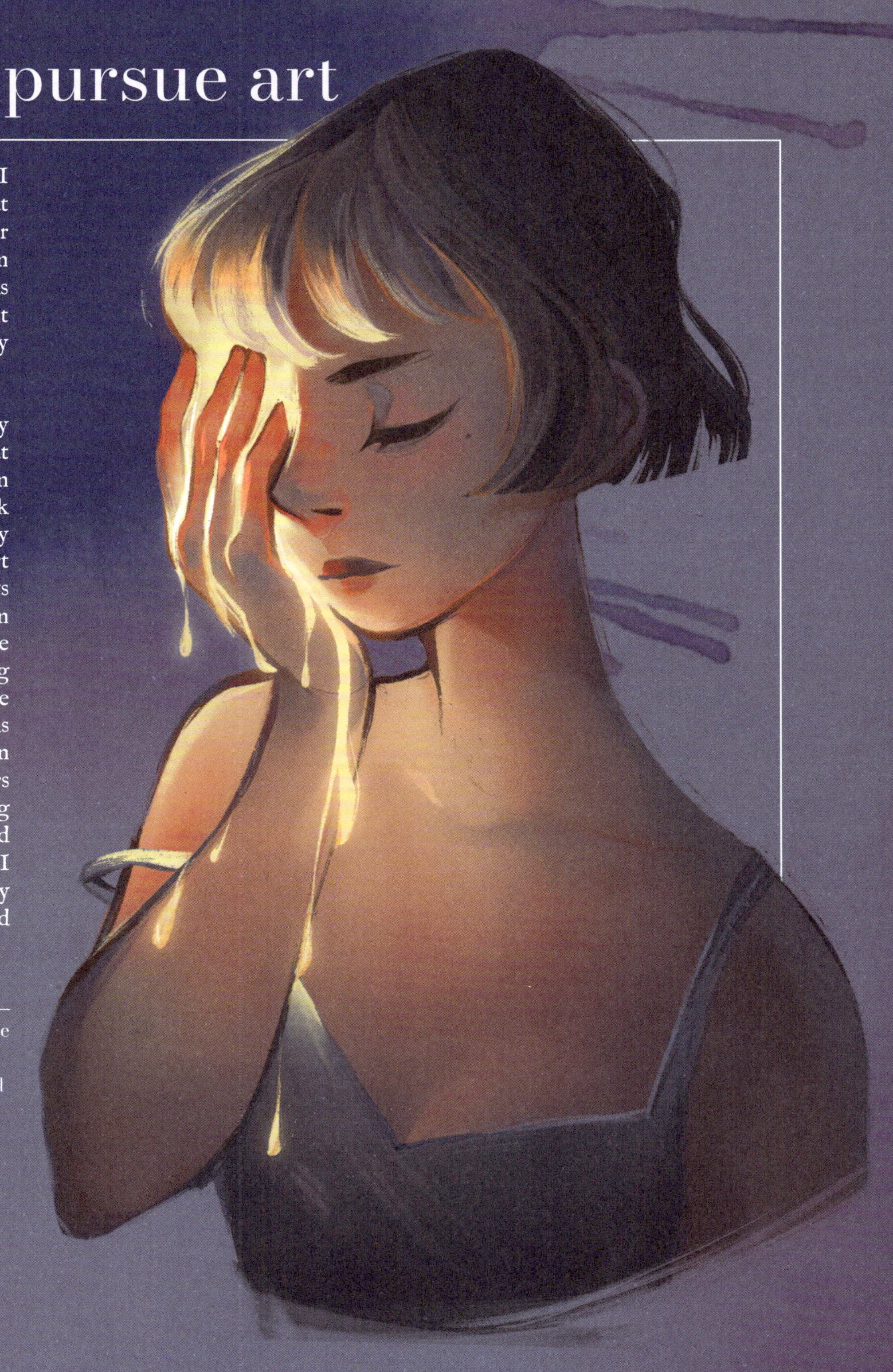

Opposite page: This piece is from a series where I explored fictional ailments from a medical point of view. Stomach butterflies may be a real phenomenon, but not quite this literally!

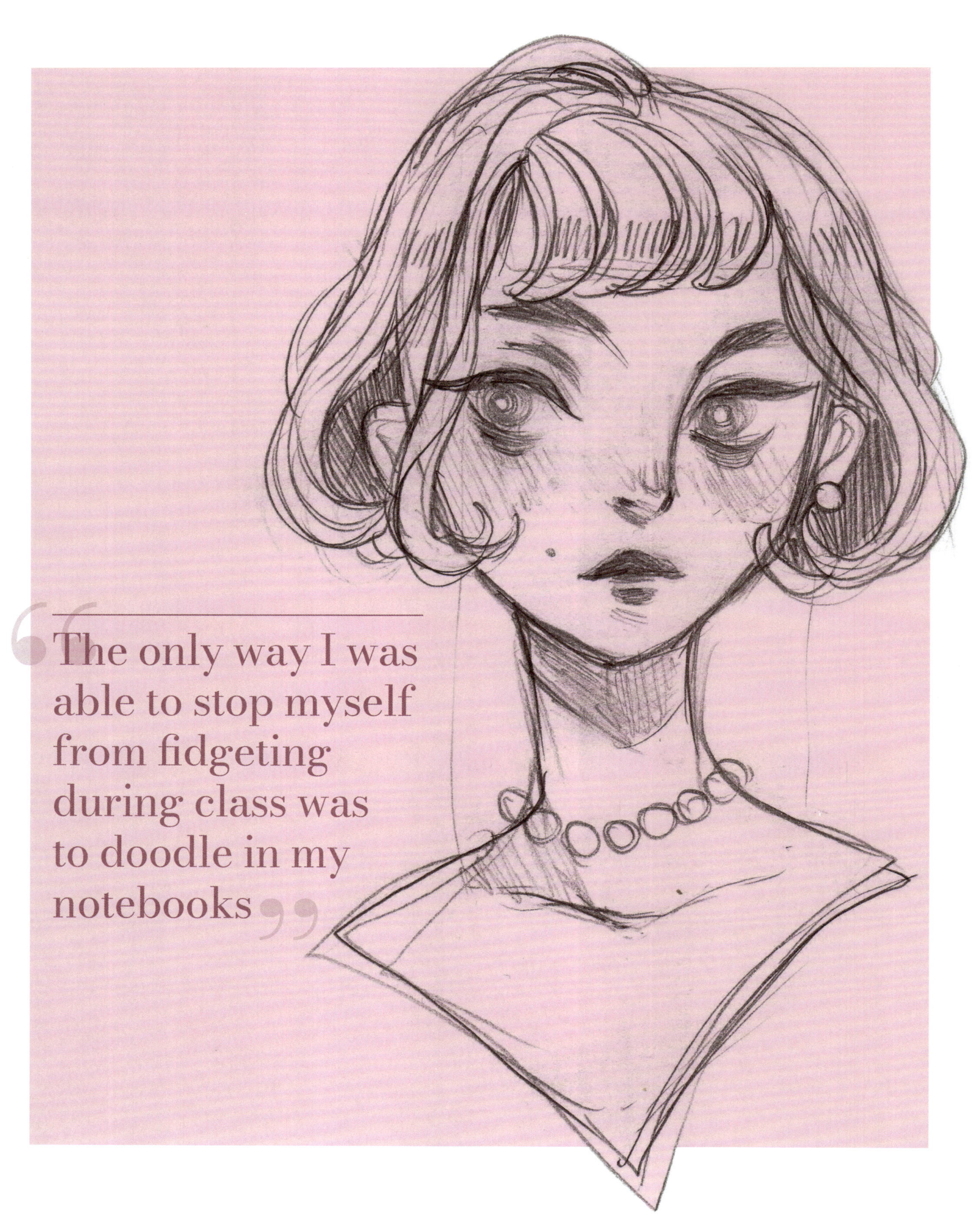

> "The only way I was able to stop myself from fidgeting during class was to doodle in my notebooks"

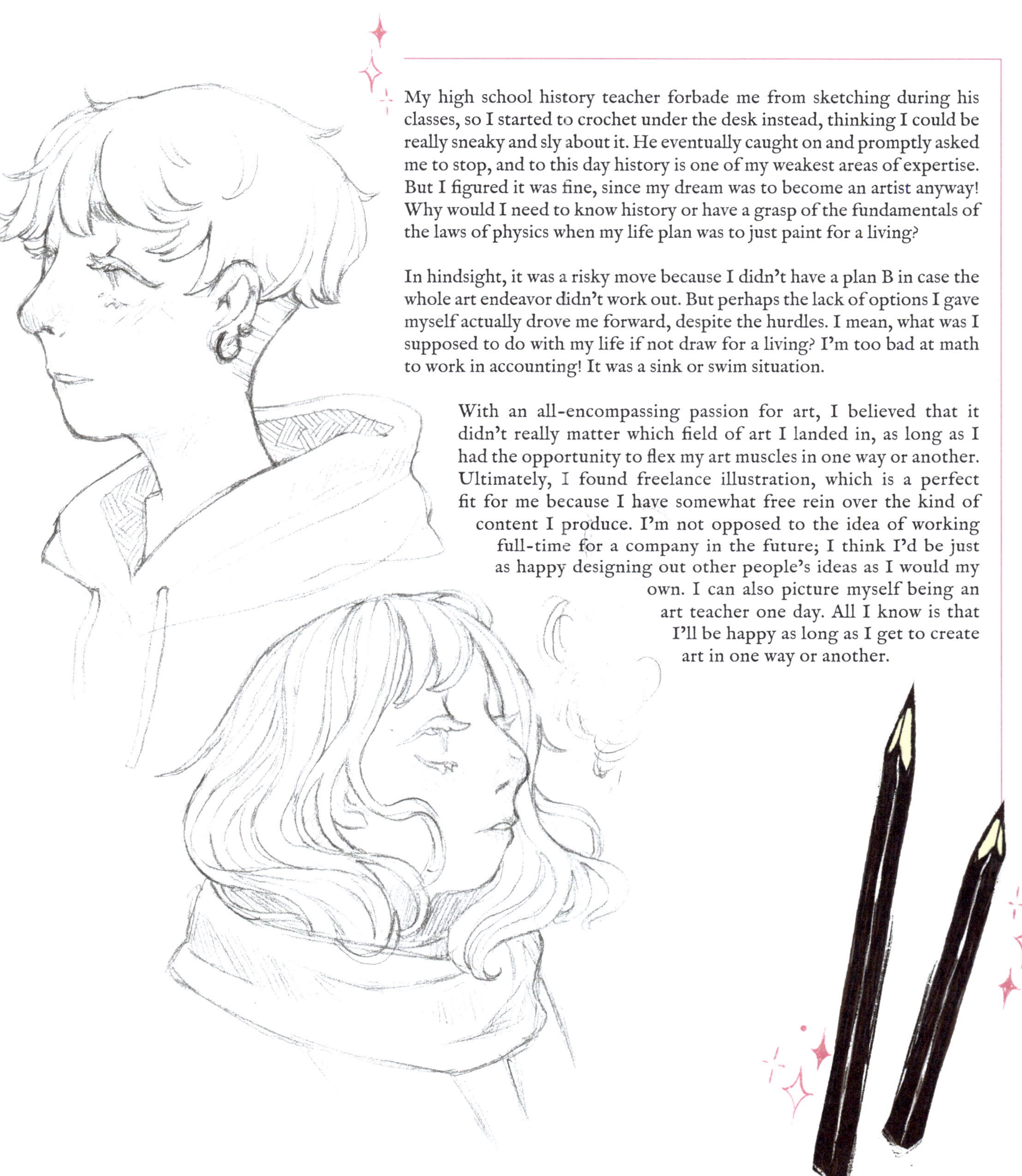

My high school history teacher forbade me from sketching during his classes, so I started to crochet under the desk instead, thinking I could be really sneaky and sly about it. He eventually caught on and promptly asked me to stop, and to this day history is one of my weakest areas of expertise. But I figured it was fine, since my dream was to become an artist anyway! Why would I need to know history or have a grasp of the fundamentals of the laws of physics when my life plan was to just paint for a living?

In hindsight, it was a risky move because I didn't have a plan B in case the whole art endeavor didn't work out. But perhaps the lack of options I gave myself actually drove me forward, despite the hurdles. I mean, what was I supposed to do with my life if not draw for a living? I'm too bad at math to work in accounting! It was a sink or swim situation.

With an all-encompassing passion for art, I believed that it didn't really matter which field of art I landed in, as long as I had the opportunity to flex my art muscles in one way or another. Ultimately, I found freelance illustration, which is a perfect fit for me because I have somewhat free rein over the kind of content I produce. I'm not opposed to the idea of working full-time for a company in the future; I think I'd be just as happy designing out other people's ideas as I would my own. I can also picture myself being an art teacher one day. All I know is that I'll be happy as long as I get to create art in one way or another.

Origins

My work is very much influenced by Japanese pop culture. I am of Japanese descent so it was sort of inevitable. I was born to a Japanese father and a Swedish mother in a small village called Aoki located in Nasushiobara, Japan. My mom moved me and my older brother to Sweden when I was three, due to the less-than-perfect family environment in Japan. I don't blame her at all for leaving Japan and I know it can't have been an easy decision. I also had a great time being raised in Stockholm! But I lost all sense of my Japanese identity once I became accustomed to life there – three-year-old children aren't exactly known for their long-term memory after all.

My dad joined us in Sweden the year I turned nine, but before the move he would always send over videos of children's anime that he had recorded from the TV in Japan. So, I grew up watching shows including *Doraemon* and *Ojamajo Doremi,* and Studio Ghibli films, and the magic depicted in those shows struck a chord in me. It was great growing up surrounded by the whimsical aspects of Japanese culture, and due to all the anime exposure, my fascination with everything cute, sparkly, and big-eyed took root at an early age.

My father passed away from cancer recently, so it's comforting to see the traces of him in my work. Despite having a Western upbringing, I can see that the cultural heritage passed down to me is echoed in my creations.

Digital illustration made in 2021.

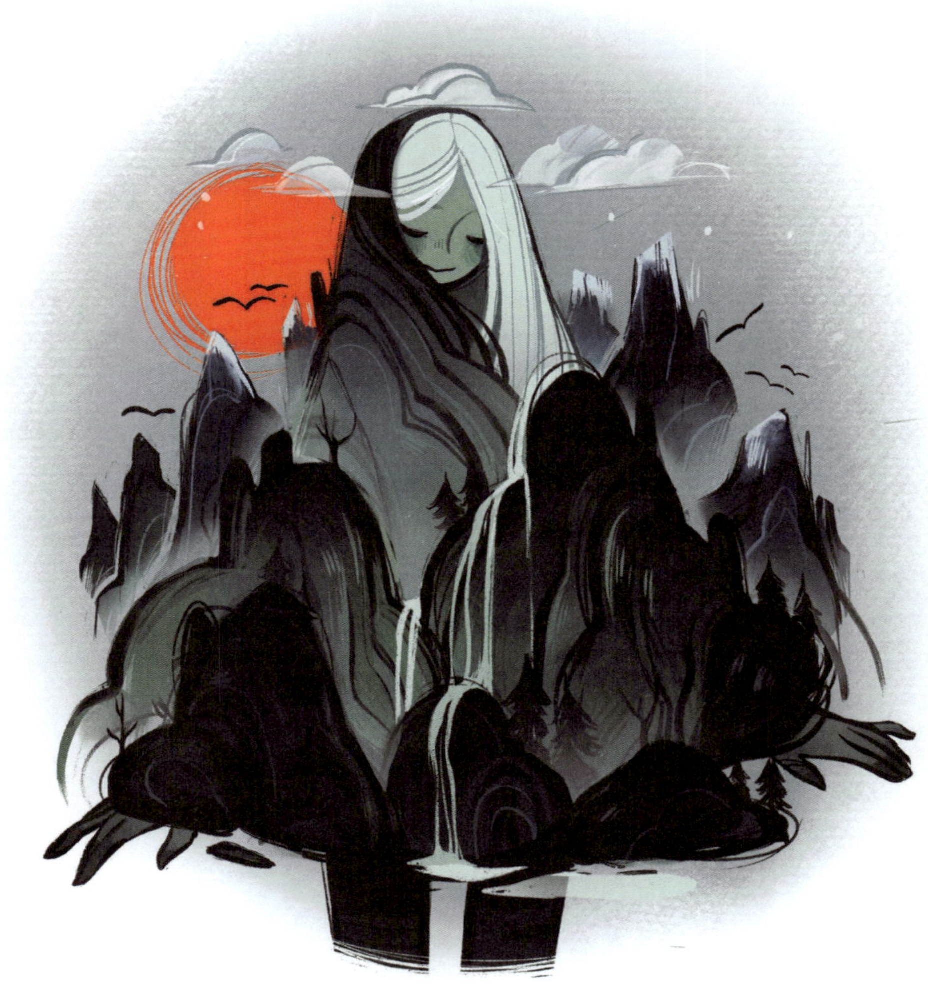

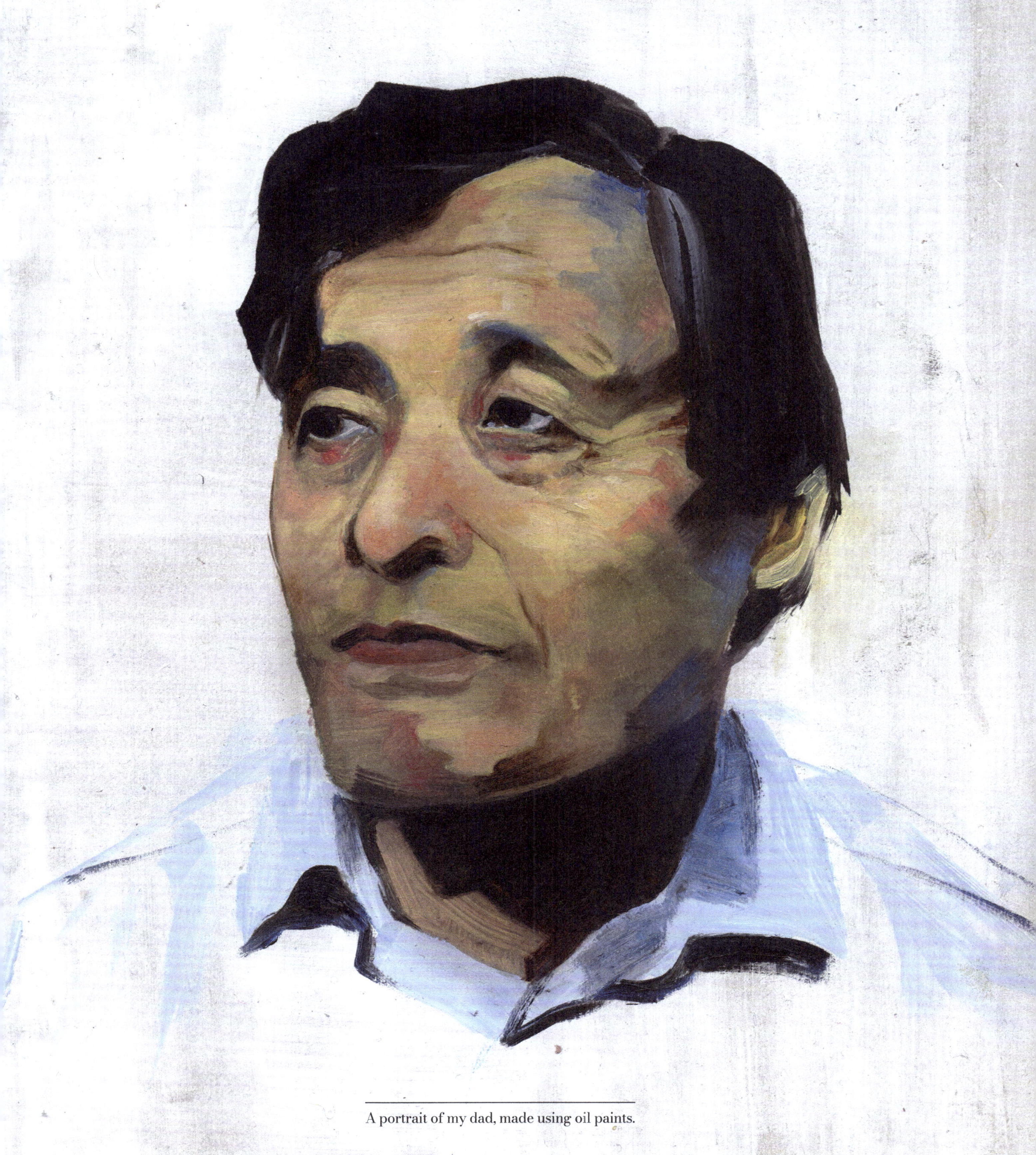

A portrait of my dad, made using oil paints.

Art education

My favorite teacher of all time was my primary school art teacher. His name was Jonas and besides being really skilled at drawing, he was also just a really cool dude. I think it's incredibly important to nurture and care for the creativity of young children, and he certainly fulfilled that role by being encouraging and supportive of my aspirations. He lent me how-to-draw books, taught me how to draw dragons, and instilled confidence in me that I still benefit from today.

I wasn't really sure which direction to head toward after graduating high school, and so I made the big mistake of entering an art school dedicated to fine art. The vast majority of art schools in Sweden are focused on teaching fine art, so it felt like the obvious option due to the lack of alternatives. Fine art is more about expression and conveying personal truths and emotions rather than what is aesthetically pleasing. It's a lovely subject and approach, but it didn't align with what I wanted to learn. I hoped attending art school would help me to improve my technical abilities and learn the fundamentals of art, such as anatomy, composition, and how to paint in different mediums. Fine art teaching however, puts more emphasis on providing a realm where one can delve deeper into one's psyche in order to better learn how to provoke thought and interpretation. Now that's not a bad thing, but it was never the right fit for me.

"... art doesn't have to carry a deeper message in order to be valid, creating something purely for the way it looks is completely valid"

I was used to, and most comfortable, drawing for the sake of aesthetics, and I had honed my technical skills to a point where I was quite content with my art. But I found that simply creating something pretty doesn't give you much credibility in the world of fine art. In the eyes of a fine artist, my creations lacked depth and meaning. I remember an art school teacher walking into my shared studio space to talk with a classmate. He casually picked up my copy of an Alphonse Mucha art book and while flipping through the pages, off-handedly commented, "Can you imagine creating something this soulless?" Alphonse Mucha was, and will always be, one of my biggest inspirations, and he probably didn't intend to be mean as he had and had no idea the book was mine, but it stuck with me.

Mucha? Soulless? The fact that the art teacher believed he had any authority on Mucha's validity demonstrates his disregard for anything figurative and his clear bias toward modernism. Not to mention embarrassing himself by trying to disrespect a world-renowned artist who defined an art movement. It's also a culturally blind comment to the historical and cultural importance Mucha brought with his depiction of the Slavic epic. As you can tell, I'm still angry about it.

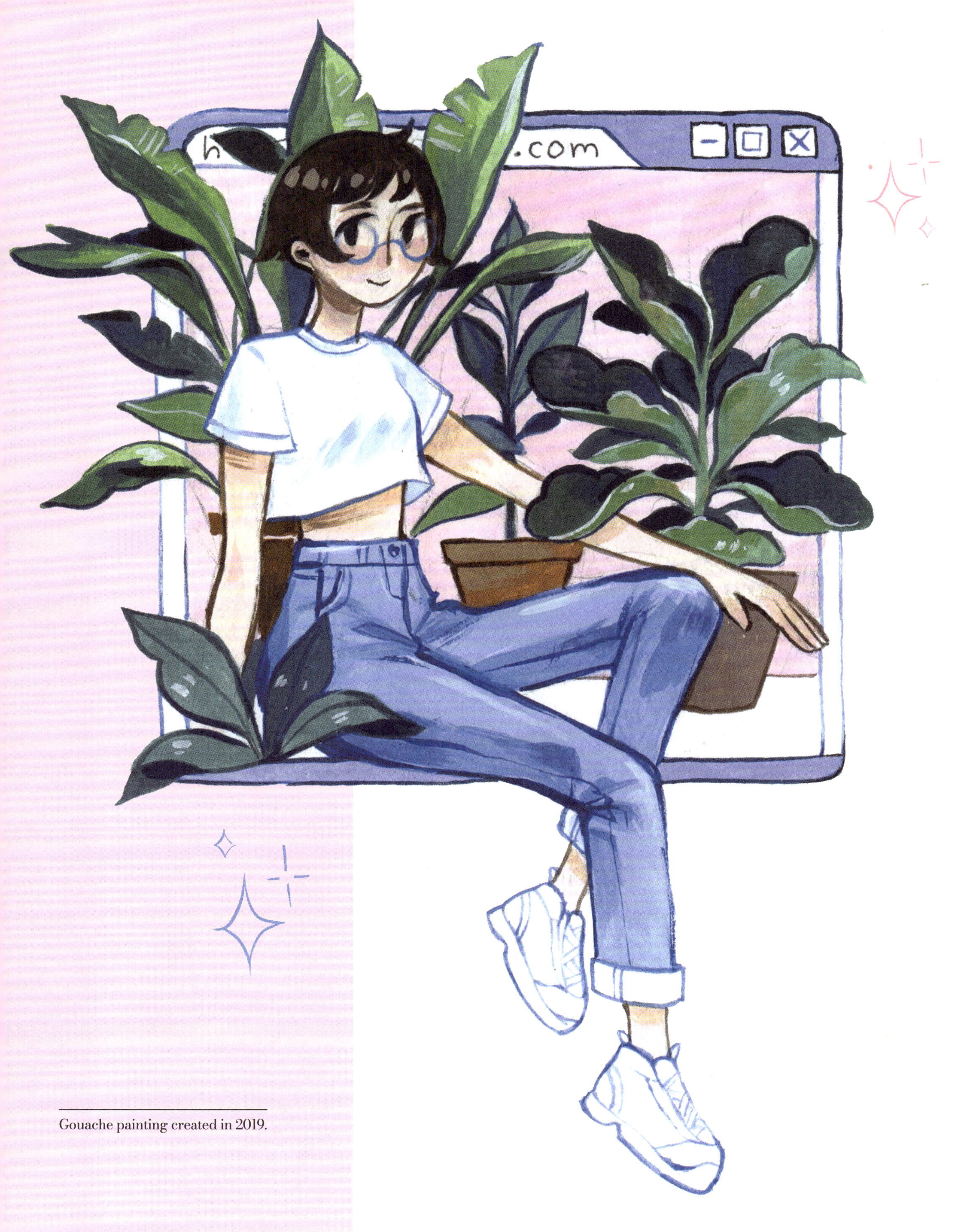

Gouache painting created in 2019.

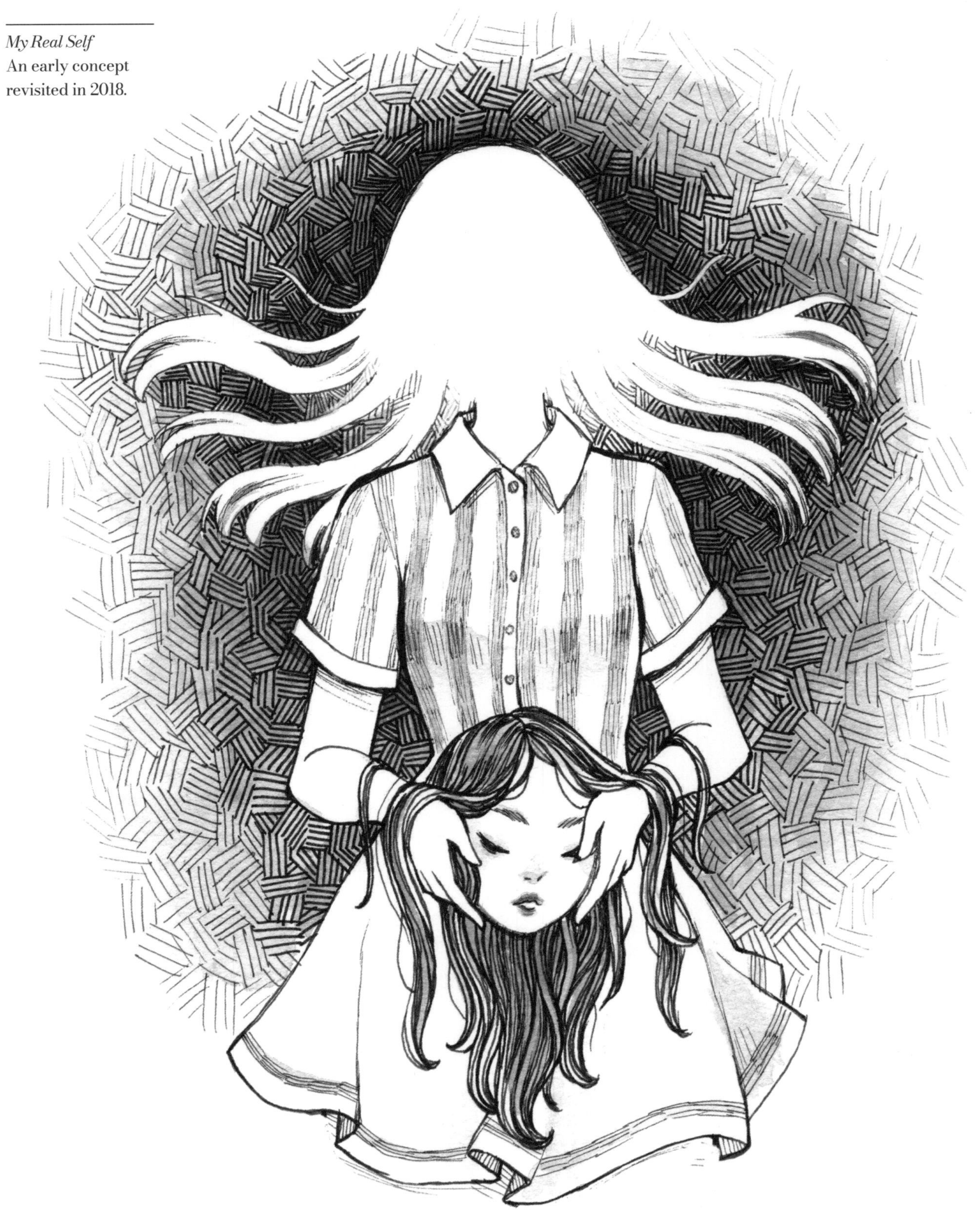

My Real Self
An early concept revisited in 2018.

Put off by my teacher's hurtful comment and faced with rigid attitudes I disagreed with, I left art school. I then spent a year rebuilding my confidence and eventually questioning why it was so essential for art to carry a hidden, deeper message in order to be deemed as meaningful. Why is it perceived as negative or shallow for a piece of art to be made for aesthetic purposes? A contemporary artwork that evokes something deep within is great, but so is a traditional skillfully painted portrait. I believe that art doesn't have to carry a deeper message in order to be valid; creating something purely for the way it looks is completely valid too. Painting is a visual medium, so I question why it is negative to enjoy it from a purely visual sense. Since leaving art school, I continued to hone my creative practice through experimentation and following my intuition.

"I continued to hone my creative practice through experimentation and following my intuition"

If I could go back in time, I would have applied to study at a school focused on illustration or graphic storytelling instead of fine art. A curriculum that prioritized teaching technique rather than expression and that had more structure would have benefited my way of working.

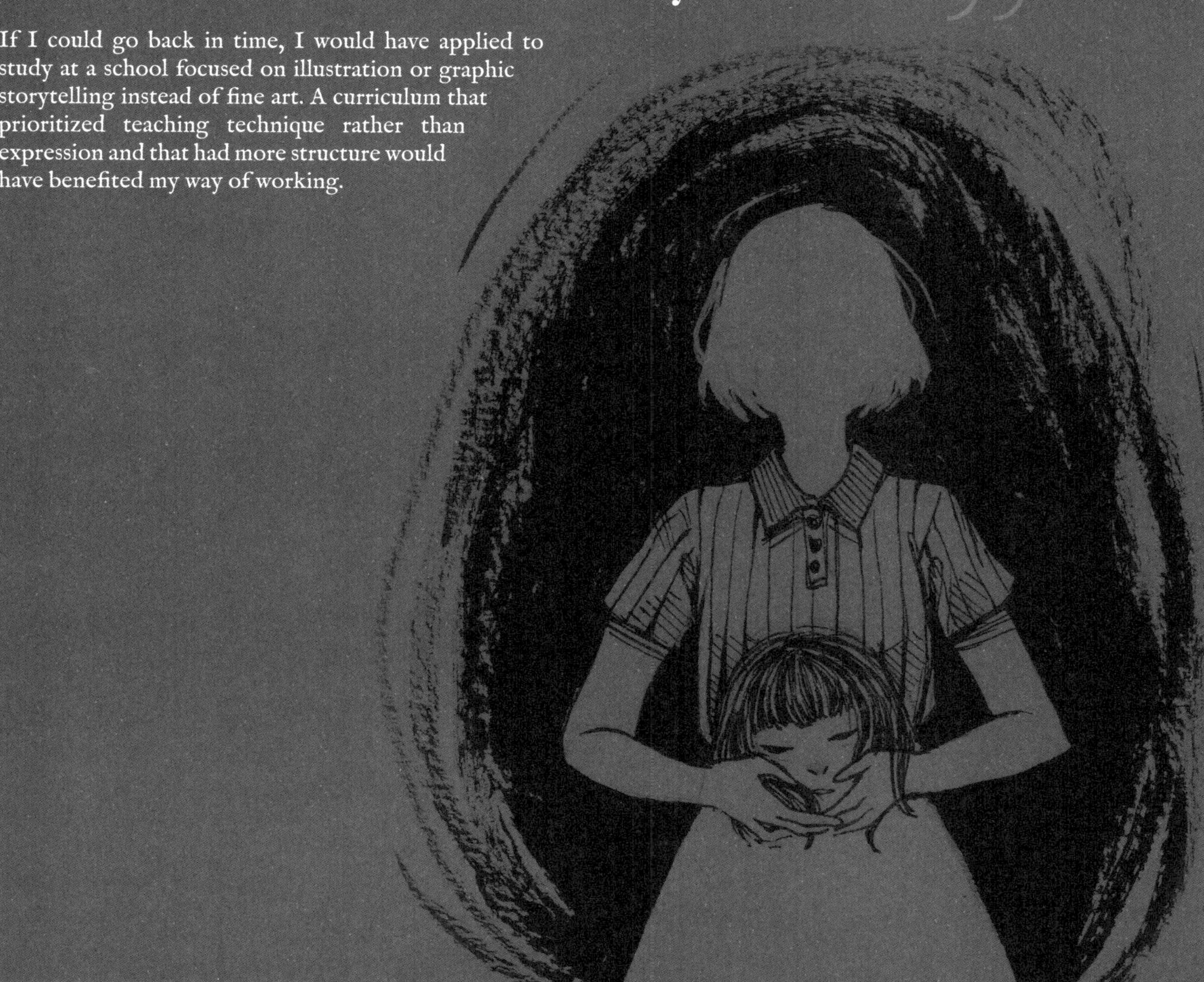

Original concept, designed in 2016.

Creative development timeline

2009 age 14

A pencil drawing I created while in school. I remember being very happy with it.

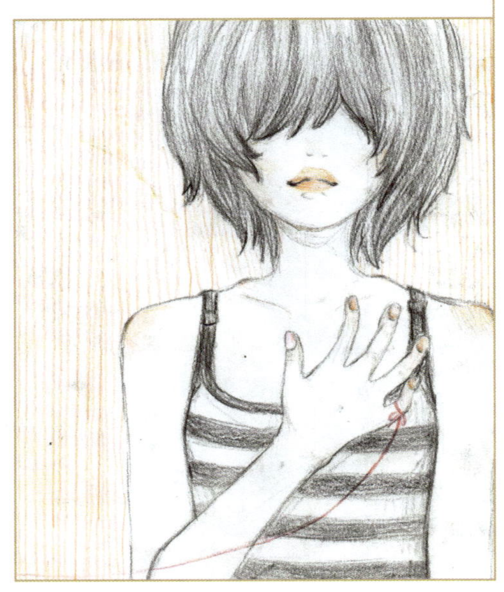

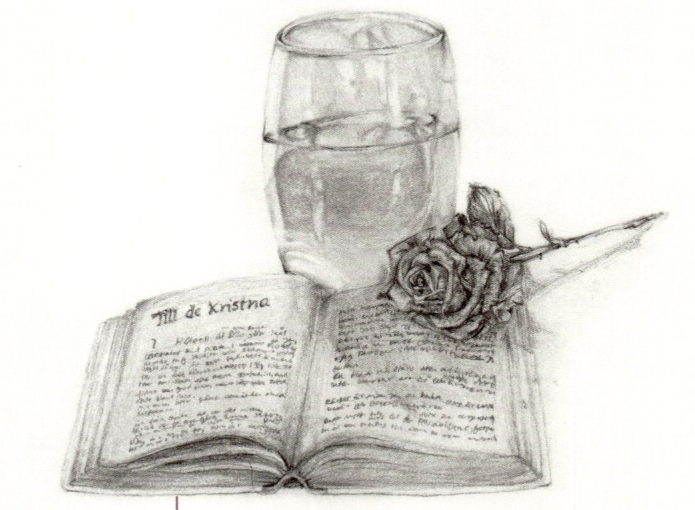

2011

age 15–16

A still life study in graphite.

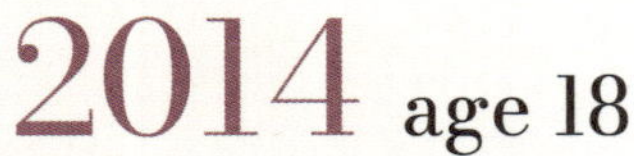

2014 age 18

An imagined dystopian cityscape becoming reclaimed by nature. I was so proud of this piece! The perspective is all over the place, but I still hold a fondness for it.

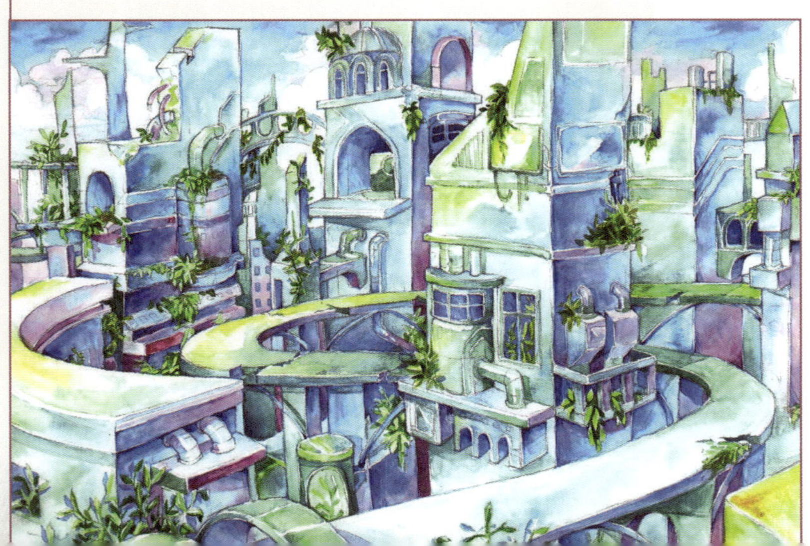

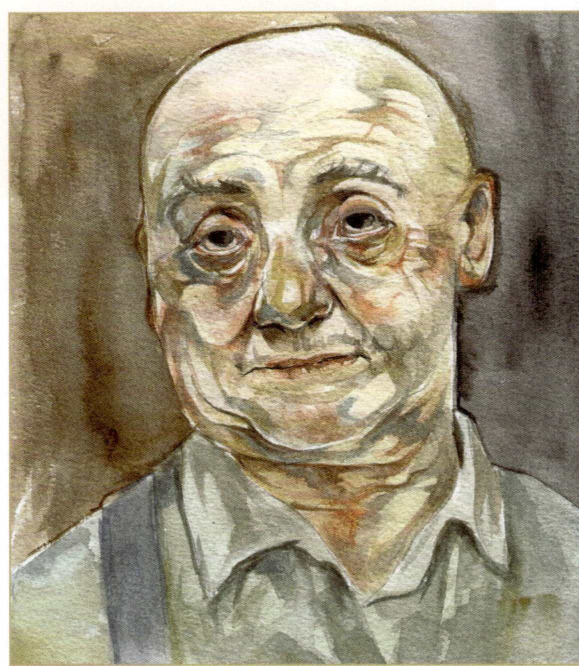

2014 age 19

I painted this during my enrollment in art school. At the time I felt I should make more gritty art in order to be taken seriously.

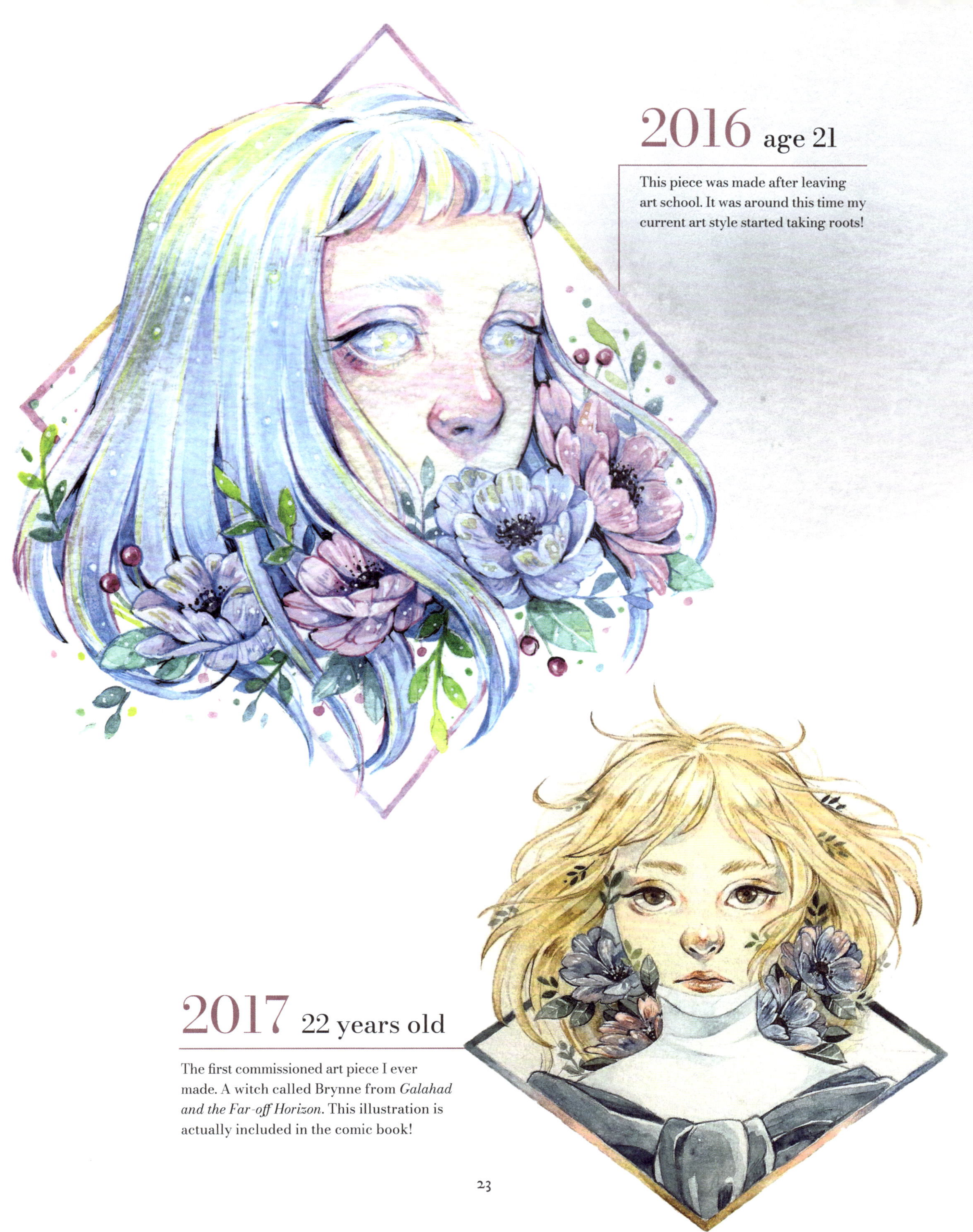

2016 age 21

This piece was made after leaving art school. It was around this time my current art style started taking roots!

2017 22 years old

The first commissioned art piece I ever made. A witch called Brynne from *Galahad and the Far-off Horizon*. This illustration is actually included in the comic book!

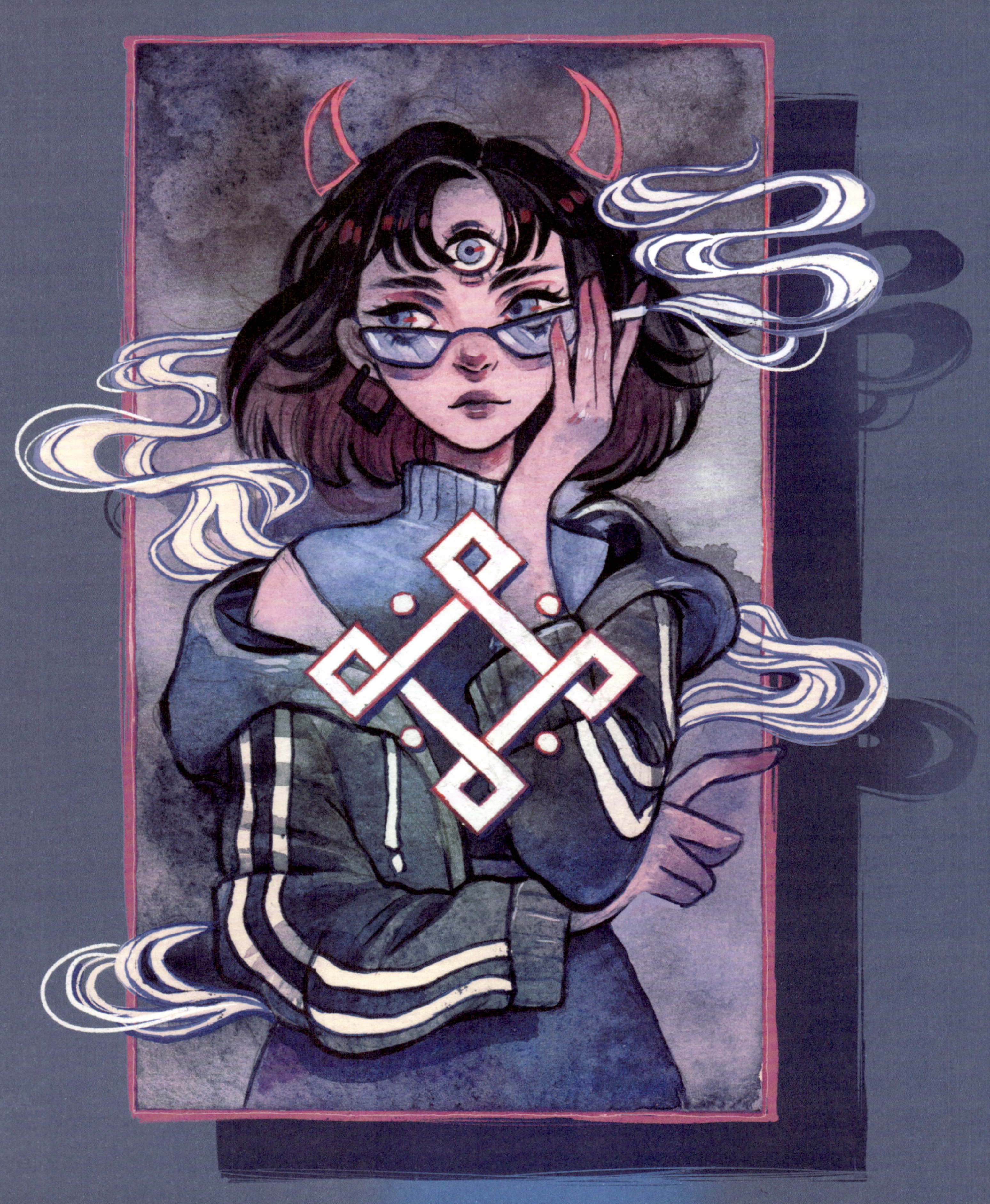

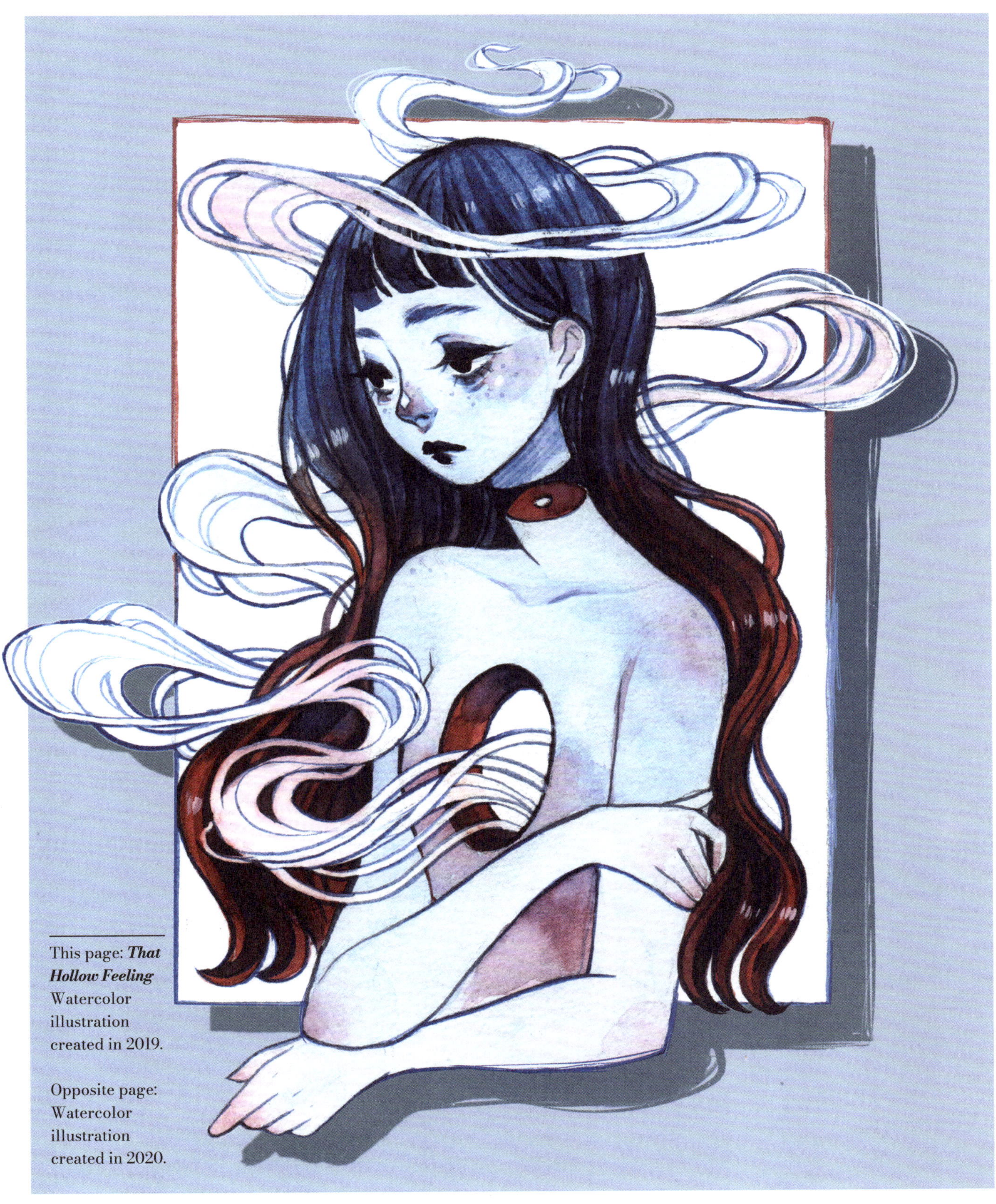

This page: ***That Hollow Feeling***
Watercolor illustration created in 2019.

Opposite page: Watercolor illustration created in 2020.

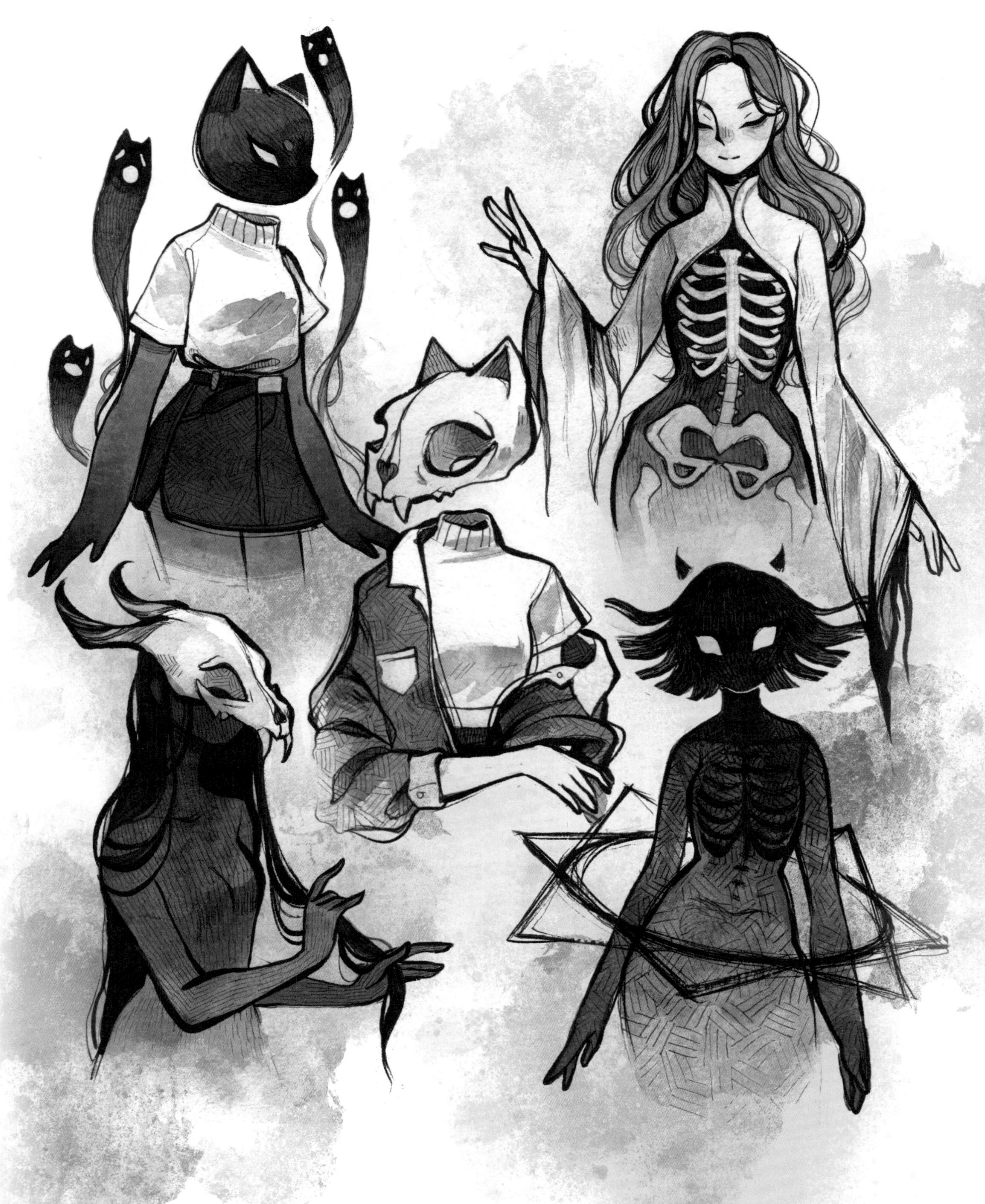

Style & Philosophy

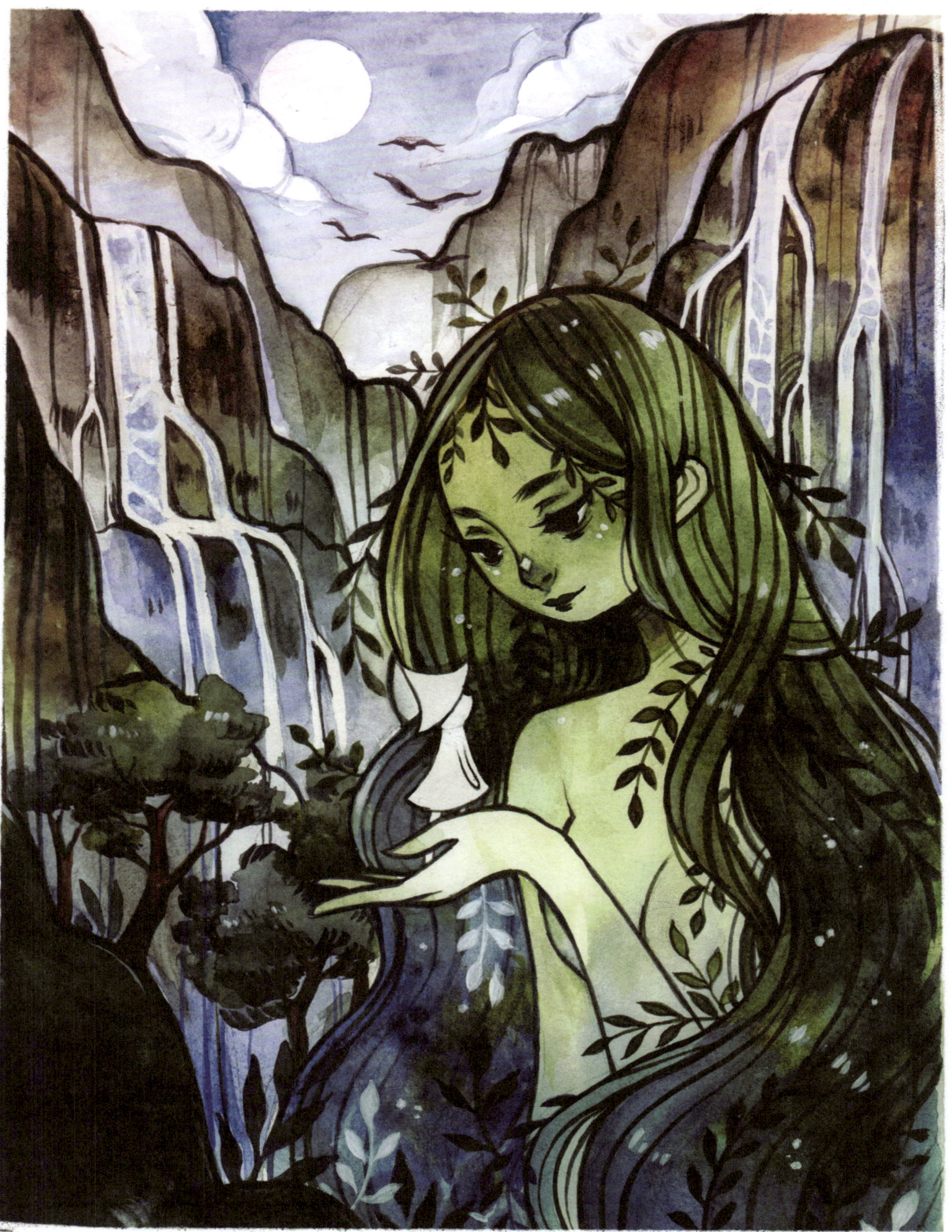

What does it mean to be an artist?

I've always found it strange how all genres of art are lumped together as if they are all one thing. I call myself an artist, but it can really mean anything creative since it's such a broad term. It can refer to a graffiti artist, a cake artist, or a sound artist that specializes in ambient whale noises. I sometimes think of myself as a craftsperson rather than an artist, because ultimately my primary goal is to craft something visually appealing using my learned skills, rather than capture an idea or a feeling.

Don't get me wrong, I love telling stories through my work, and for them to hold a narrative, but overridingly, I just want to create pieces that look cool!

At the core of it all, I like to think of myself as an uncomplicated person, and my ultimate goal in life is to just be happy. Creating art makes me happy, and that's the biggest reason I continue to do it. I'm content with earning a humble wage and living an unglamorous lifestyle if it means I get to spend my time doing what I'm most passionate about. That's not to say that monetizing your passion is always the best idea – it can have a wondrous way of sucking the joy out of what you do. Being an artist, a musician, or pretty much anything within the cultural sector means compromising your creative process to some extent.

I find that motivation and inspiration are unreliable sources of drive, so I have had to learn to push my way through art blocks and draw through those tough times where my brain decides to deprive me of all of my creativity. Inspiration is fantastic for creativity, but I see it more as a privilege rather than a constant presence, so for me, it's essential to be able to rely on some good old-fashioned work ethic to power me when inspiration is not available! I'm still learning the best ways to pull productivity out of myself, and while I have gotten better at it over the years, it's still a big struggle at times.

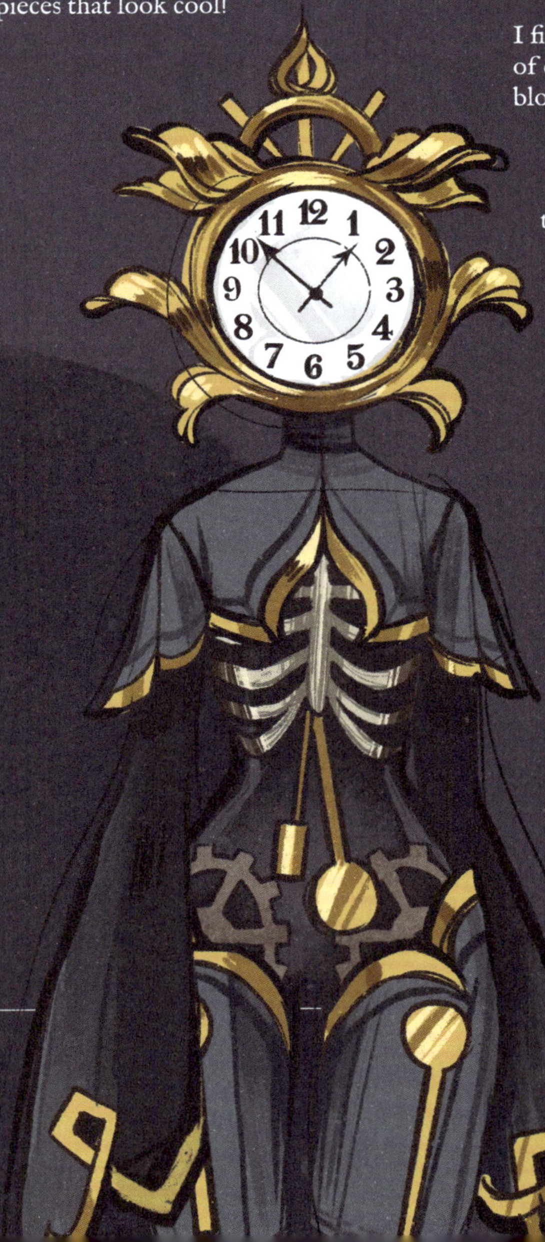

Traveler

A watercolor illustration.

Learning to draw

Drawing is something I have been doing from a young age. I never really made a conscious decision to improve, it's just a skill I have developed over the years due to the many hours I've spent performing it. If I had entered into my artistic development with a more tactical mindset and followed specific art lessons, I would probably have been a little better at drawing than I am today, but I prefer the process of learning at my own pace. I'm also a little bit stubborn when it comes to my art, to my detriment in some cases. I hate being told what to do and prefer to figure out what is right for me on my own.

Through trial and error, I've discovered what feels most comfortable for me and suits my way of working. I find that the best way to improve my skills and develop new work is to look at lots of art, observe the world around me, and simply consider how I can interpret them in different ways. If there is a particular element I'm struggling with, I tend to go online to look up references and research how other artists have tackled the same hurdle – another great wonder of the internet!

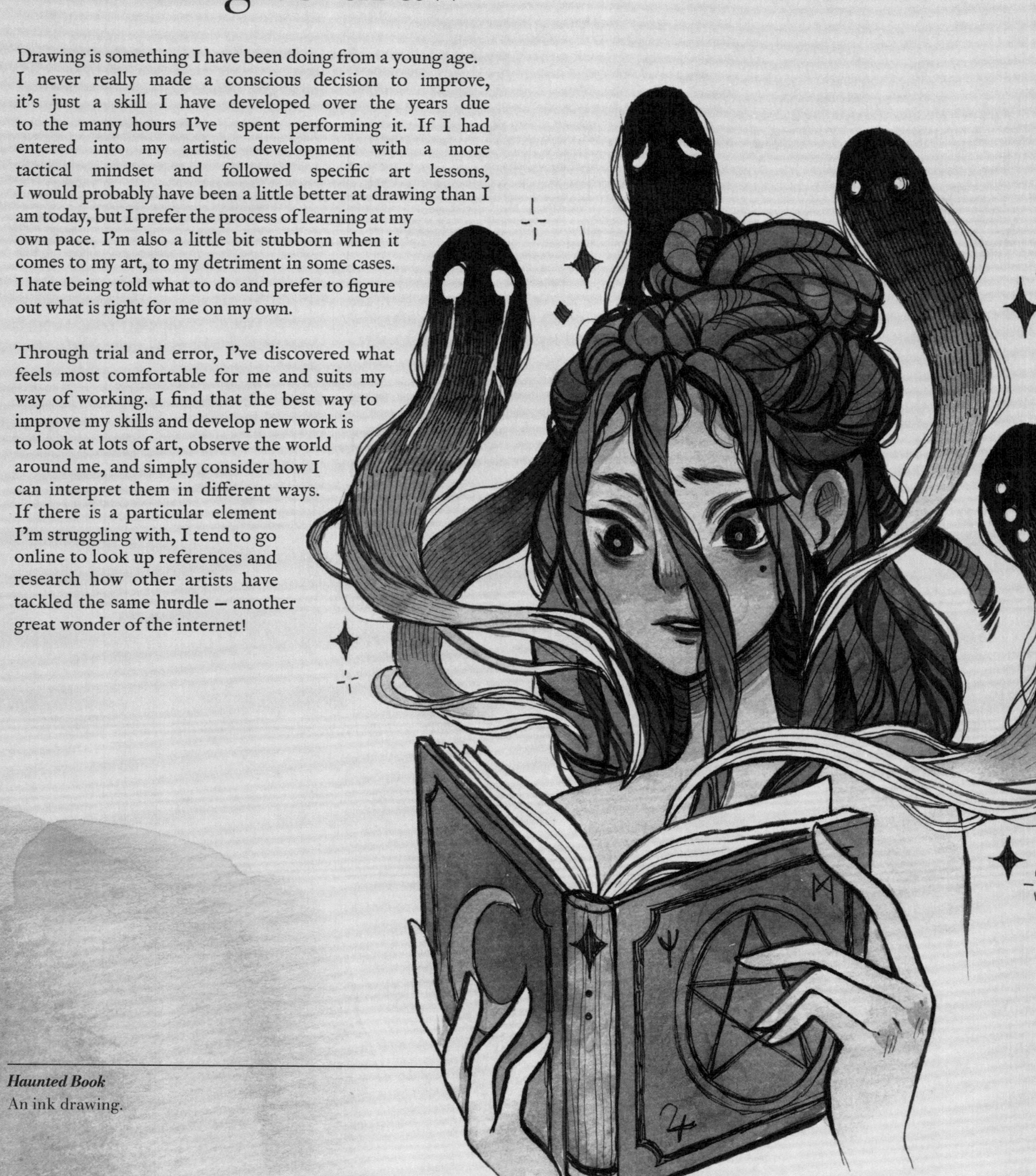

Haunted Book
An ink drawing.

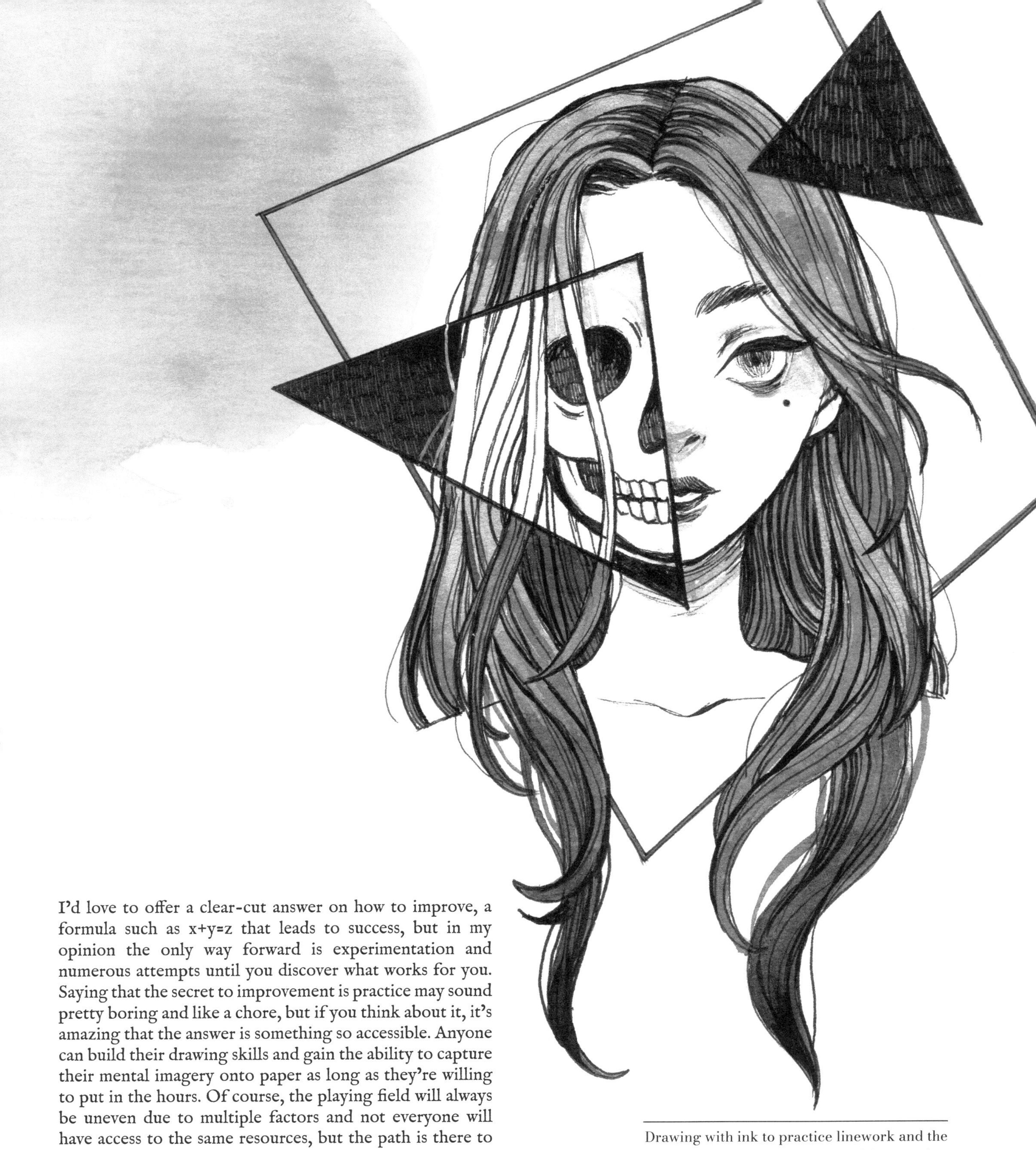

I'd love to offer a clear-cut answer on how to improve, a formula such as x+y=z that leads to success, but in my opinion the only way forward is experimentation and numerous attempts until you discover what works for you. Saying that the secret to improvement is practice may sound pretty boring and like a chore, but if you think about it, it's amazing that the answer is something so accessible. Anyone can build their drawing skills and gain the ability to capture their mental imagery onto paper as long as they're willing to put in the hours. Of course, the playing field will always be uneven due to multiple factors and not everyone will have access to the same resources, but the path is there to follow if you persevere.

Drawing with ink to practice linework and the limitations of working with one color.

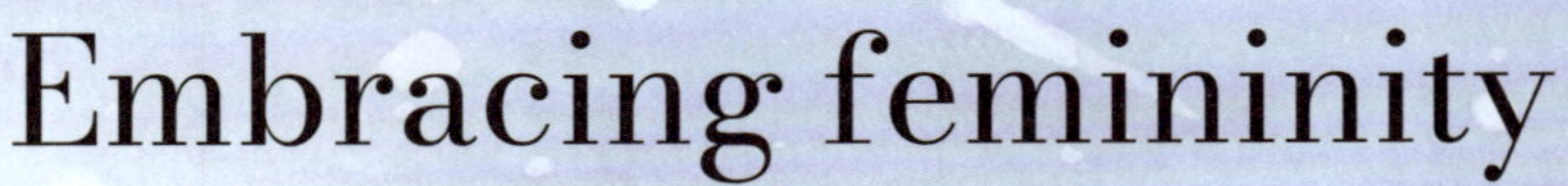

Embracing femininity

Some of my favorite subjects to draw are flowers, long flowing hair, and cute girls in skirts. I gravitate toward anything that emits a pink sparkly aura. I'm also obsessed with romance novels and had a *Twilight* fixation during my tweens – I think I read the whole series about three times. And I can't even begin to count the number of Shoujo manga books I've finished over the years. The point I'm trying to make is that I really, really love stereotypical "girly" stuff.

I have always been drawn toward things labeled as feminine, despite the bad press they often receive. Media geared toward a female audience is often looked down upon and deemed as frivolous, which has always bothered me. The aesthetic shouldn't automatically have a lower value because women enjoy it. There's also a negative implication that anything meant for a teenage-girl audience is automatically stupid, which I strongly disagree with. I believe there's power in being unapologetic in your love for all things girly!

This page: ***Head in the Clouds***
A watercolor illustration, 2019.

Opposite page: ***As Above***
Created using watercolor and digital techniques.

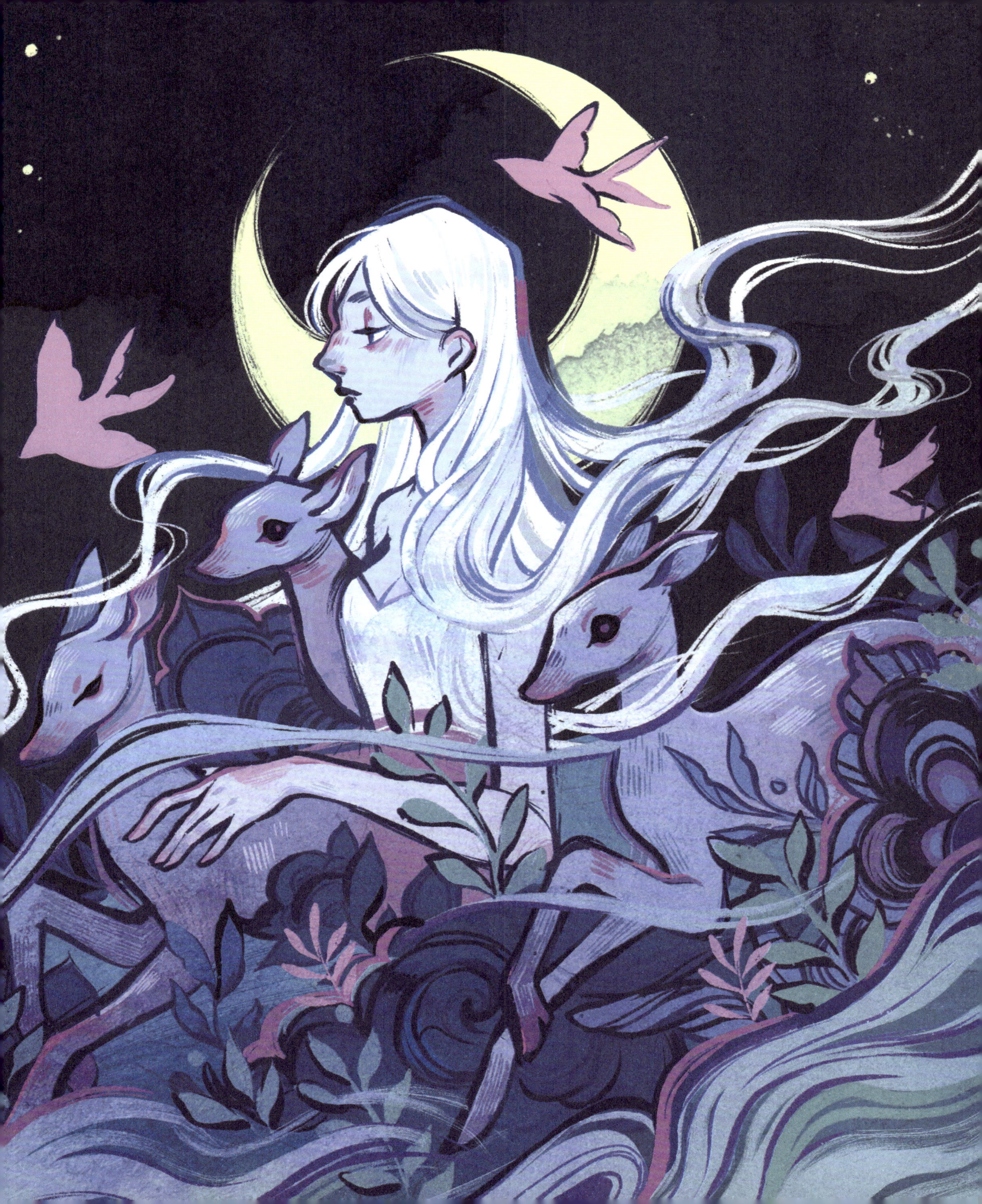

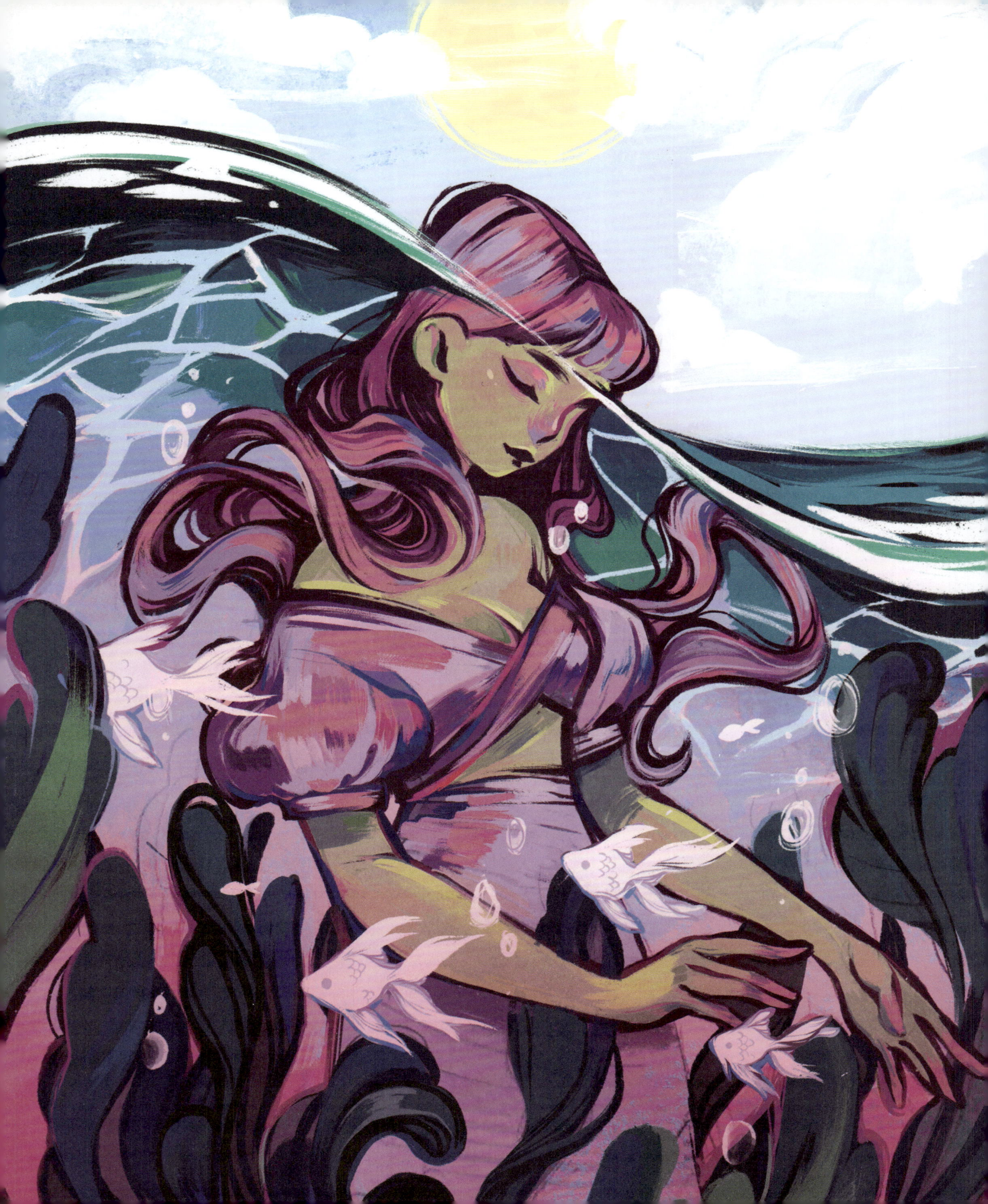

"...there's power in being unapologetic in your love for all things girly"

When I started to share my feminine-style artwork with the online community, I was initially shocked to receive such a positive response. As I'd previously received criticism surrounding my girly aesthetic from people in my private life, I didn't expect such an encouraging reaction. I really had no idea that there was such a large market for femme-oriented work, and that I happened to fit within that field like a missing puzzle piece.

Although over the years I have occasionally steered my artwork into a gritty and serious direction, I always return to the girly aesthetic because it's what I enjoy making and seeing most. And now I'm happy I didn't succeed in changing it!

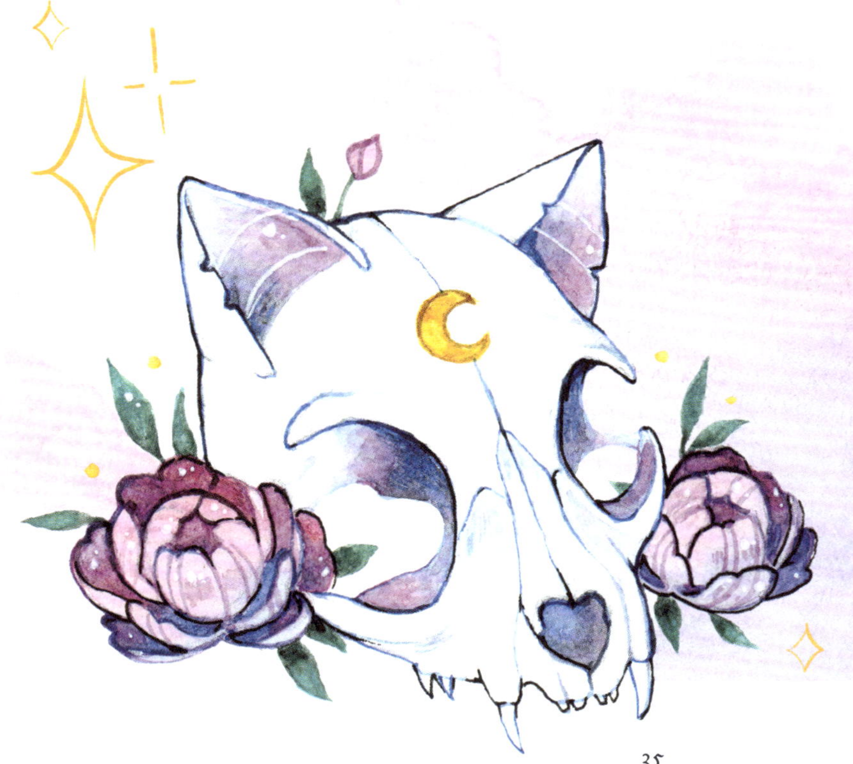

This page: ***Cat Skull***
Cat skulls don't really have ears attached to them, but it would be cuter if they did. Evolution, take note!

Opposite page: ***So Below***

Morbid curiosity

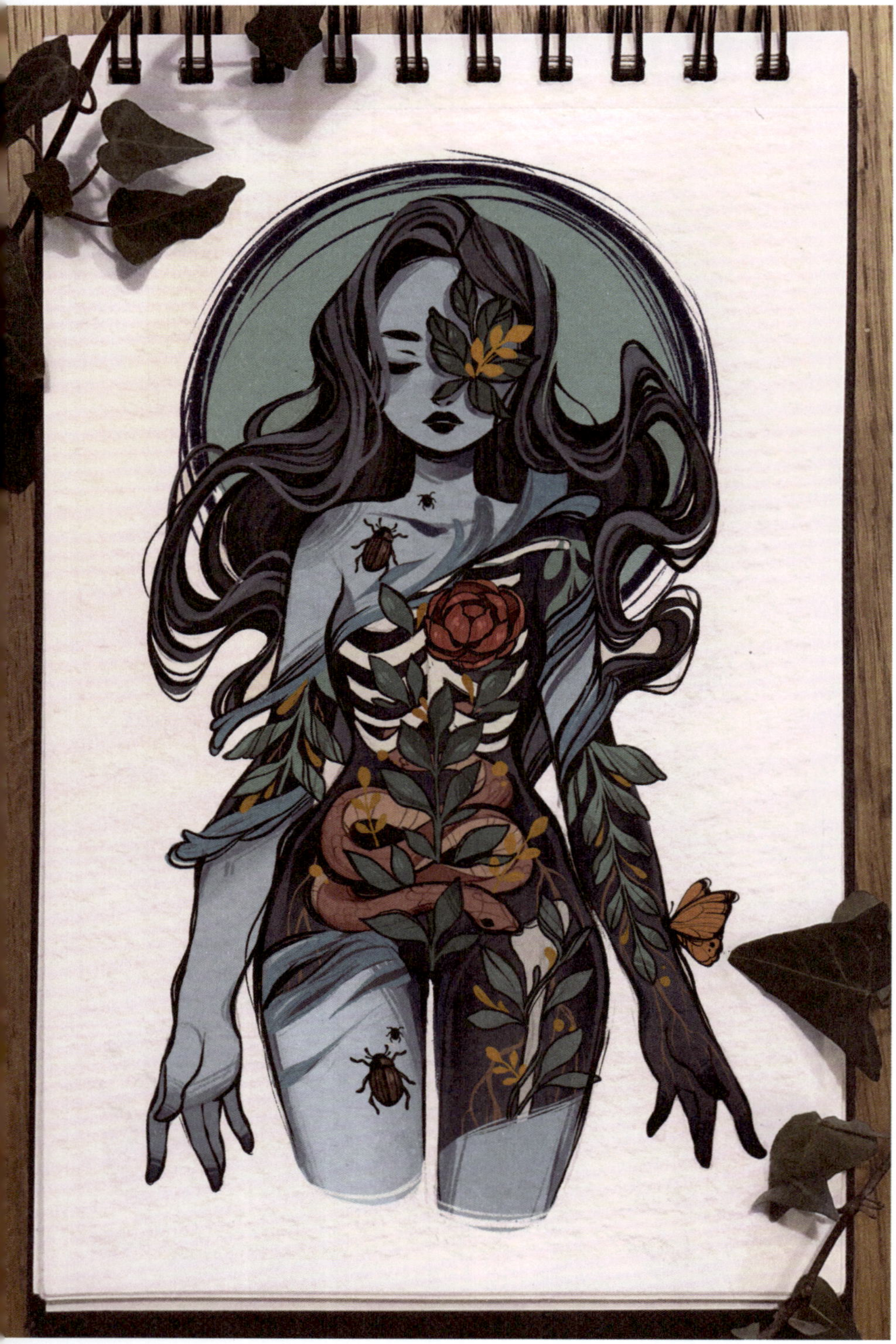

I have a fascination with death. And I think many people share this sentiment, as my more morbid pieces always seem to engage my audience on social media. I guess it's just part of human nature to carry a curiosity for life beyond, or lack of.

Death can be beautiful in many ways. We often fear it as it marks the end of life and everything we've ever known, and we have no idea of what to expect afterwards. I don't think it deserves all the negative press it has been getting; it's a natural experience, and the only certainty life has to offer. Don't get me wrong, I love life and I'm happy to be here, but death is a part of life and I think it deserves some love and attention as well.

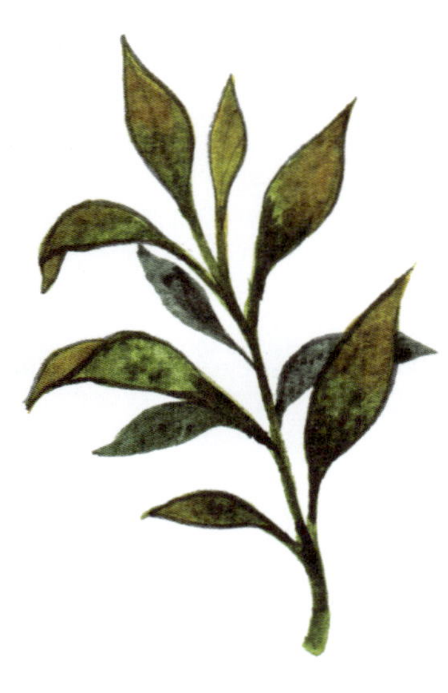

This page: ***Rose for a Heart***
Opposite page: ***Return to the Forest***

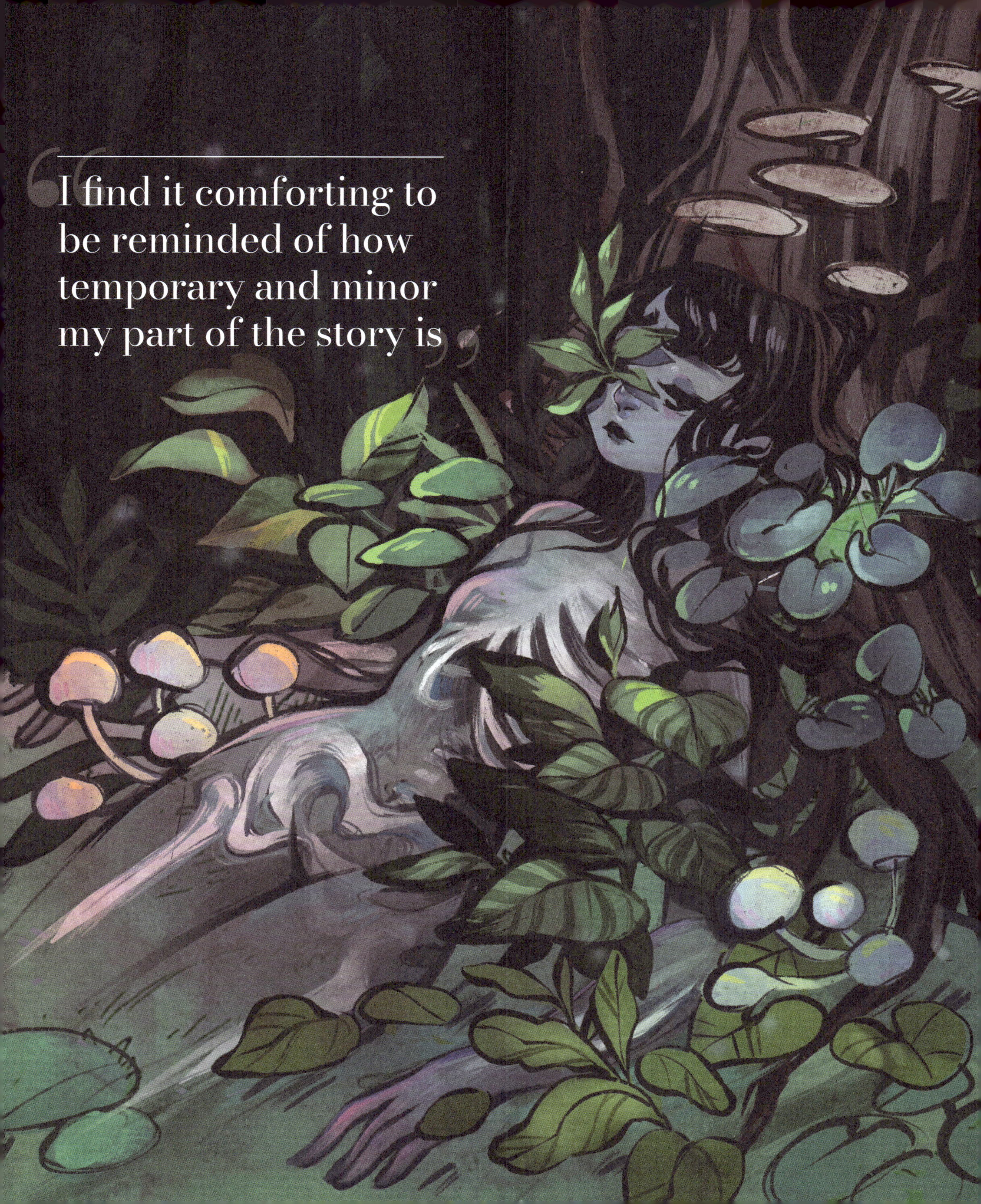
"I find it comforting to be reminded of how temporary and minor my part of the story is"

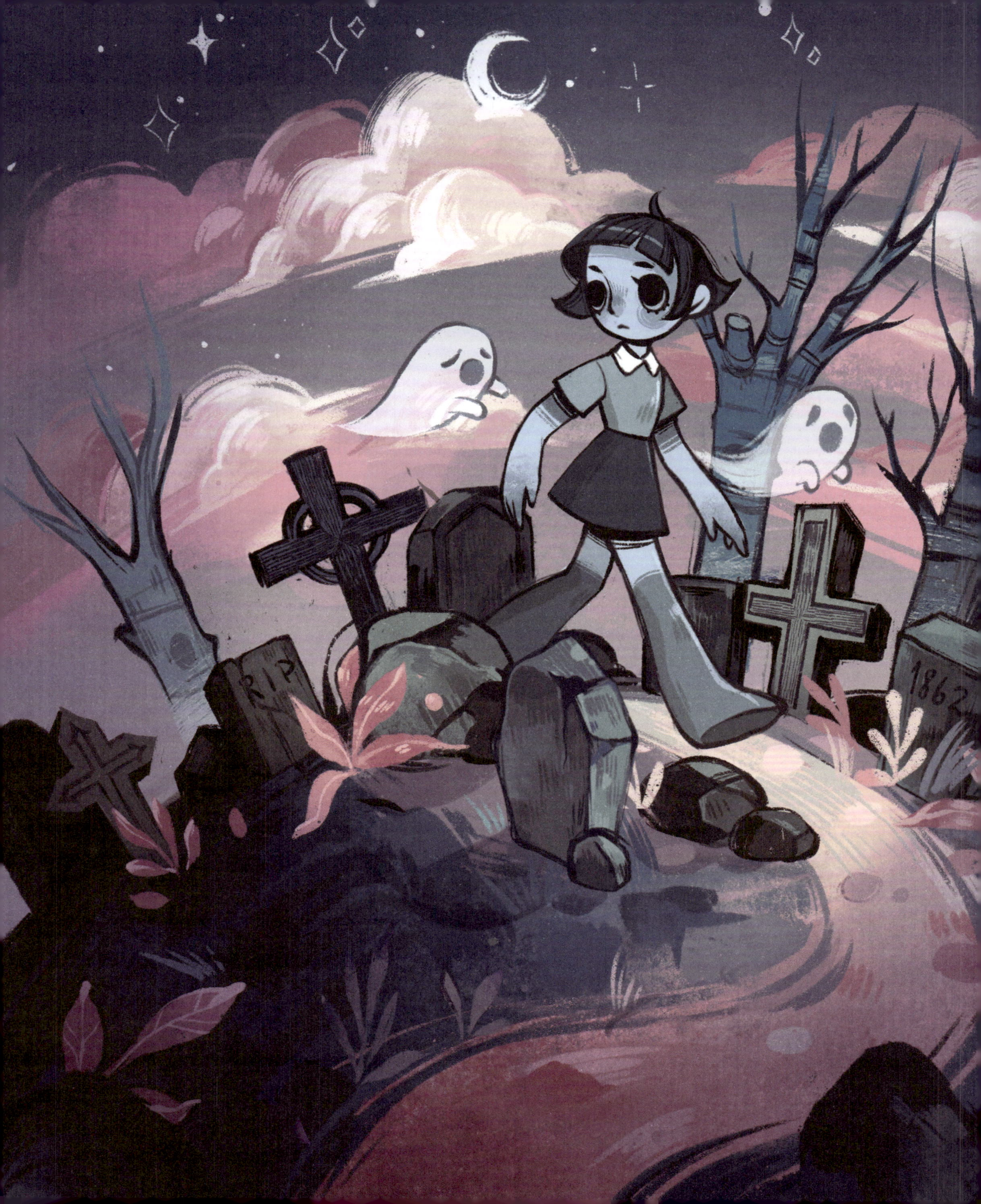
RIP
1862

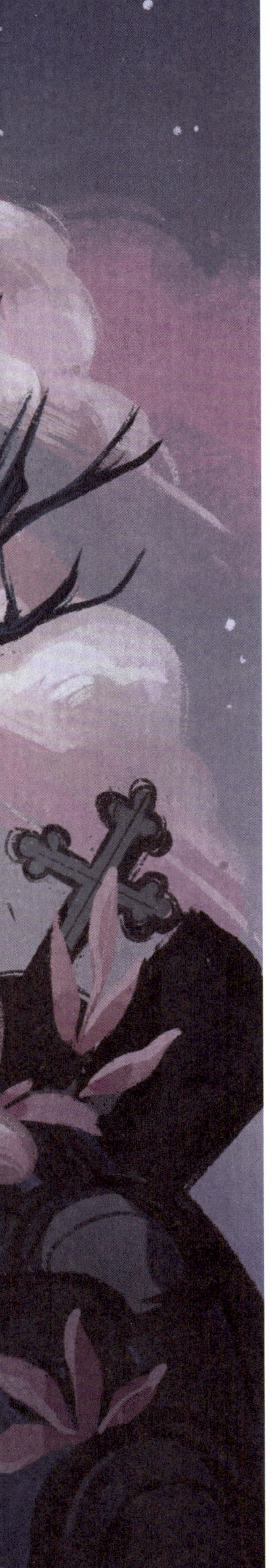

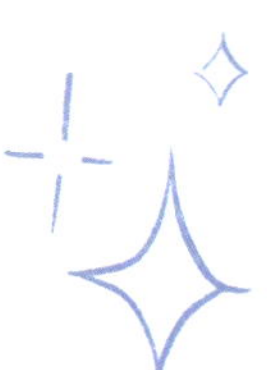

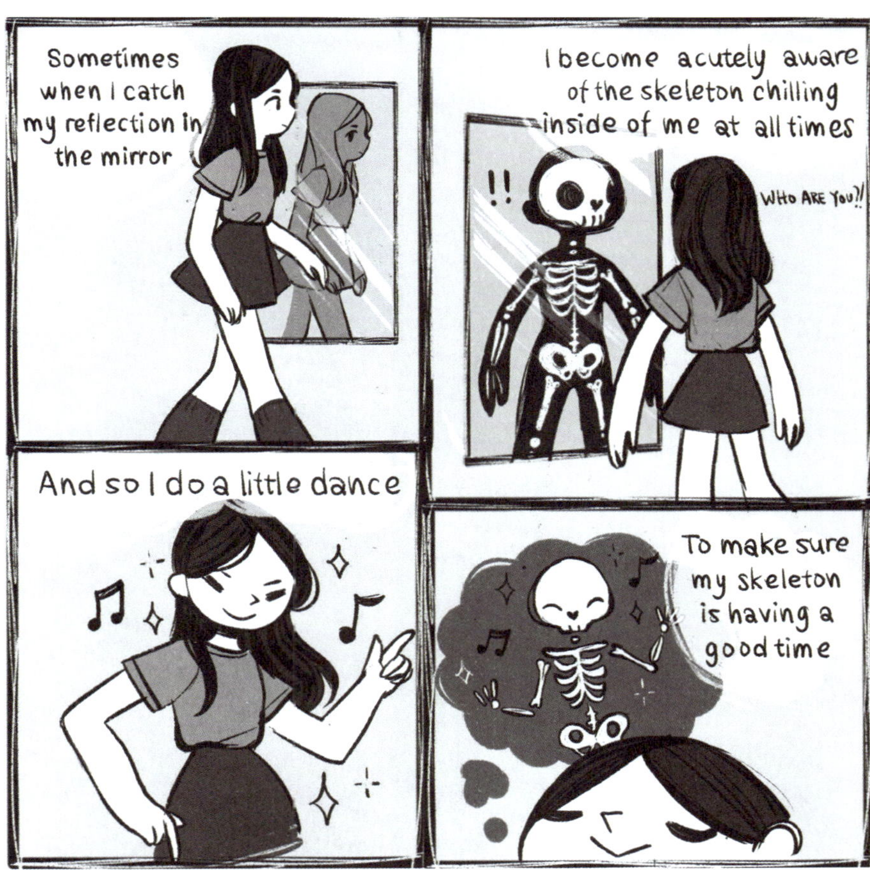

I sometimes get overwhelmed when pondering the vastness of space and so I find it comforting to be reminded of how temporary and minor my part of the story is. I feel as though I've been granted a small glimpse of existence, really just a speck of awareness in the grand scheme of things, and it's up to me to do what I can with it. Life can feel so overwhelming at times and as if you're carrying the burdens of the world on your shoulders, but in the end we will all be united with the earth and the cycle will continue forward.

That's why I love creating pieces that feature an existence between life and death, the middle ground between being and ceasing. It can be perceived as scary and disturbing, or it can be looked at as a gentle reminder to enjoy the limited time we have on this special blue/green rock. I could probably write several more pages on my thoughts on mortality and optimistic nihilism, but this is an art book so I will spare you the lecture!

This page: ***My Bones and Me***
Opposite page: ***Graveyard Stroll***

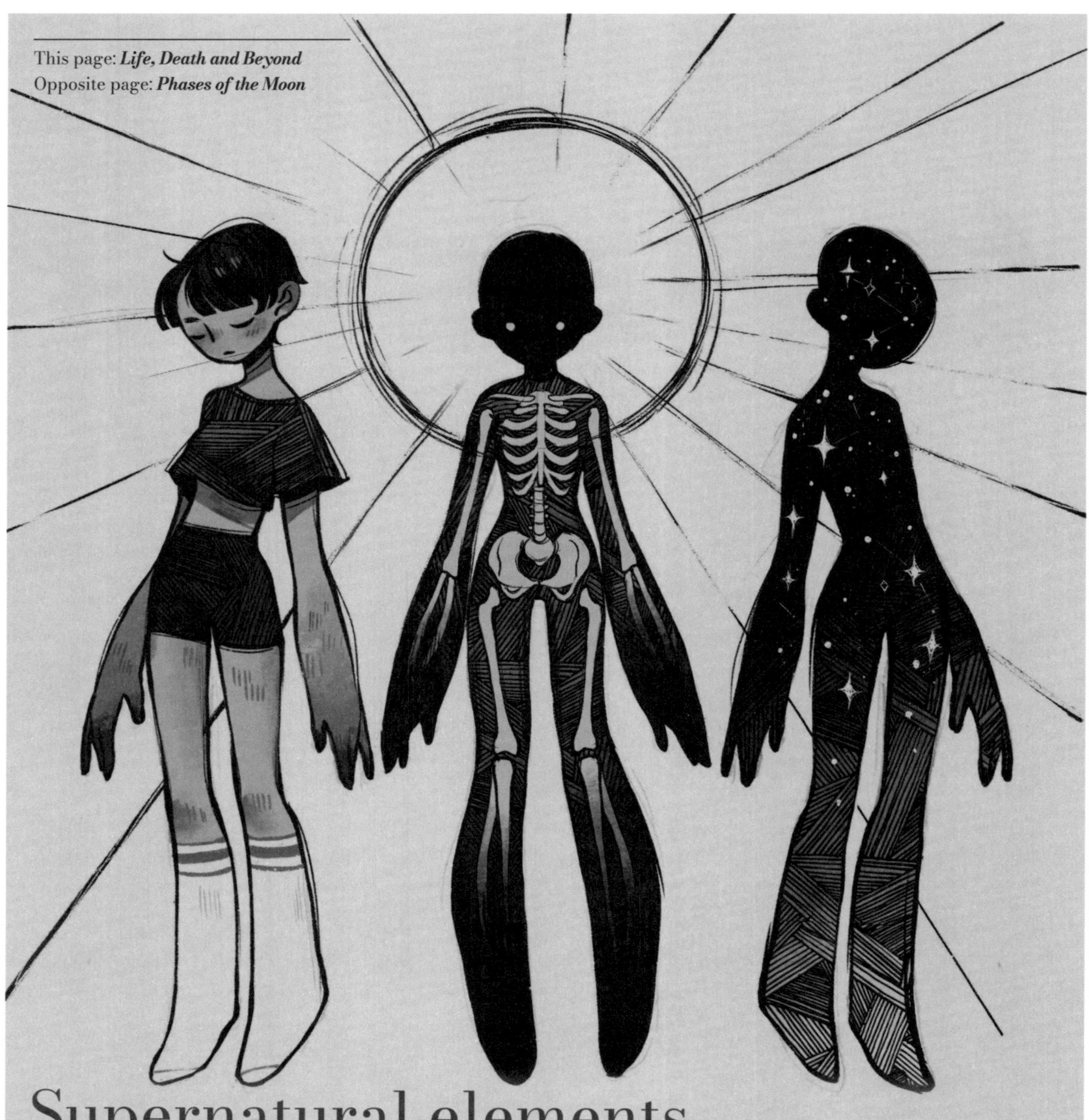

This page: ***Life, Death and Beyond***
Opposite page: ***Phases of the Moon***

Supernatural elements

I gravitate toward portraying elements of a supernatural nature because I find that I can generate much more exciting ideas when I'm not constrained to draw only what is possible and exists in our reality. I see it as a way to explore a parallel world; where reality can be adjusted to suit aesthetics! Tarot, space, and otherworldly themes often creep into my work as they offer a form of escape to another universe. While I enjoy expanding existing ideas, I also revel in the challenge of creating a new fantastical idea. I spend a lot of time pondering different concepts and considering which elements and compositions I could combine to conjure up something fun and alternative.

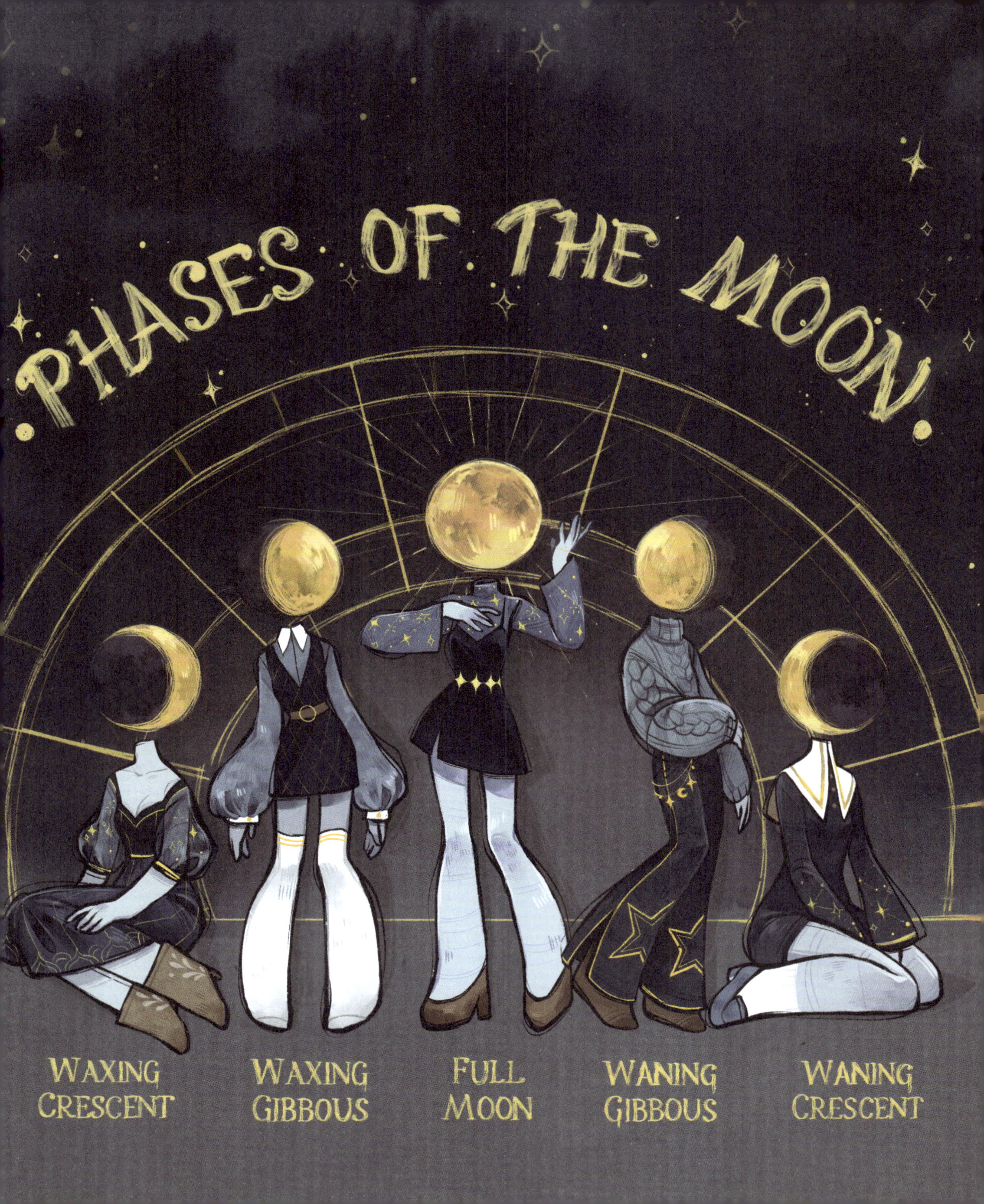

PHASES OF THE MOON

WAXING CRESCENT

WAXING GIBBOUS

FULL MOON

WANING GIBBOUS

WANING CRESCENT

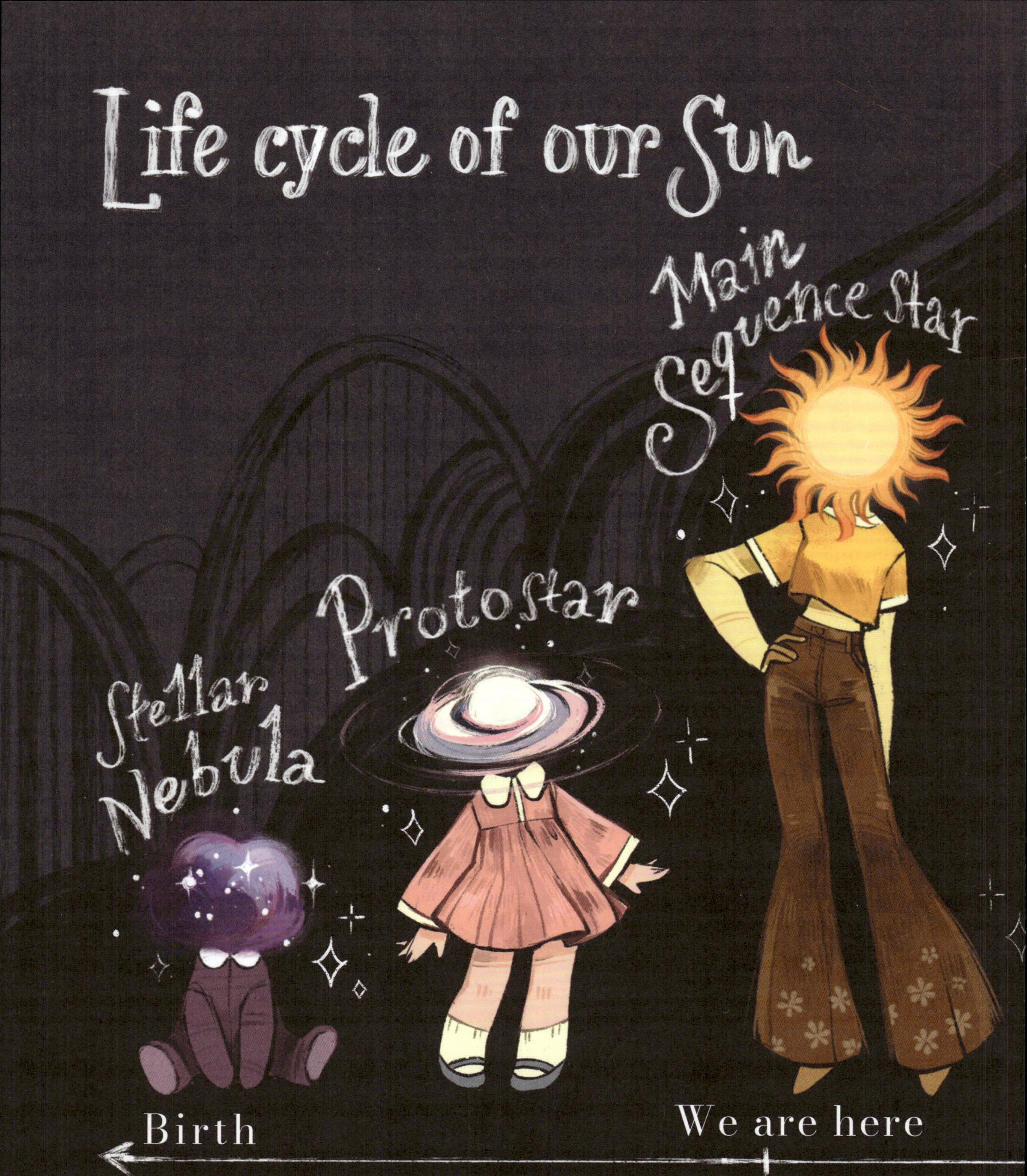

Life cycle of our Sun

Main Sequence Star

Protostar

Stellar Nebula

Birth

We are here

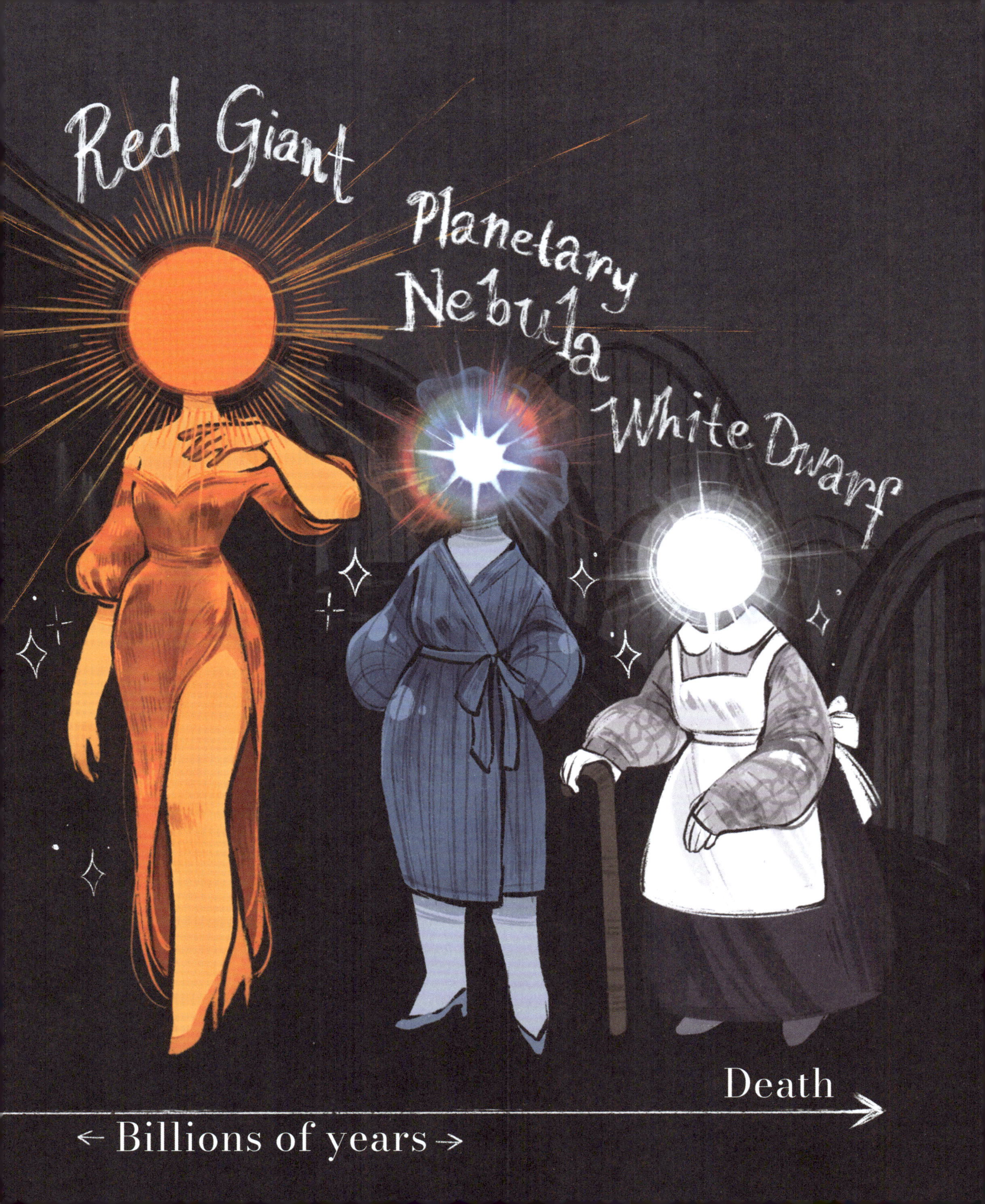

Red Giant

Planetary Nebula

White Dwarf

Death

← Billions of years →

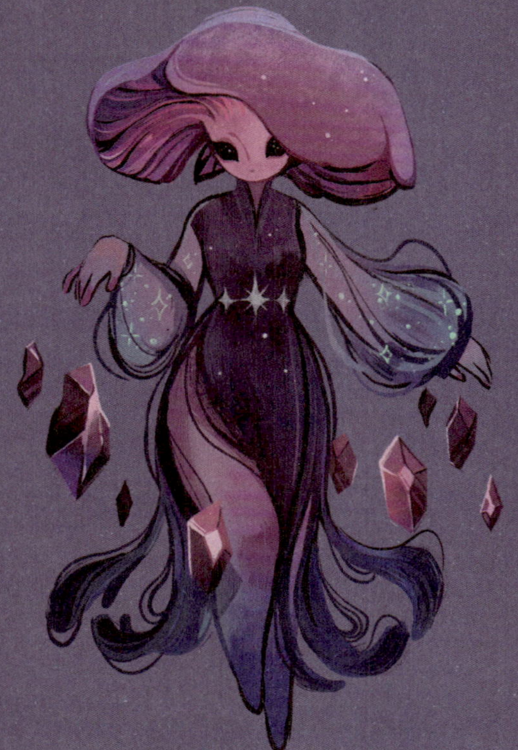

Character design

Conjuring up character designs is a big passion of mine, because I really enjoy the process of breathing life into something new. I often think about their origin, their traits and quirks, and how those aspects play into their final design. Although I rarely draw the same character more than once, I still want them to appear as if they originate from their own universe and have their own stories to tell.

I often find inspiration from the most miscellaneous of sources – it can really be anything. Sometimes when I'm out of ideas, I look around and pick a random item near my vicinity and base my concept around that! I then consider what they would wear and what their personalities might be like. It's one of my favorite ways of overcoming art block because it challenges me to think outside the box while also providing me with a point of reference.

My characters often heavily reference nature, or play on an existing concept. I like to keep my designs relatively simple so that their beautiful natural elements can shine through. I want them to be reincarnations of their source material, not just a design based on them!

For example, if I'm designing a character based on dandelions and I aim for my character to appear as if it is a manifestation of that flower, I'll try to incorporate key details of the source material into the final design so that the end result properly portrays who and what they are. There's a difference between a character design based on a dandelion and a character that *is* a dandelion!

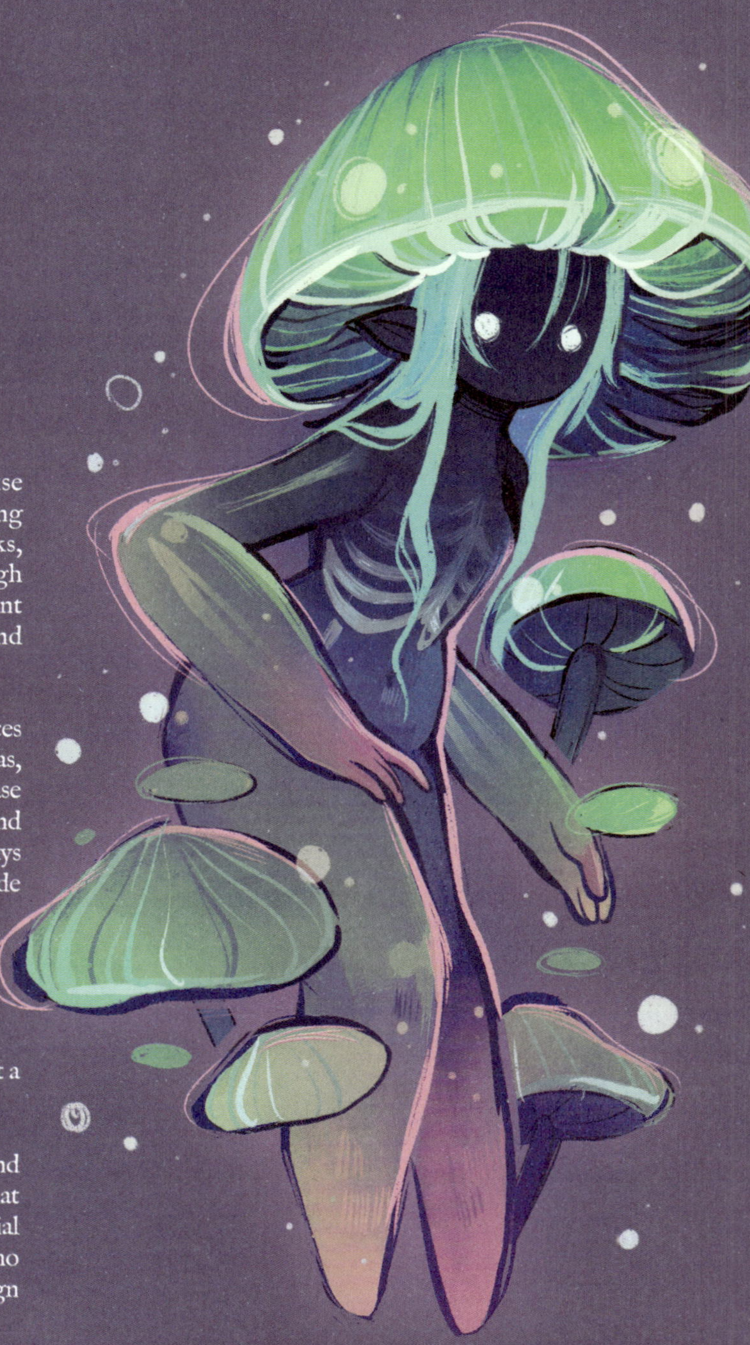

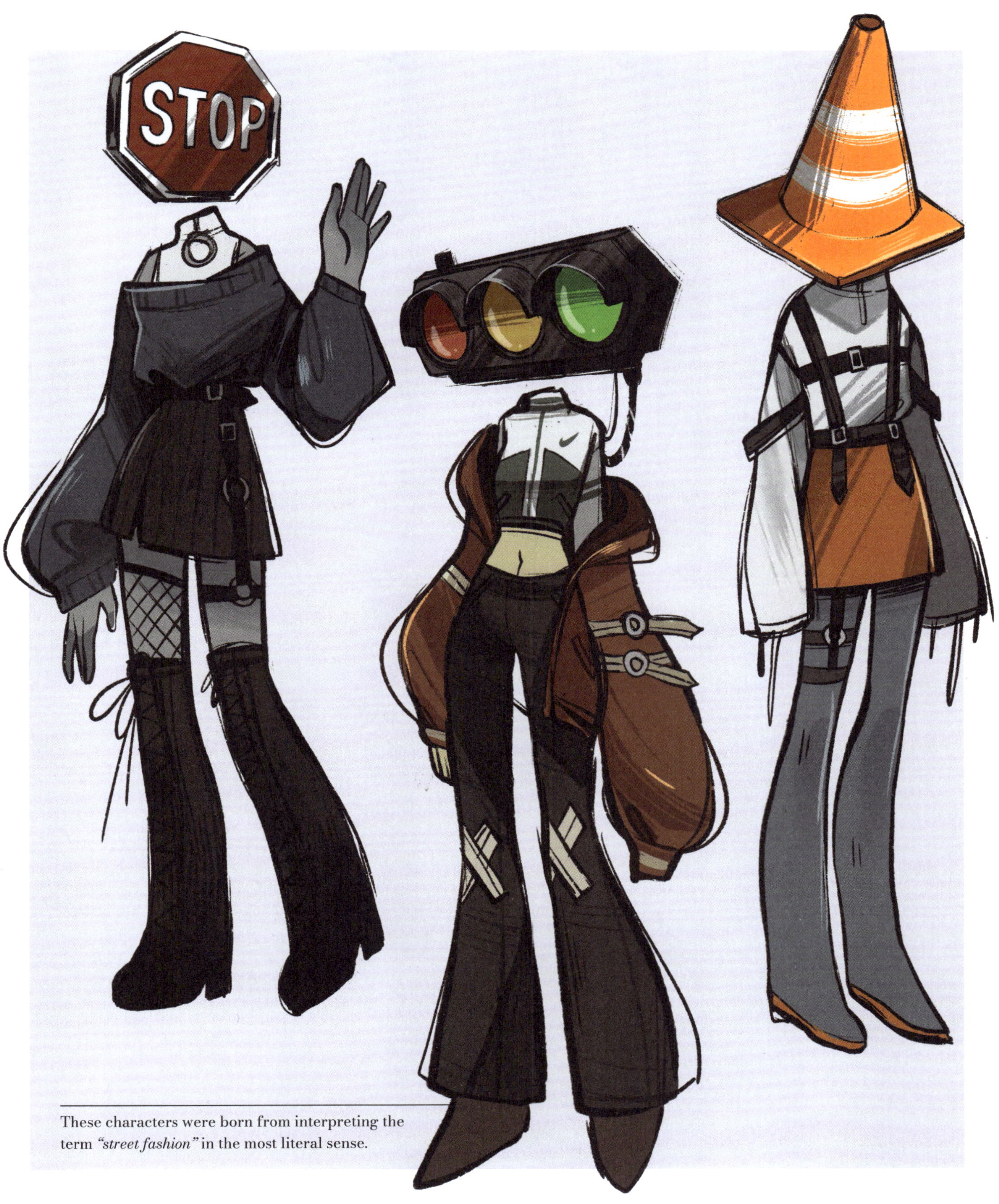

These characters were born from interpreting the term *"street fashion"* in the most literal sense.

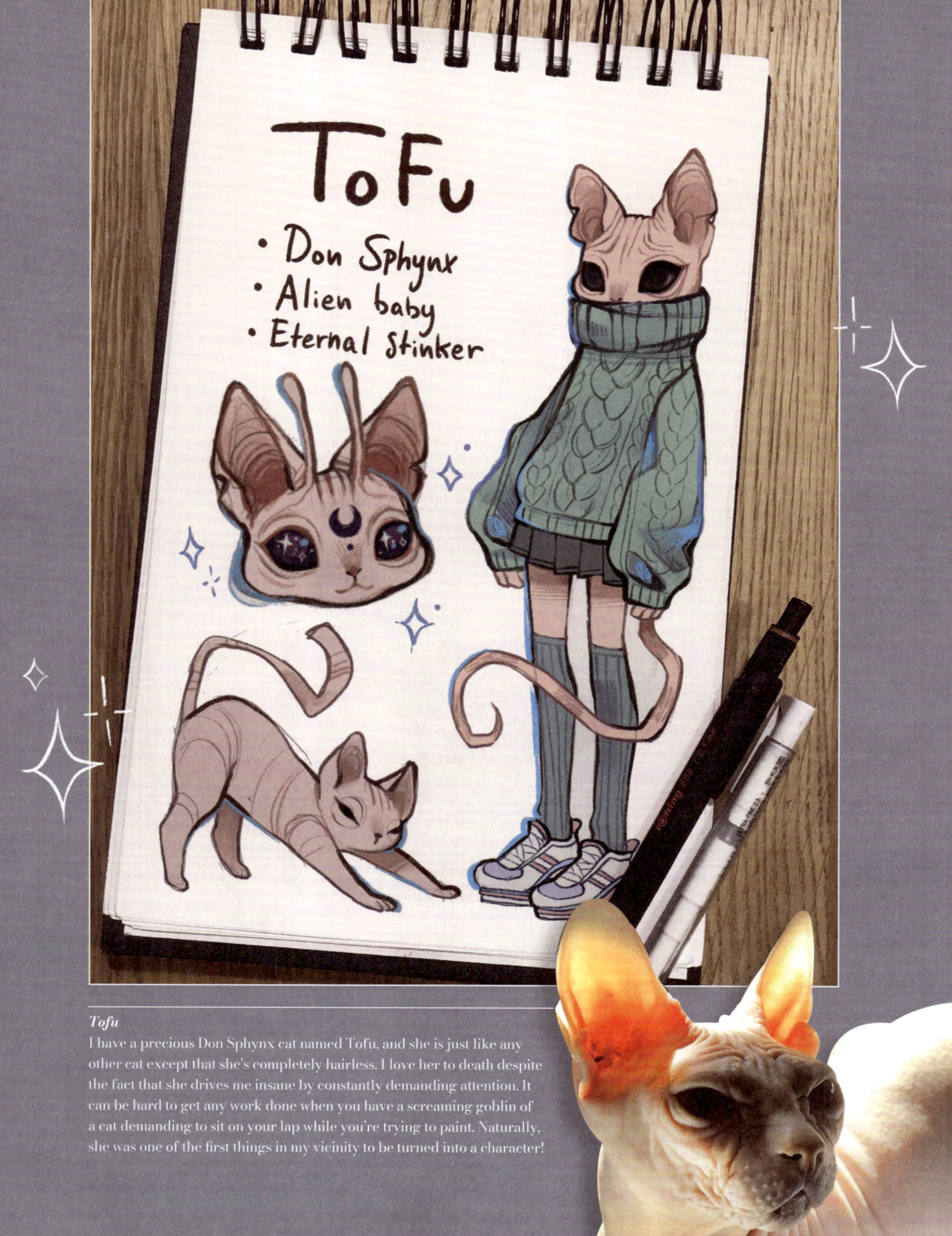

Tofu

I have a precious Don Sphynx cat named Tofu, and she is just like any other cat except that she's completely hairless. I love her to death despite the fact that she drives me insane by constantly demanding attention. It can be hard to get any work done when you have a screaming goblin of a cat demanding to sit on your lap while you're trying to paint. Naturally, she was one of the first things in my vicinity to be turned into a character!

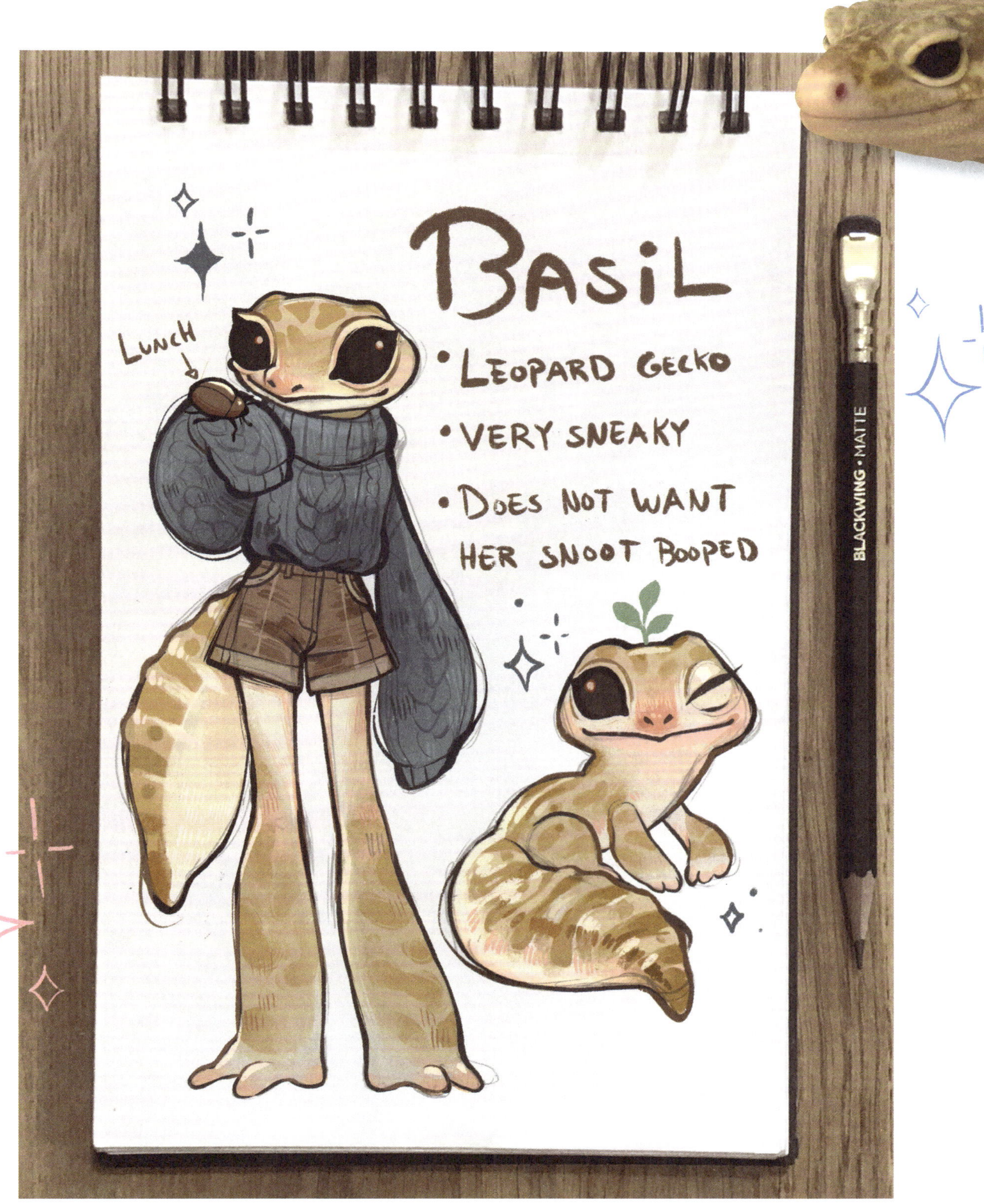

Basil

After designing a Tofu character, I created a character sheet for my friend's leopard gecko as well!

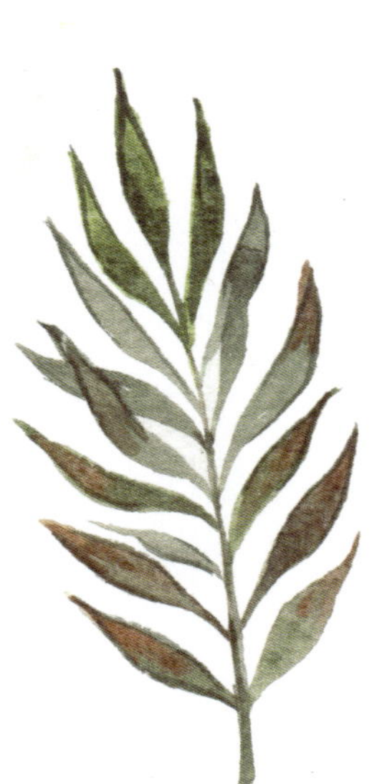

Growth

Watch as these various species from the flora and fungi kingdom grow and change throughout the cycles of life – from tiny plantling into an old and wise mother plant. From baby spore into sage mushroom matriarch.

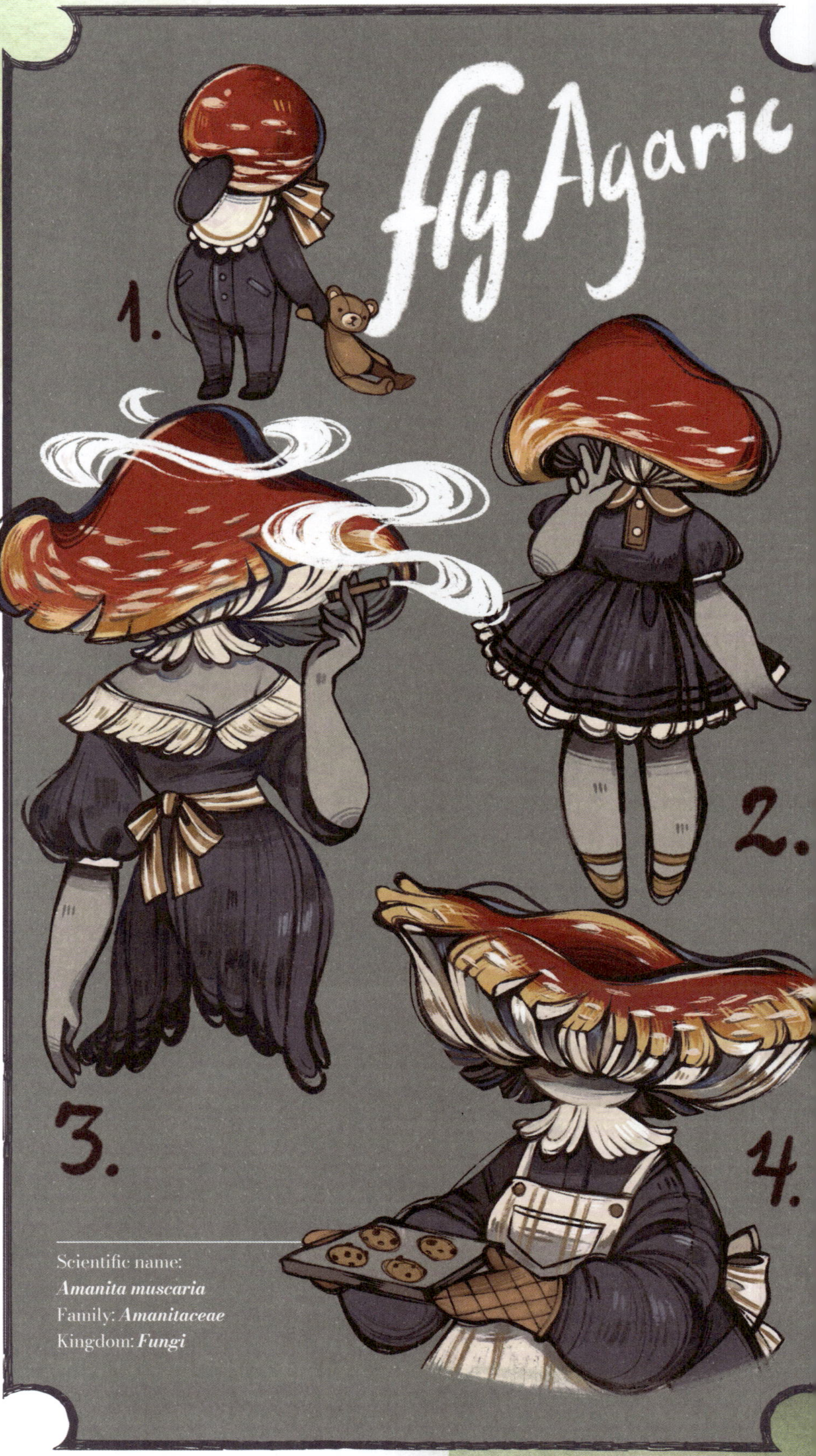

Fly Agaric

1.

2.

3.

4.

Scientific name:
Amanita muscaria
Family: ***Amanitaceae***
Kingdom: ***Fungi***

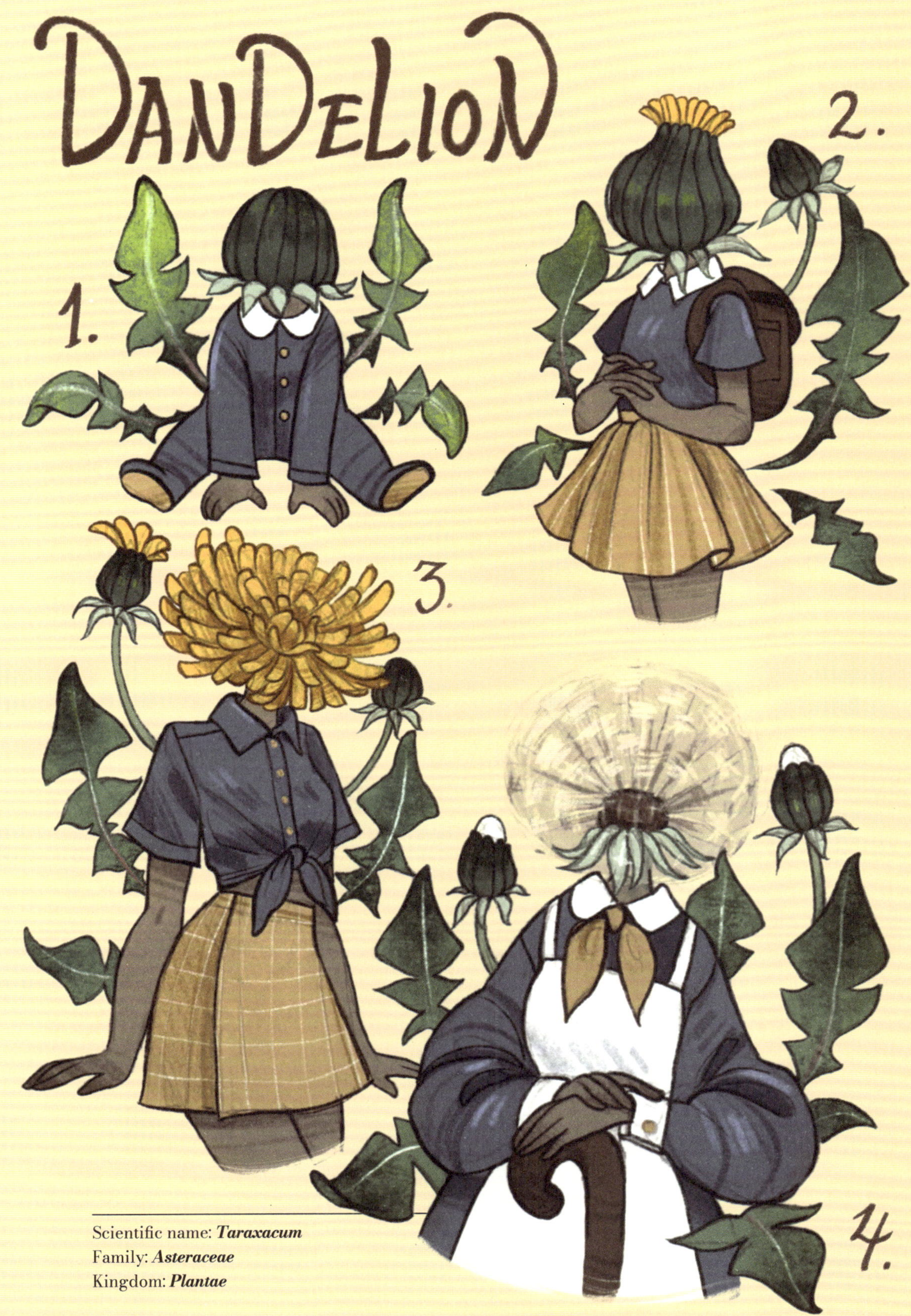

Scientific name: ***Taraxacum***
Family: ***Asteraceae***
Kingdom: ***Plantae***

STRAWBERRY

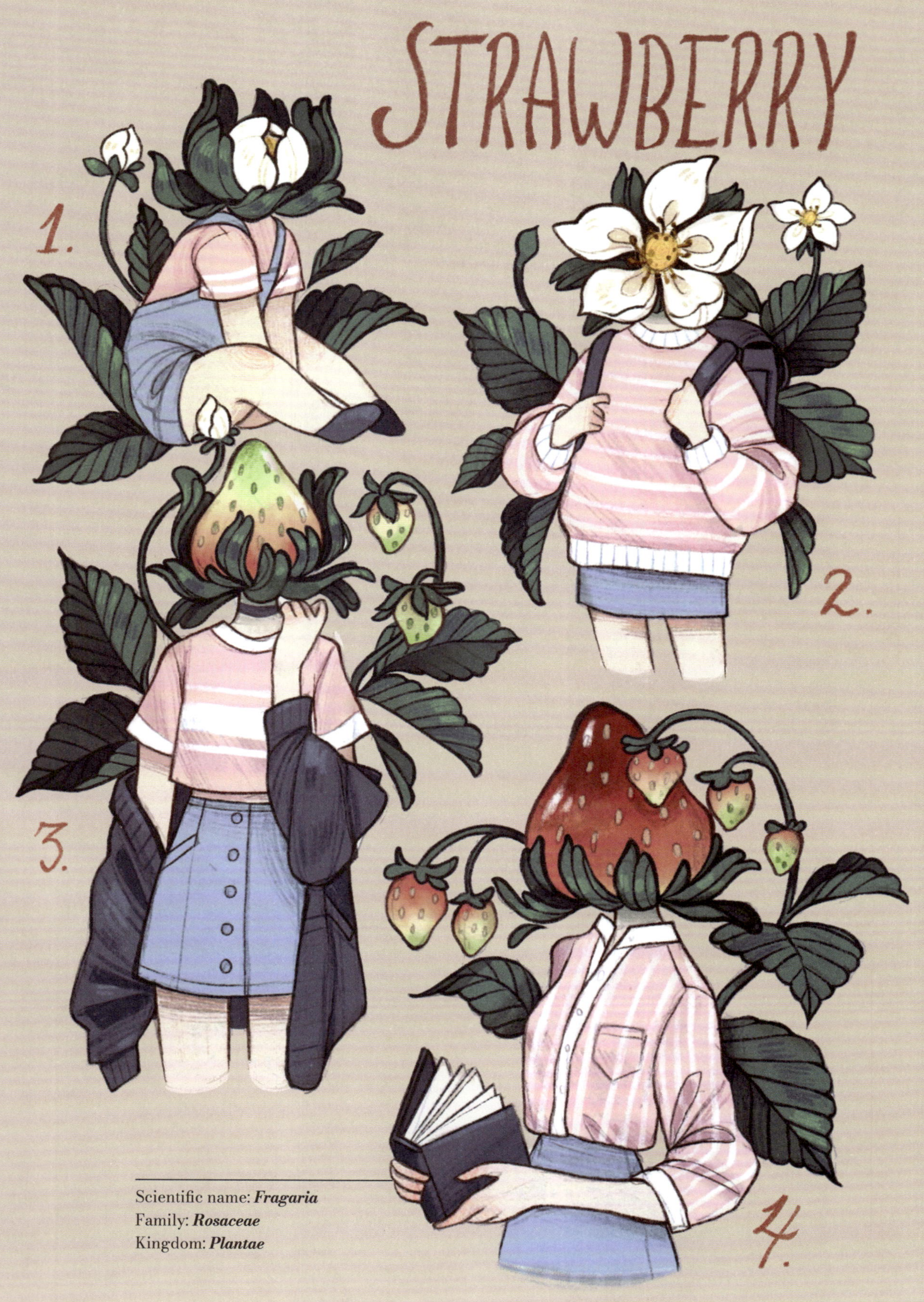

Scientific name: ***Fragaria***
Family: ***Rosaceae***
Kingdom: ***Plantae***

Oyster Mushroom

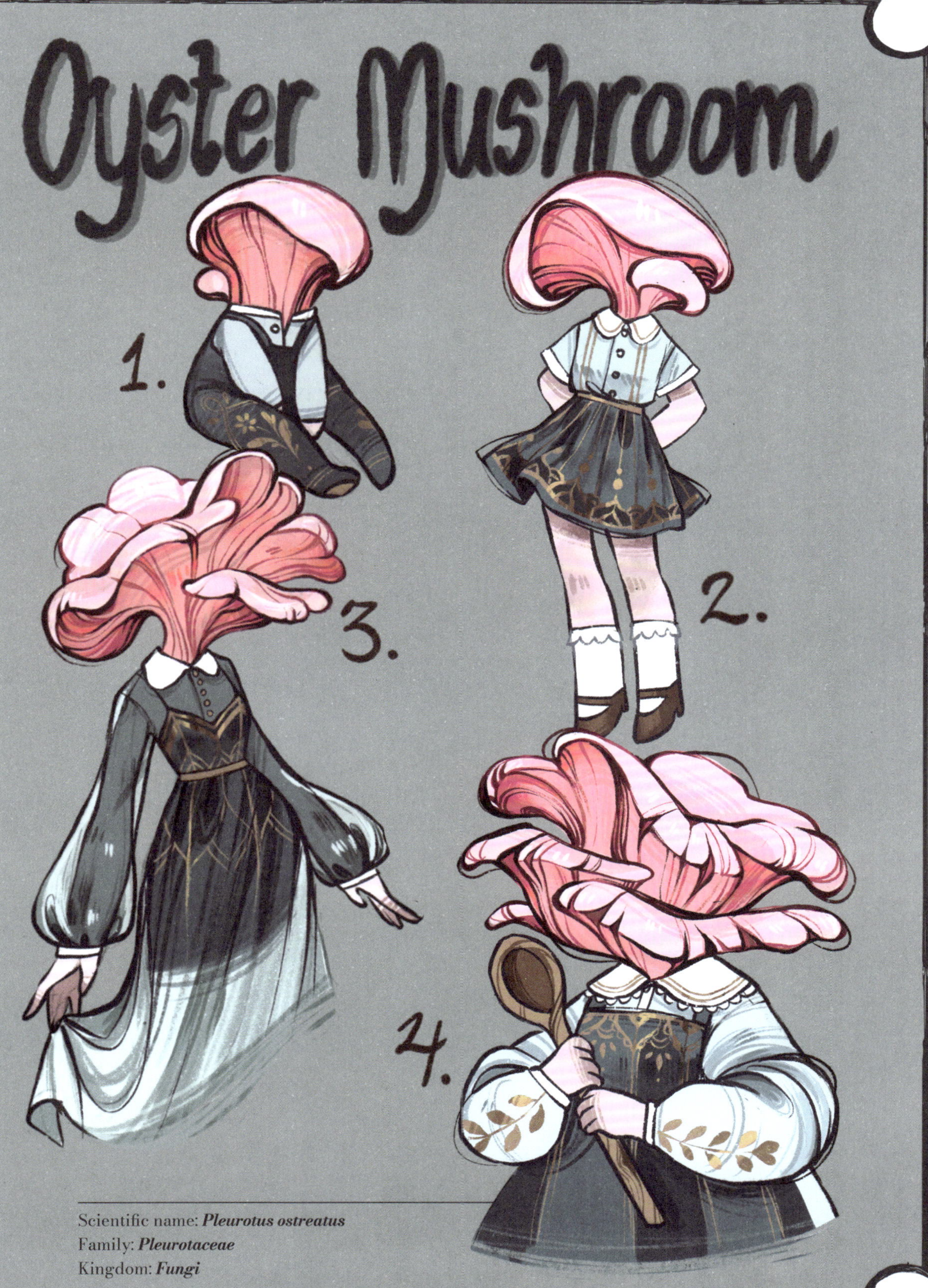

Scientific name: ***Pleurotus ostreatus***
Family: ***Pleurotaceae***
Kingdom: ***Fungi***

HONEY FUNGUS

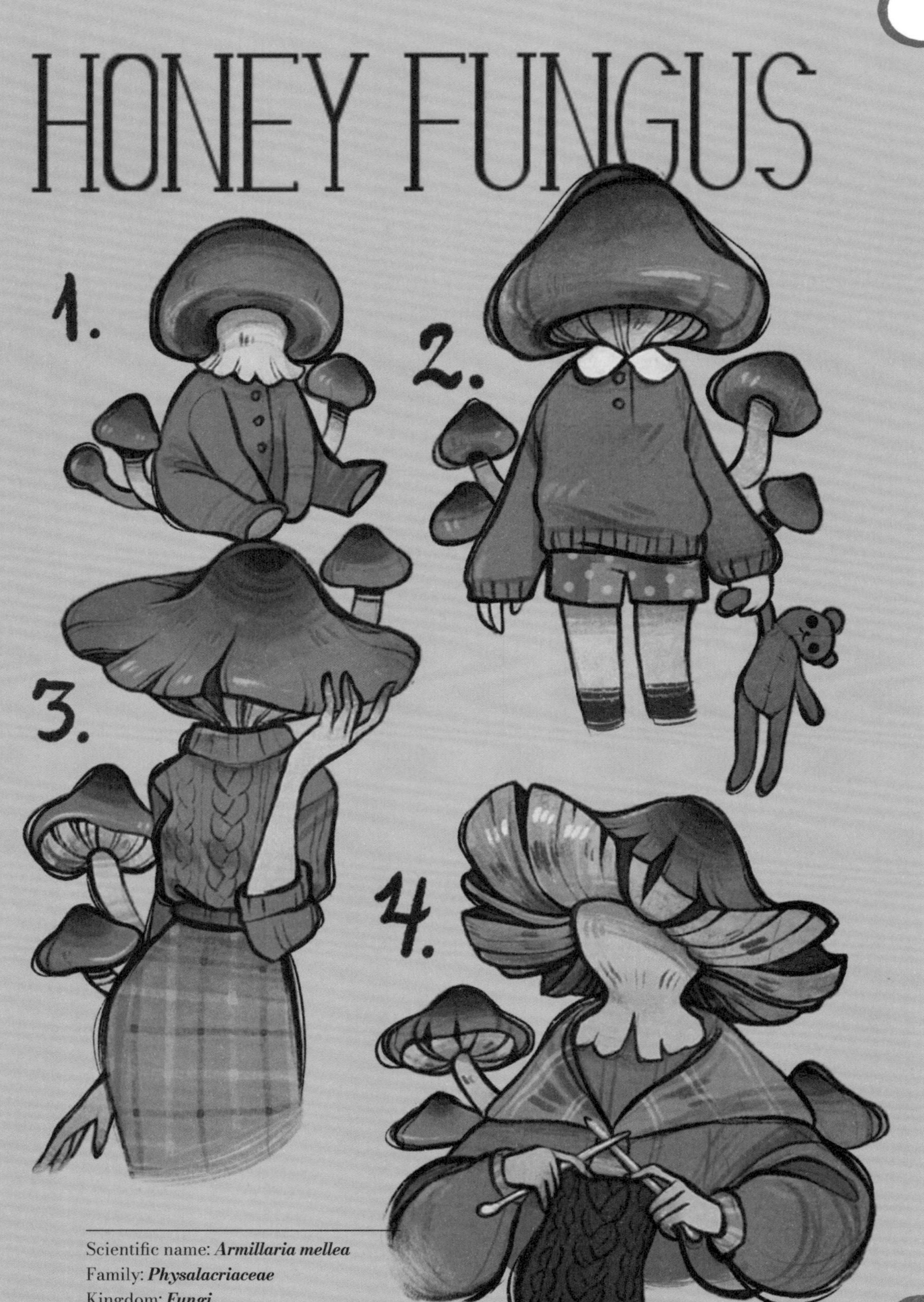

Scientific name: ***Armillaria mellea***
Family: ***Physalacriaceae***
Kingdom: ***Fungi***

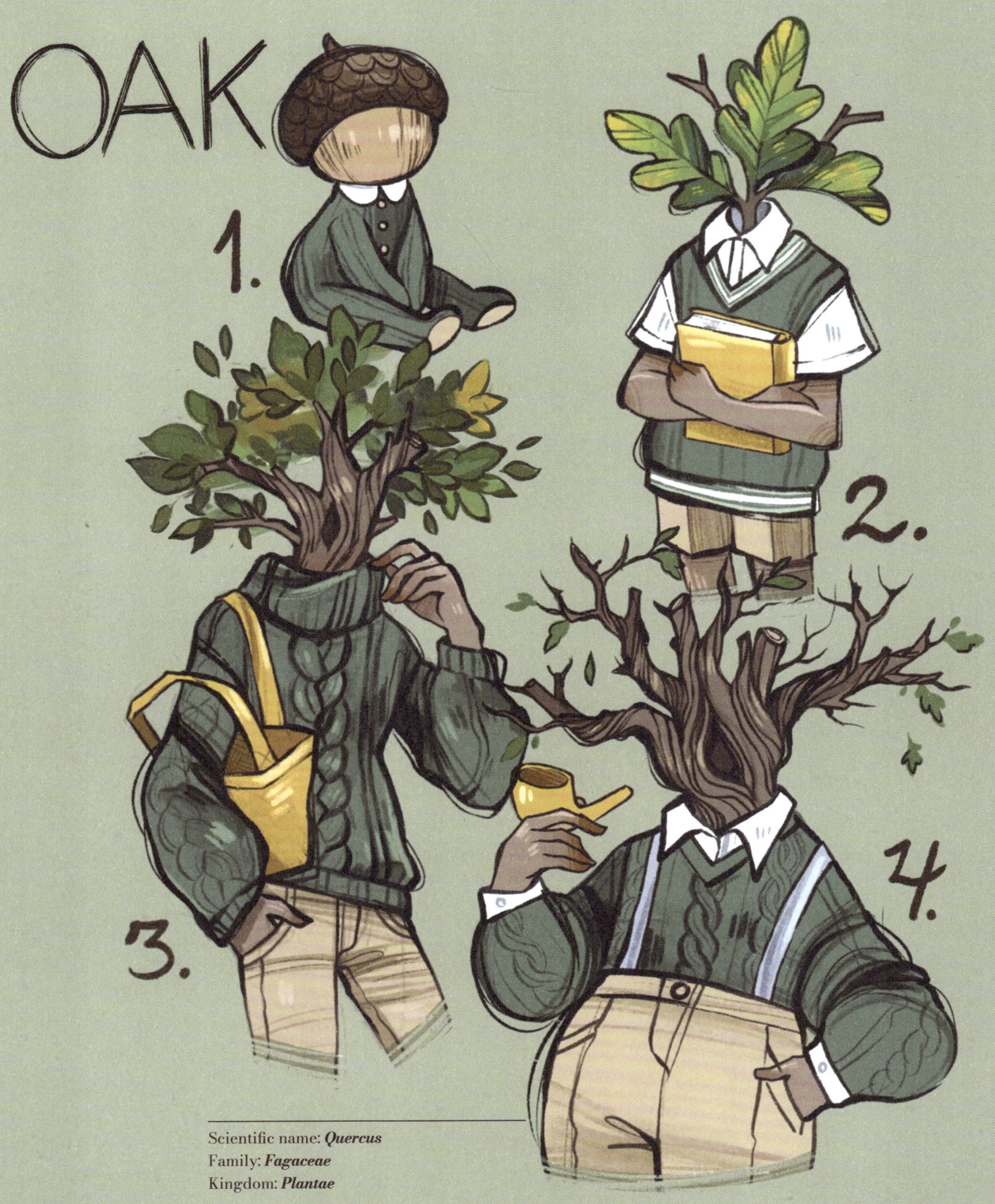

Scientific name: ***Quercus***
Family: ***Fagaceae***
Kingdom: ***Plantae***

INKY CAP

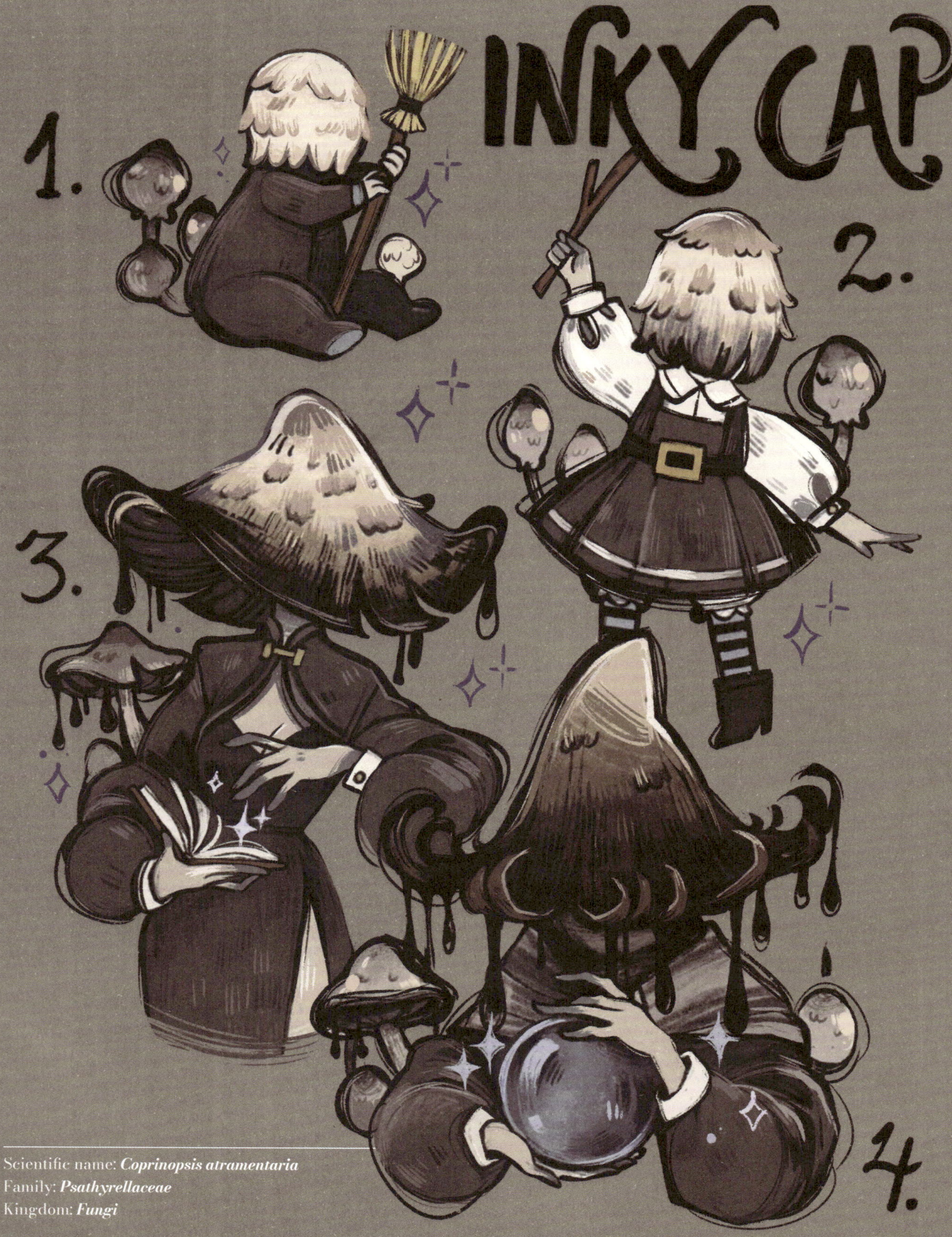

Scientific name: ***Coprinopsis atramentaria***
Family: ***Psathyrellaceae***
Kingdom: ***Fungi***

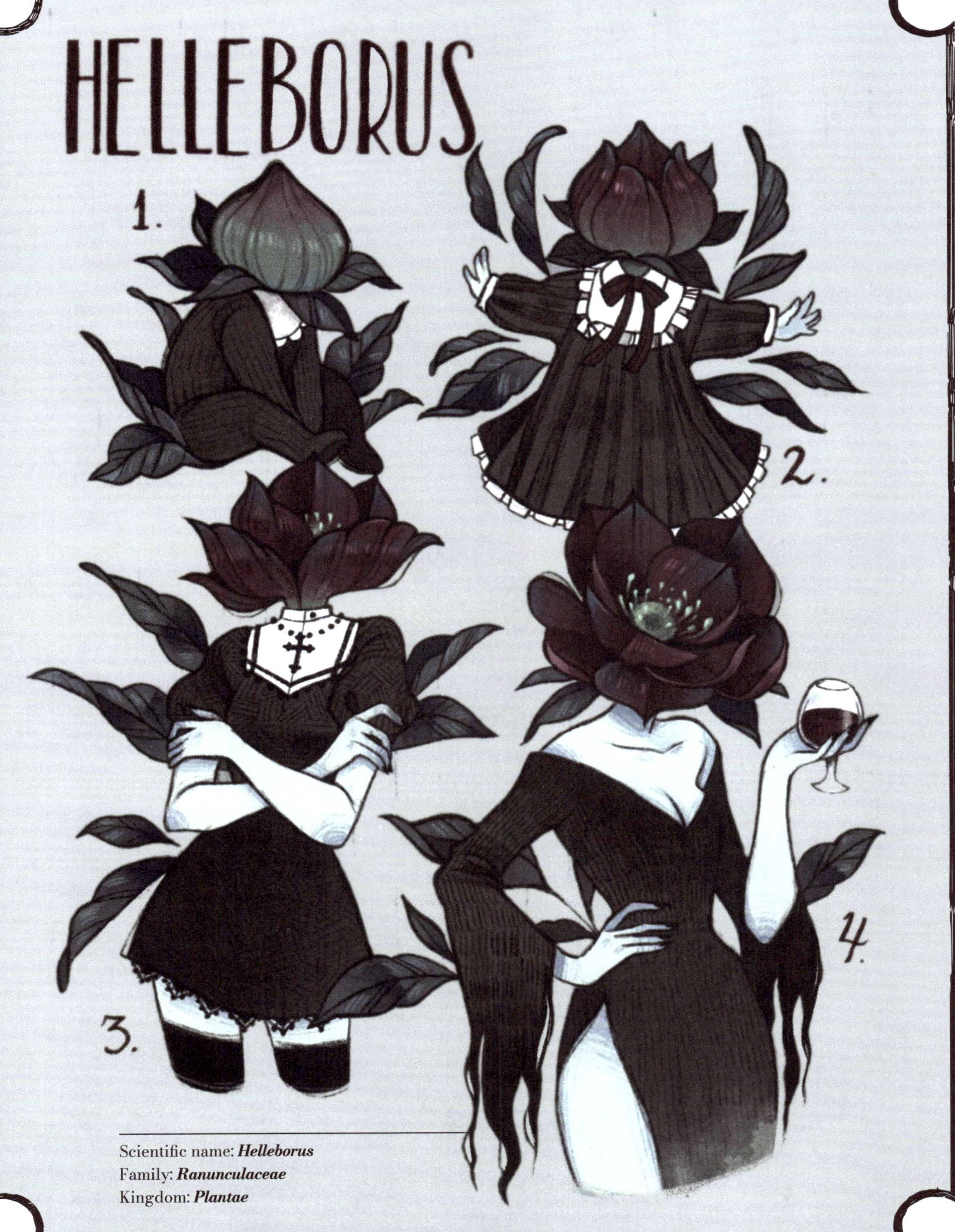

Scientific name: ***Helleborus***
Family: ***Ranunculaceae***
Kingdom: ***Plantae***

> "I find myself using the same two colors over and over – pink and blue"

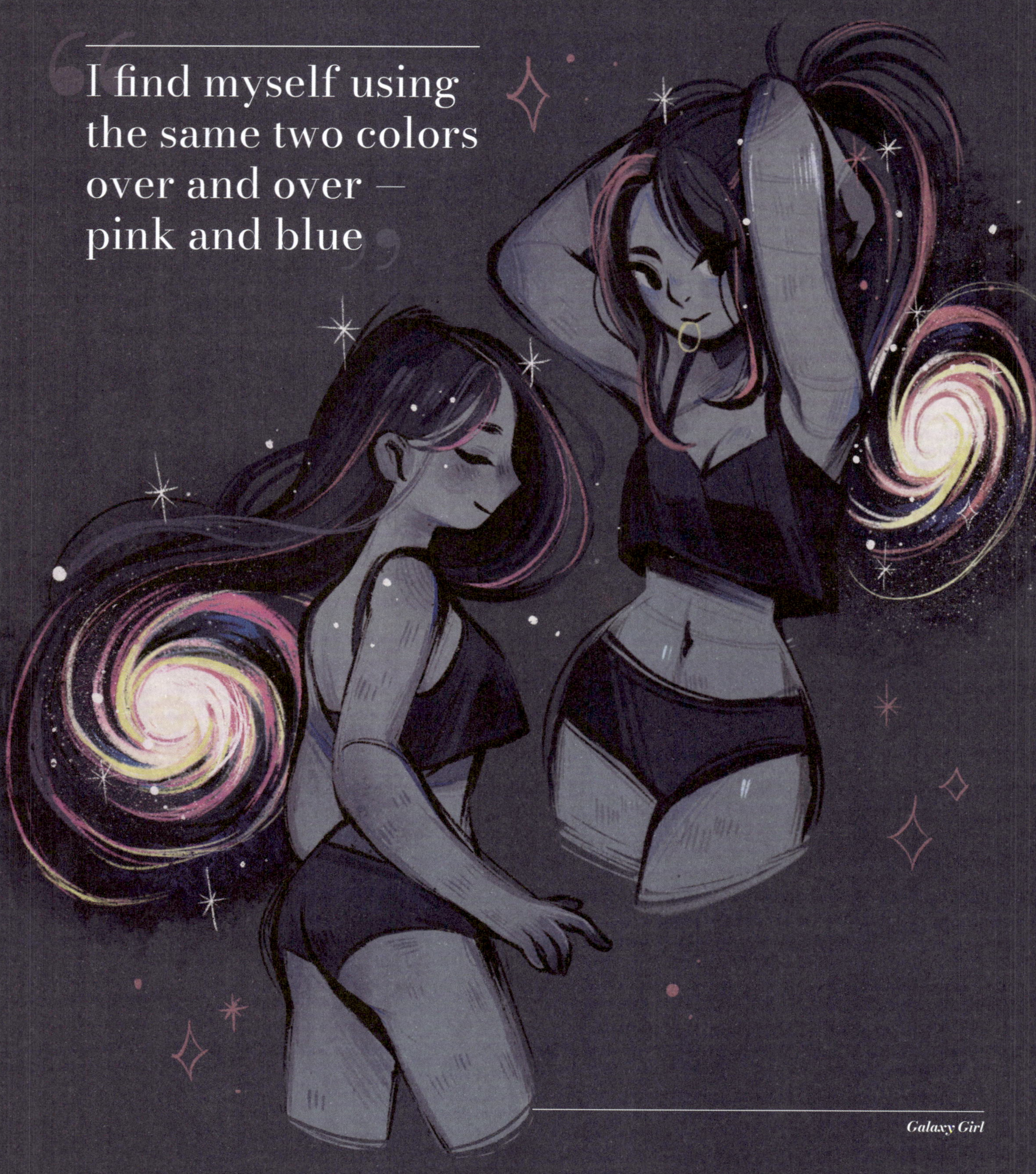

Galaxy Girl

Color

Ahh, colors. So vibrant, evocative, and enchanting, in an endless variety of hues. Did you know that the mantis shrimp possess sixteen color receptors, whereas humans only possess three (blue, yellow, and red)? Still, it's pretty amazing that we're able to discern so many colors, since we're really just witnessing light being reflected off objects.

Despite this, I find myself using the same two colors over and over – pink and blue. I don't know what it is about blue and pink in a combined color scheme, but I am always drawn to them. Bubblegum pink is fun and playful, while blues are deep and celestial – everything I could ever want! I could probably limit myself to exclusively using these two colors for the rest of my life and be fully satisfied. But alas, I know my audience would tire of my art very quickly if I did, so I at least attempt to use other colors in my work besides these two!

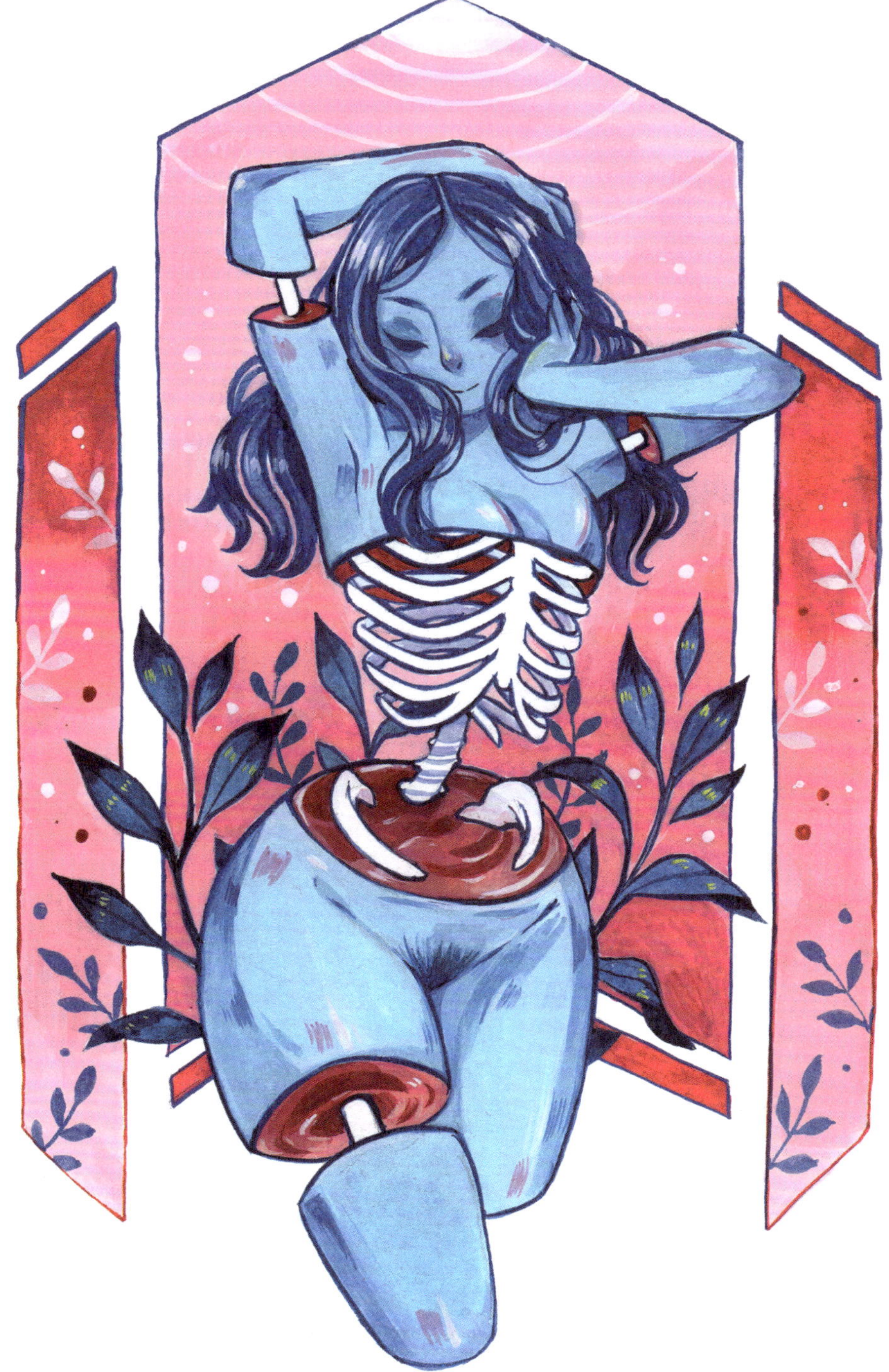

Cut
A gouache painting built around a powerful pink and blue palette.

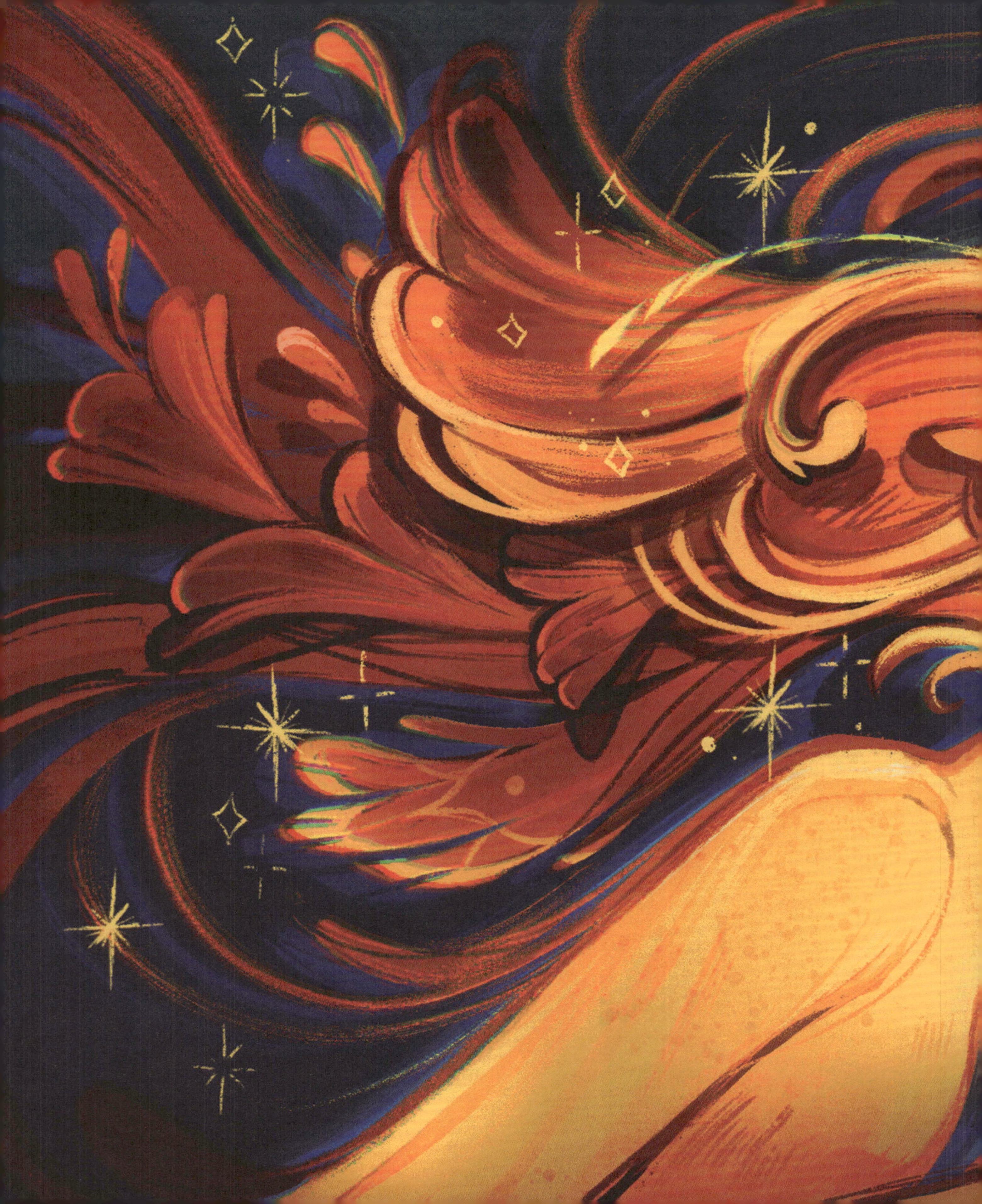

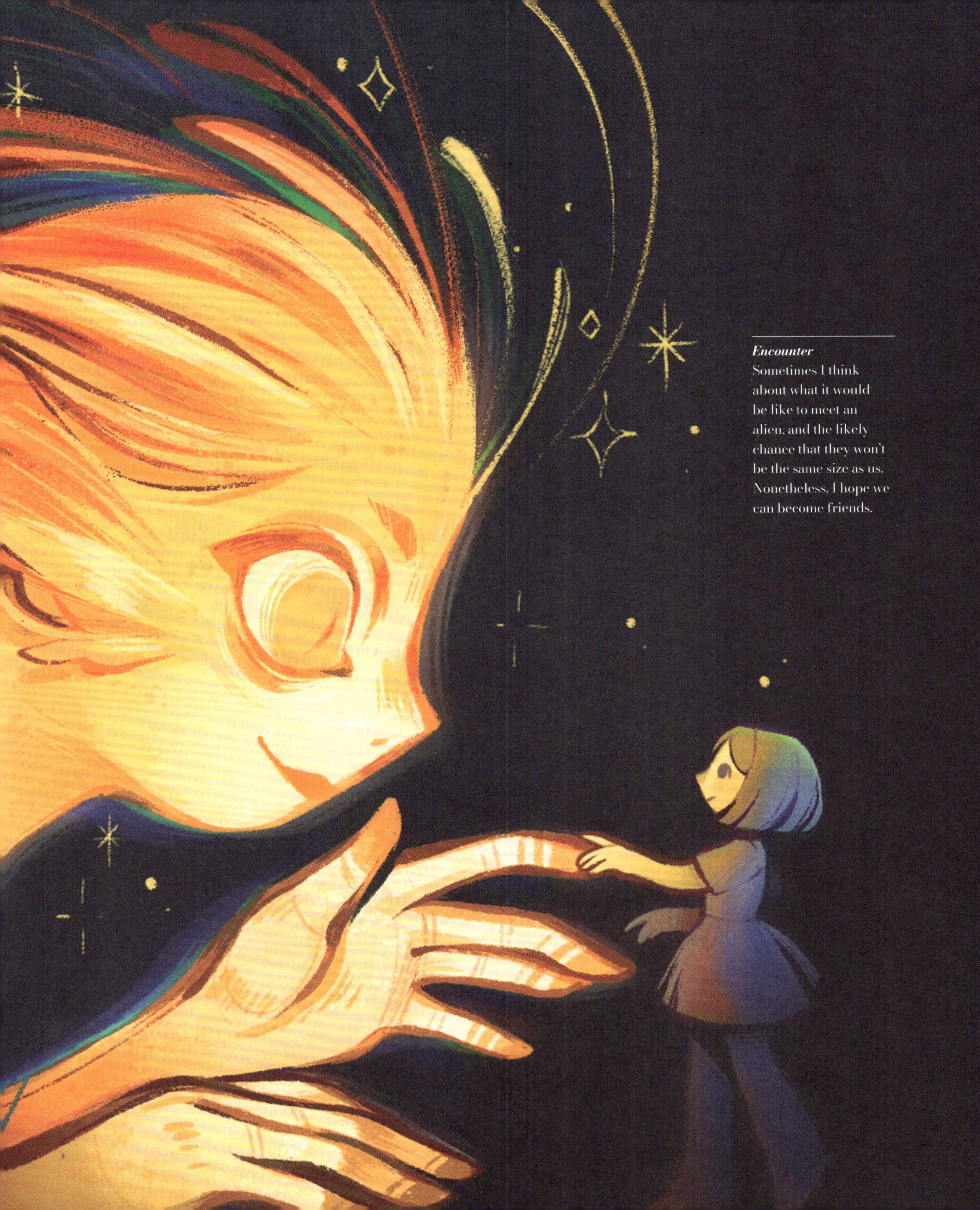

Encounter
Sometimes I think about what it would be like to meet an alien, and the likely chance that they won't be the same size as us. Nonetheless, I hope we can become friends.

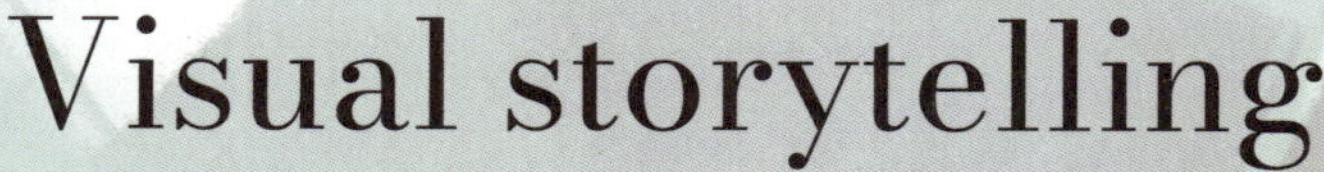

Visual storytelling

My recipe for a compelling art piece is a mixture of skill and storytelling. I like creating art that carries a narrative and that sets a scene in an alternate realm, but I also want it to be beautifully crafted and painted with a palette that sets a nice mood.

The chosen narrative doesn't need to be controversial or especially powerful; it can simply offer a sense of intrigue and wonder to a piece for the viewer to indulge in.

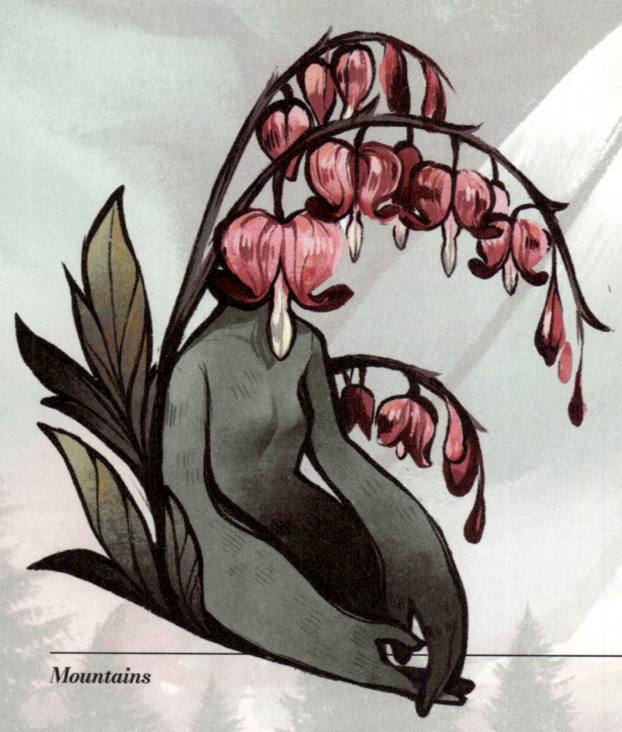

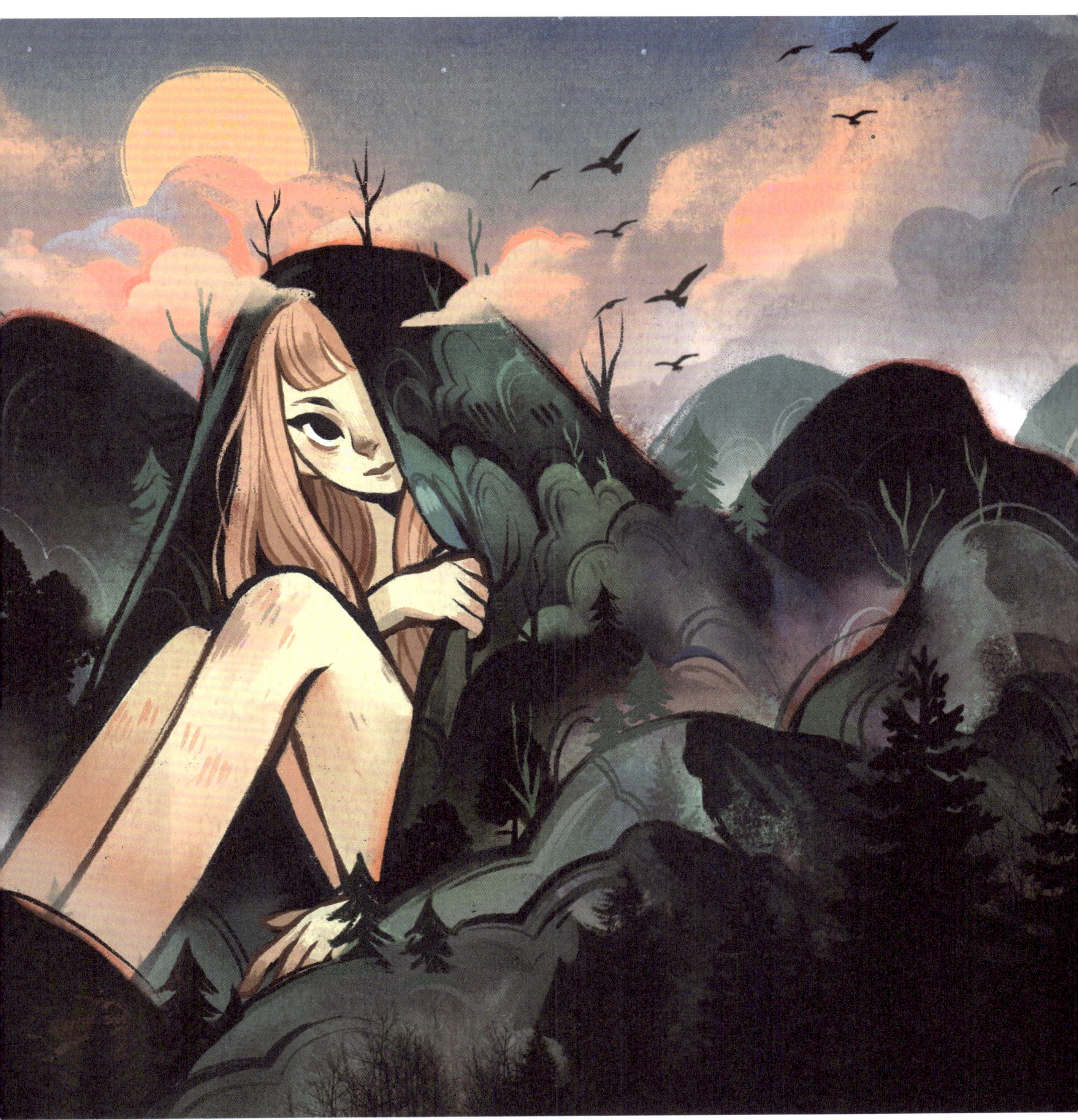

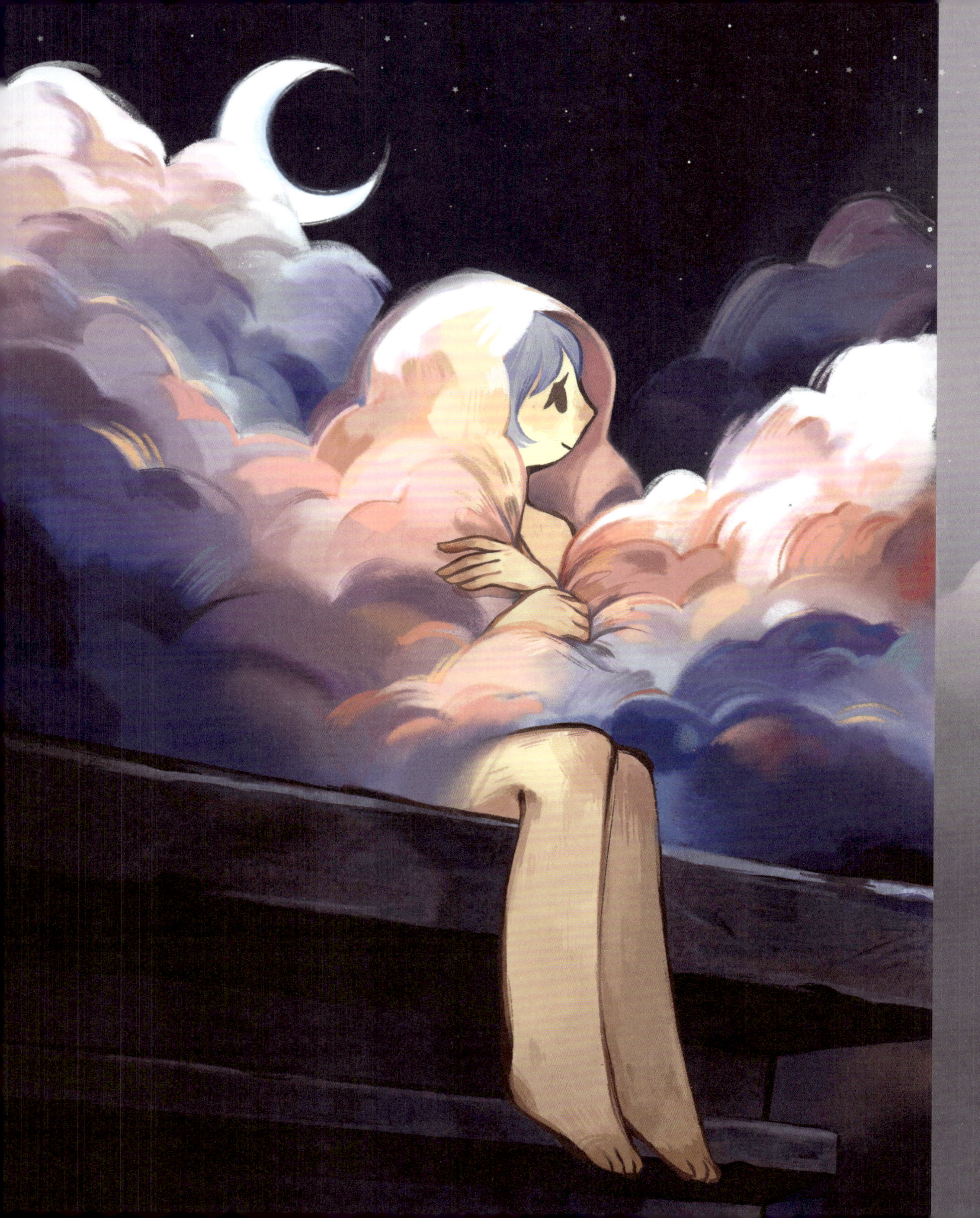

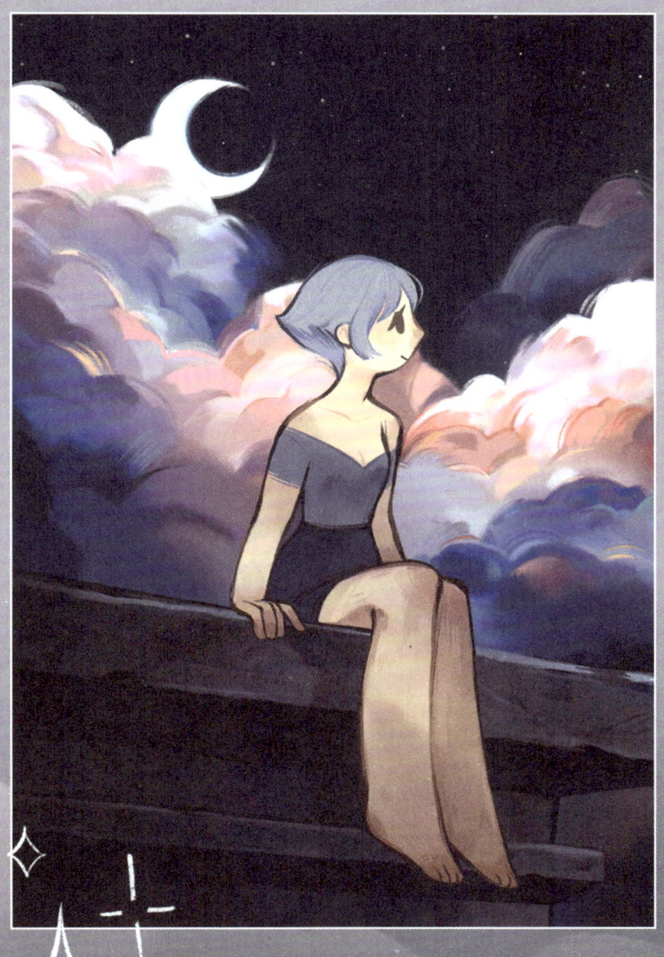

For example, think of a girl sitting on a ledge against a backdrop of fluffy clouds, appearing to be completely serene. It's nice to look at and has a calming vibe to it, but it doesn't offer much further insight into the story.

Now, imagine that same picture but instead of the clouds merely acting as a background, they form a fluffy blanket, wrapped around the main character. Clouds are made out of water vapor and would not make suitable blankets; this makes absolutely no sense and this scenario now appears to be completely bizarre and surreal.

By making simple adjustments you can bend reality to make for a more compelling and fantastical image. Suddenly, there's intrigue and magic amidst that pretty imagery! It's difficult to tell a whole narrative with a single illustration, but it can offer a small insight into an alternative realm; leaving plenty of room for the mind to wander.

Opulence
If I can't think of anything exciting I want to draw, I usually opt for drawing girls. I strongly believe that cute girls in sparkly shirts make the world go around.

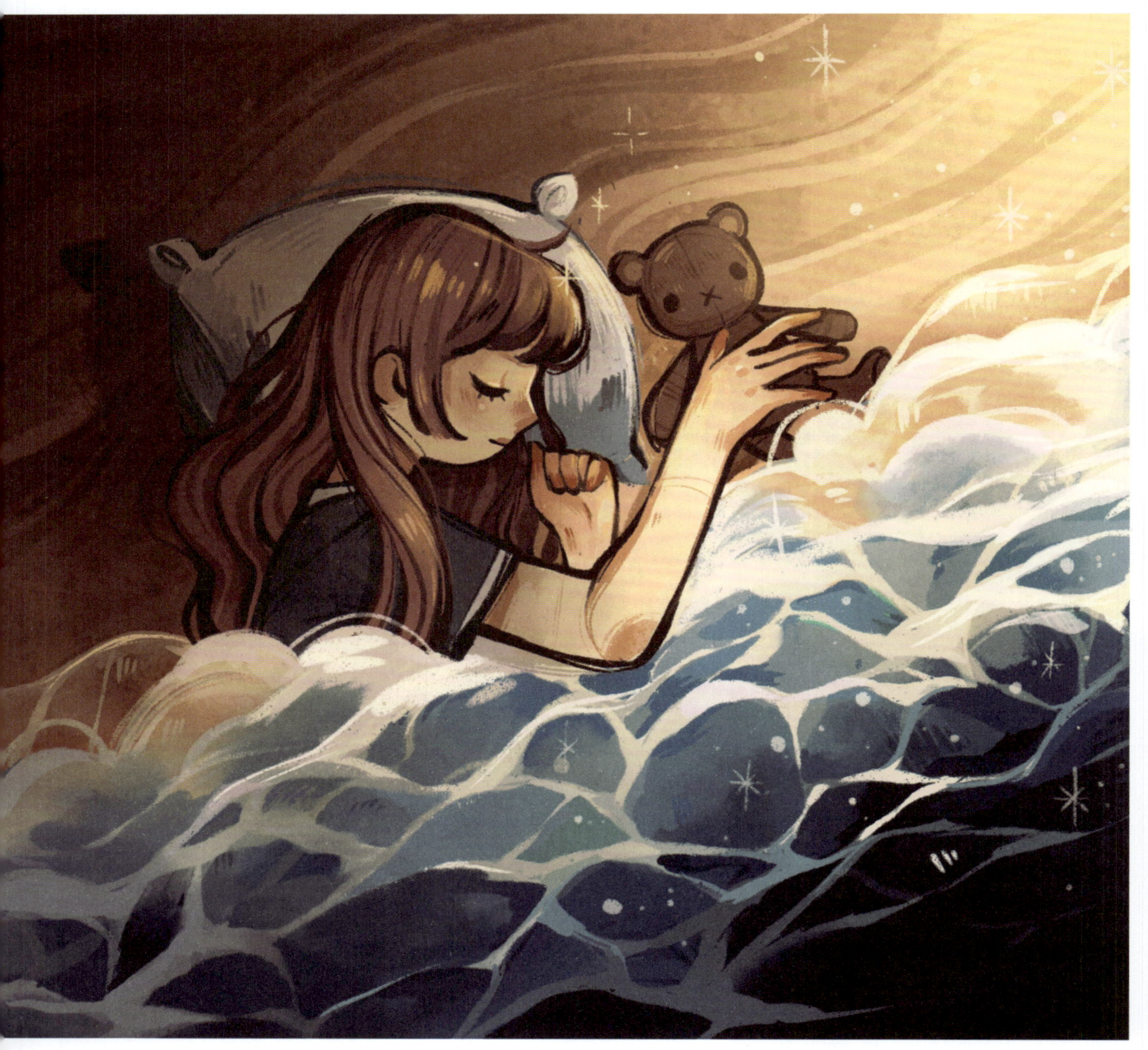

This page: ***Beach Nap***
Opposite page: ***Lava***

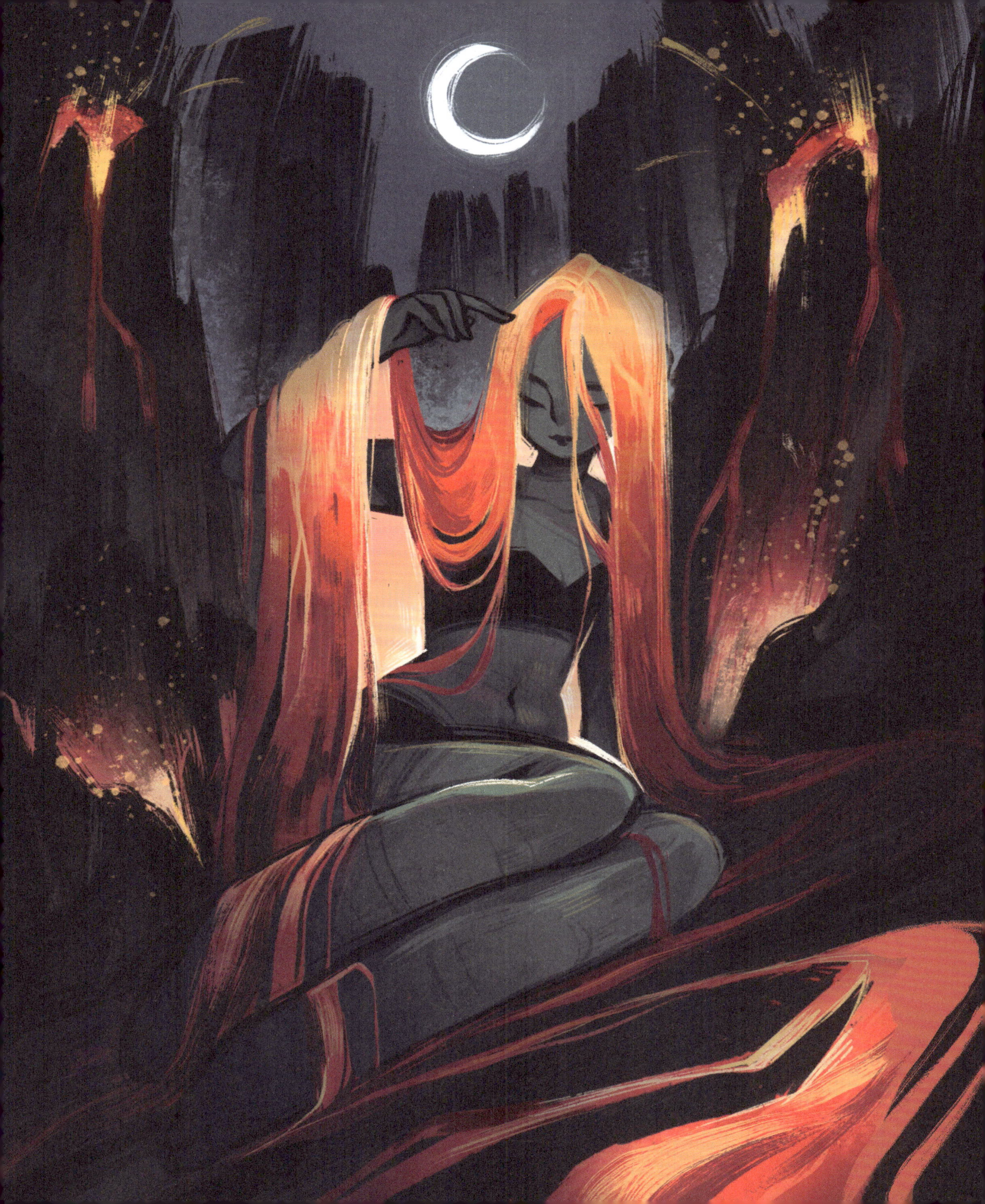

Finding your style language

The most common art-related question I am regularly asked surrounds how an aspiring artist develops their own style. There's a lot of value in an individualistic style because it distinguishes your unique brand, and who doesn't want a style so recognizable that people can instantly tell it's you behind the canvas without being told so?

I believe a key step in discovering your style is to practice drawing without a reference, and to draw as often as you can. Just doodle up a storm whenever you have a chance, and your brain will make all those little connections and shortcuts automatically as you go. As you continually sketch and keep drawing the same things over and over, you'll eventually pick up preferences and quirks along the way.

Of course, it's still important to make studies of the things you want to improve at drawing, and having useful reference material is always an excellent idea. I like to say that you have to be able to have a somewhat good grasp on reality before you can bend and manipulate it to your will!

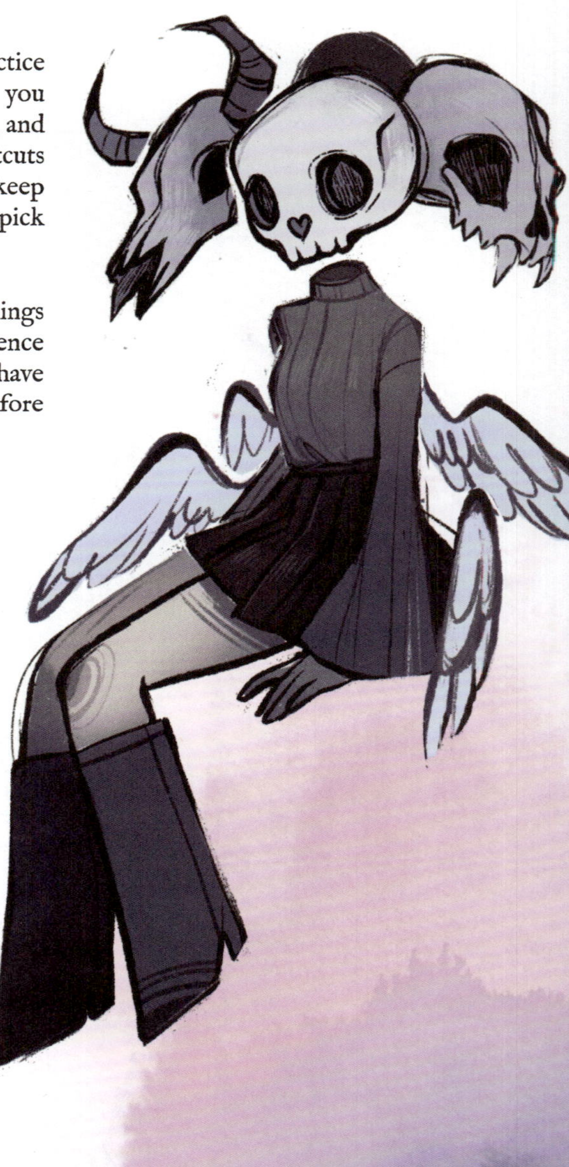

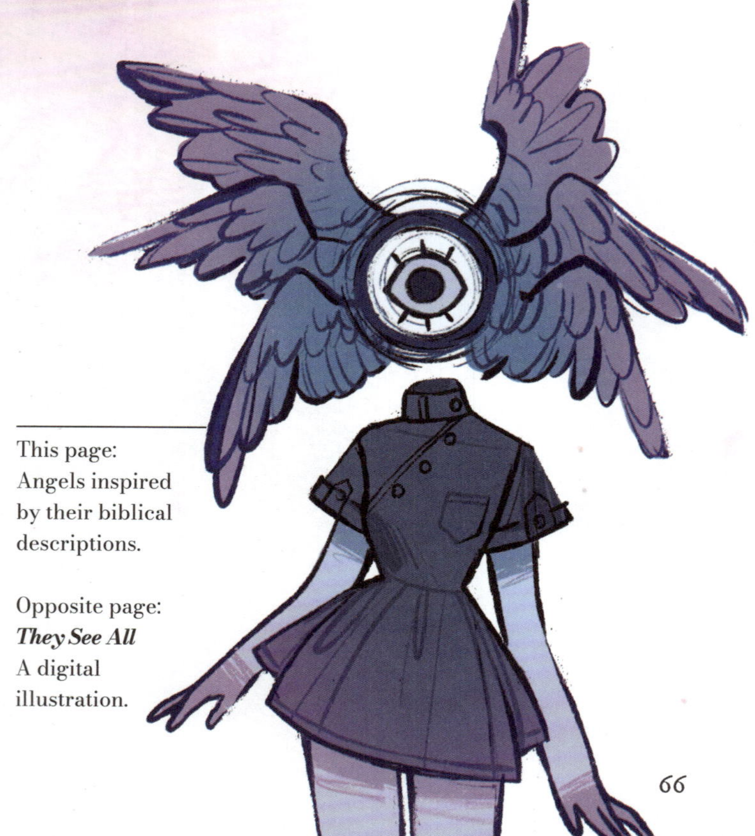

This page: Angels inspired by their biblical descriptions.

Opposite page: ***They See All*** A digital illustration.

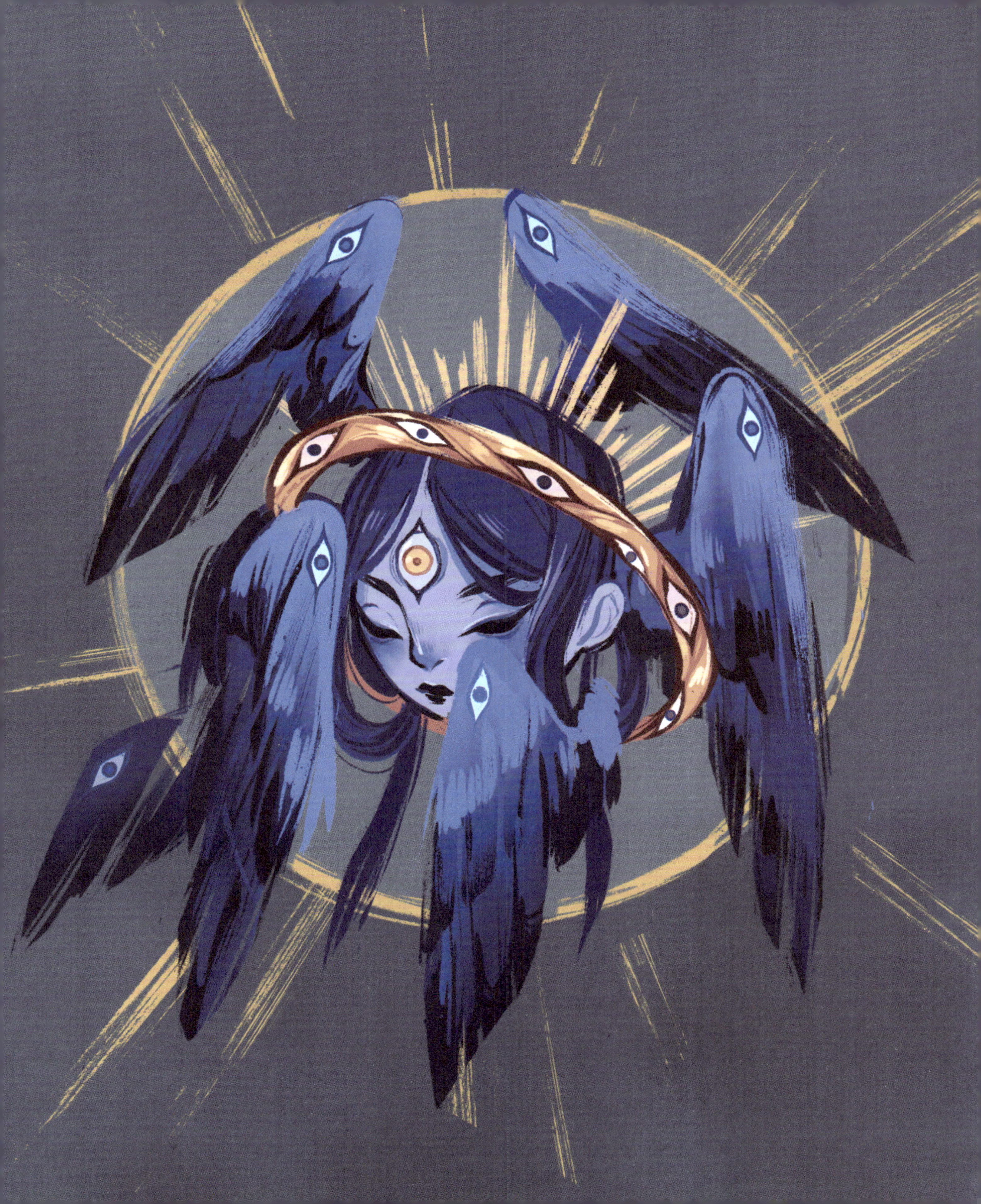

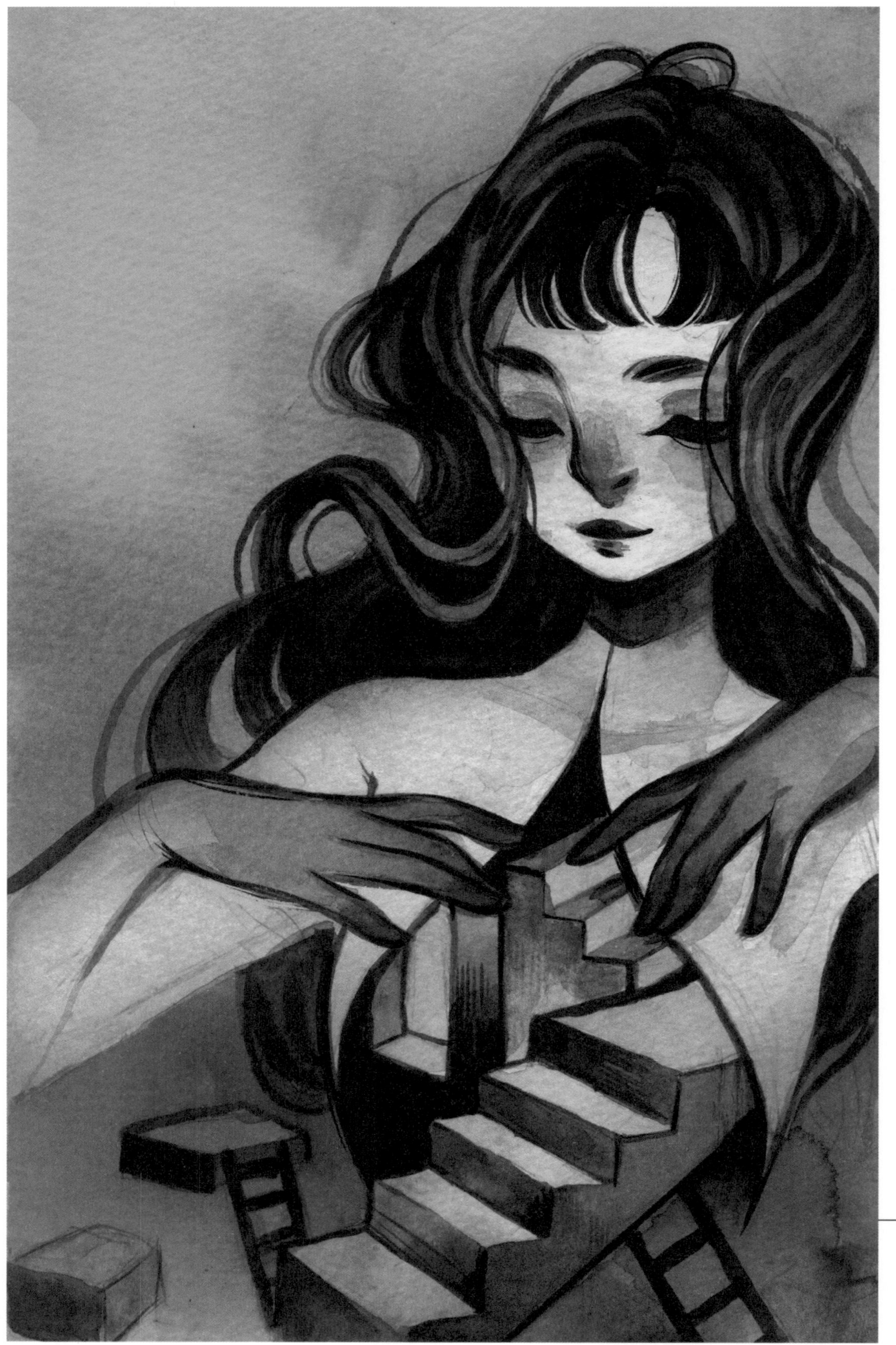

> An art style is a summary of what the artist's abilities and limitations are, and the way they look at the world

I also recommend looking at a lot of different genres of art, and considering which types of stylistic genres you gravitate toward. It's completely fine to be inspired by and take reference from other artists – just make sure you put your own twist on things. I often hear of artists being worried about taking inspiration from other artists because they don't want to steal someone else's ideas, but all artists copy each other in some capacity. When I first started painting more detailed faces, I took a lot of inspiration from others, and I basically mixed and matched various features from a number of different artists. For example, I liked a nose and lips that I saw from other artists, so I borrowed them and adapted them to fit with my style. Copying others is fine in practice, but when creating your own art, remember not to simply replicate someone else's way of drawing – it's important to interpret things in your own way.

An art style is a summary of what the artist's abilities and limitations are, and the way they look at the world. It's as individual as your personality or handwriting. It's not something to intentionally choose, but rather something to be discovered through finding little things you like and tendencies you lean toward, which eventually culminate into a unique artistic taste. A top tip from me is to not rush into selecting an art style for yourself just for the sake of acquiring one, because you will needlessly put yourself in a box. At the start of your artistic journey, you are in your experimental phase, which is a really fun place to be, so embrace it! It's also absolutely fine to have multiple ways of drawing and to dabble in a variety of styles, so there's no need to limit yourself to just one way of creating. I tend to draw differently depending on the mediums I use – I find that the limitations set by the medium very much affect my final results.

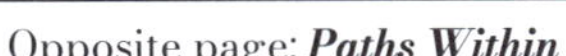

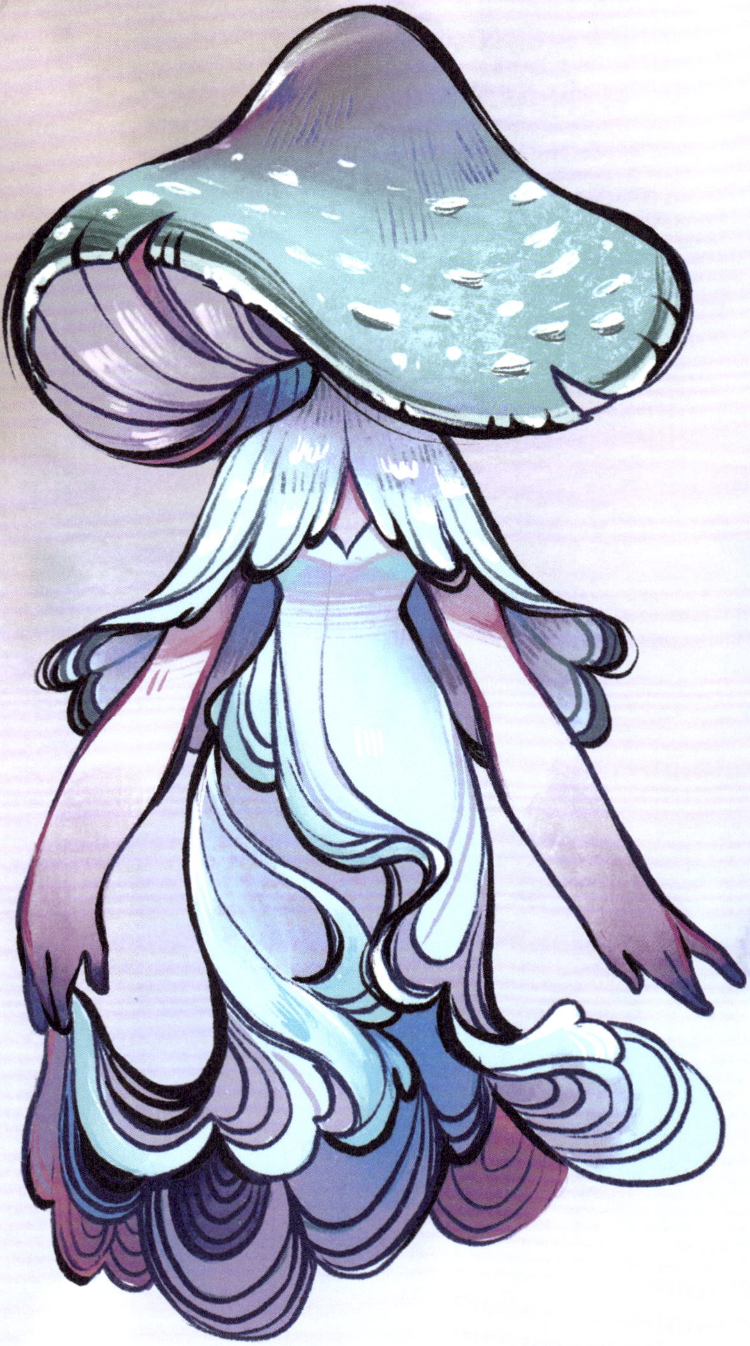

Opposite page: ***Paths Within***
A watercolor painting. Inside every human there's a metaphorical room filled with trapdoors and ladders. That's why it's difficult to steal a person's heart – there are too many steps to climb!

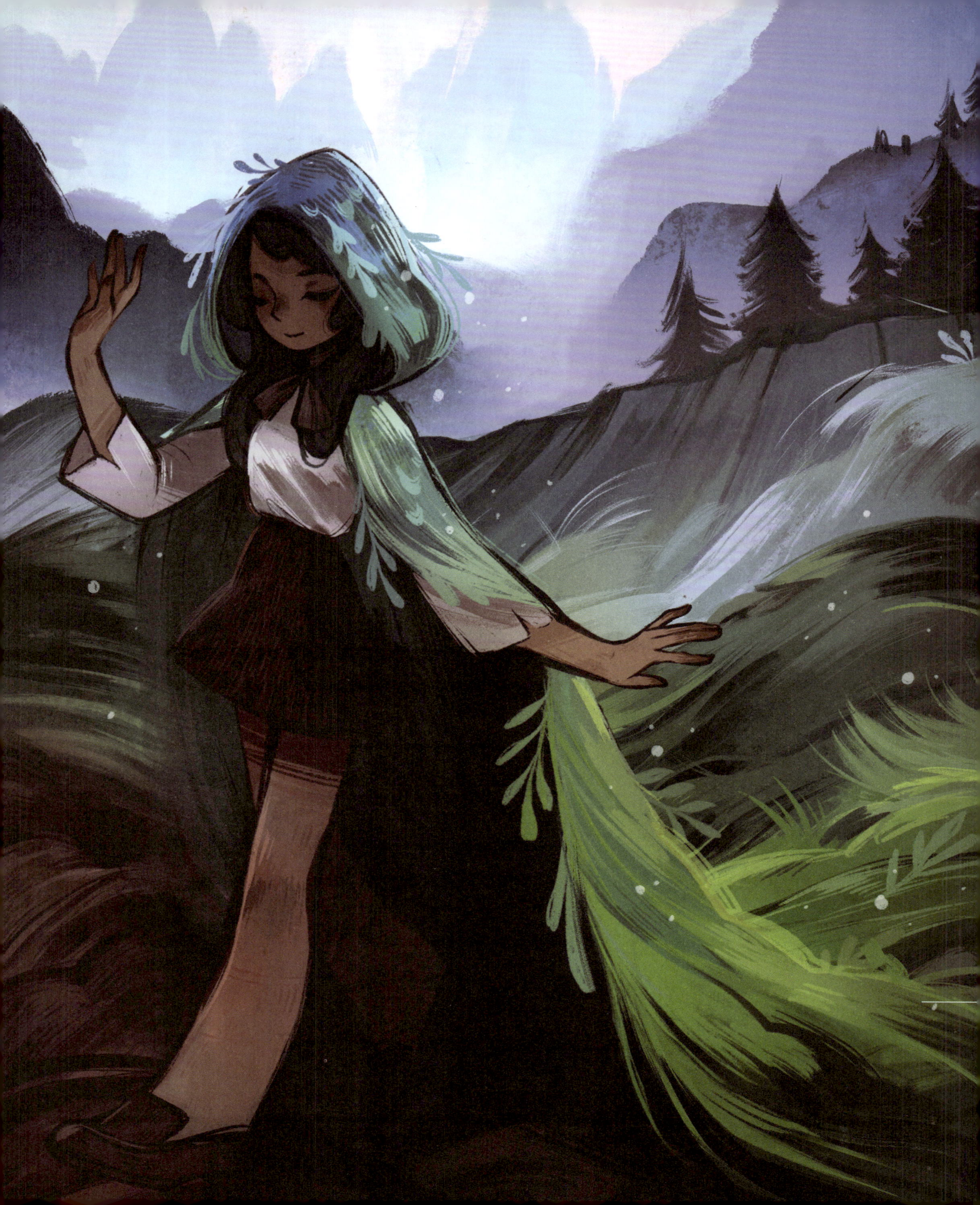

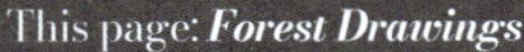

This page: ***Forest Drawings***
I felt that this forest was lacking something and looked a little bit bland. I edited the color scheme and added a few sparkles as a final adjustment, resulting in a much more exciting image. It just goes to show what a bit of editing magic can accomplish!

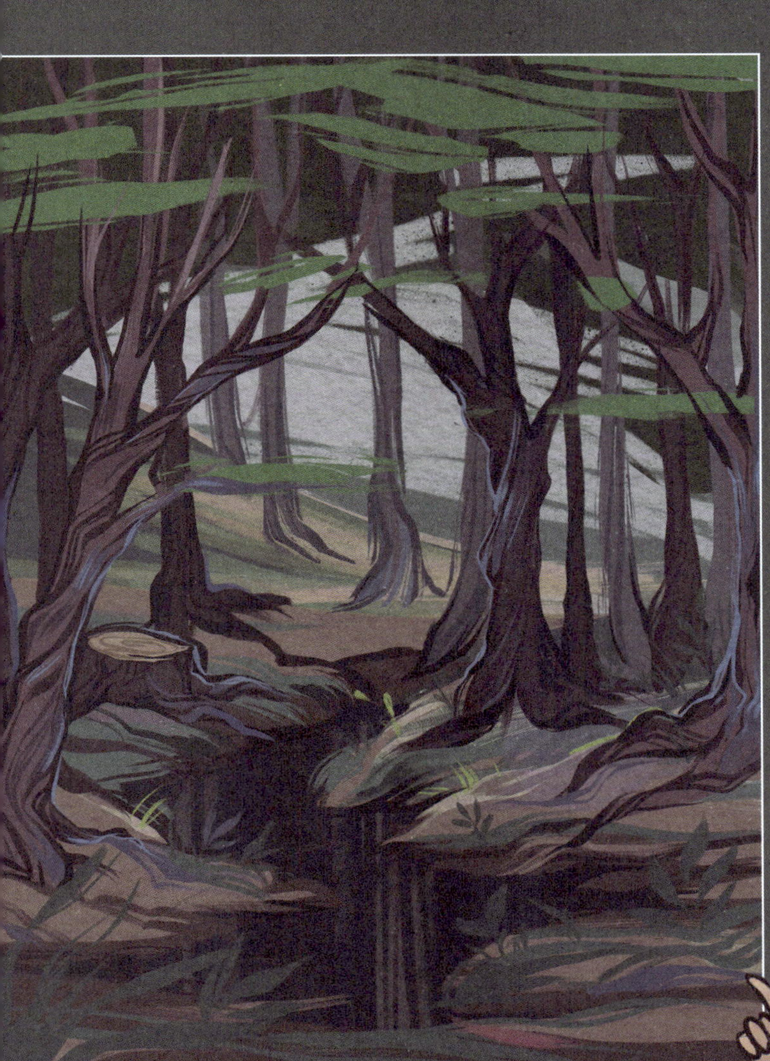

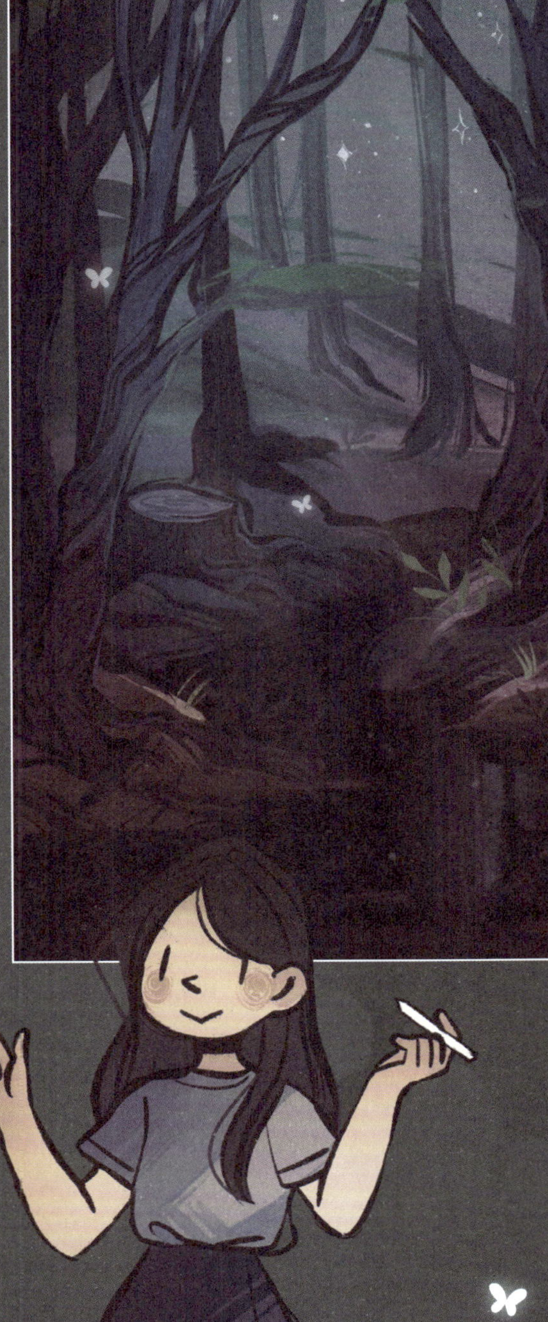

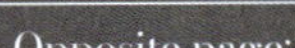

Opposite page:
Wherever She Goes, the Grass Will Grow
A young girl walks through rolling hills, covering the barren land with fields of green as she goes. She's taking the job title of landscape artist to a whole new level.

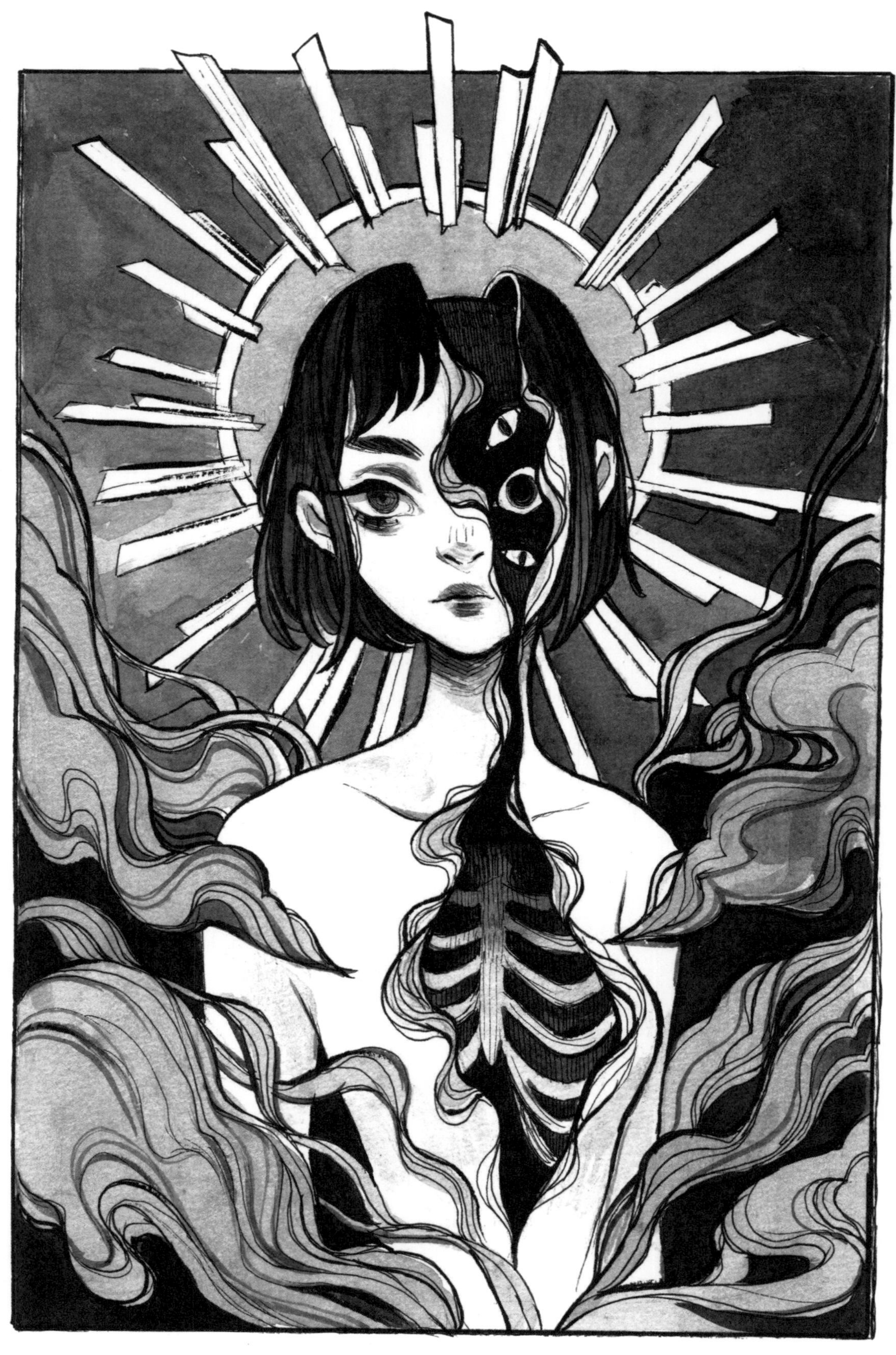

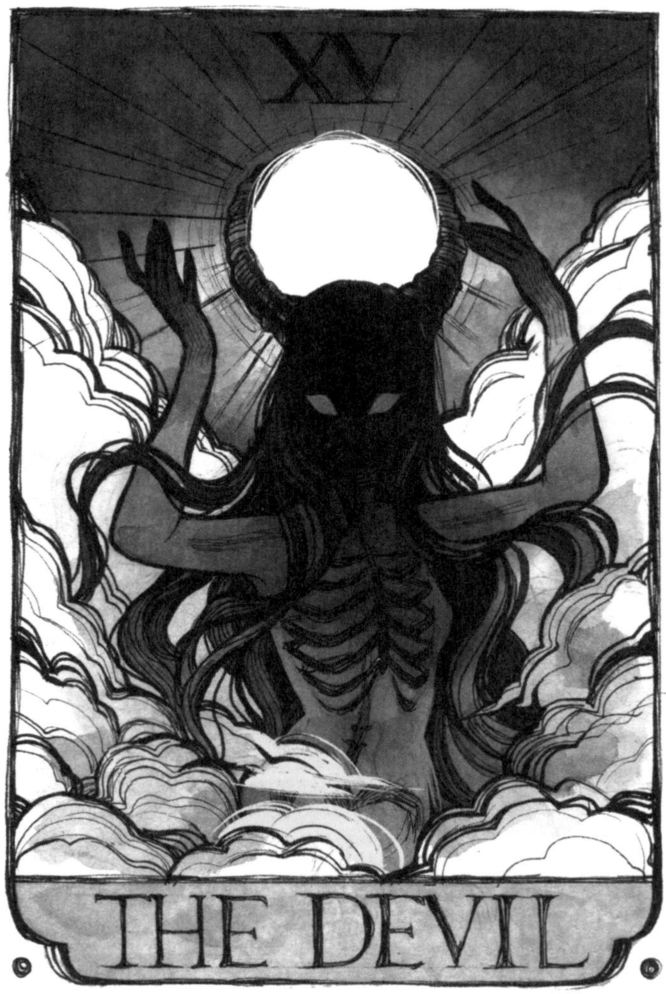

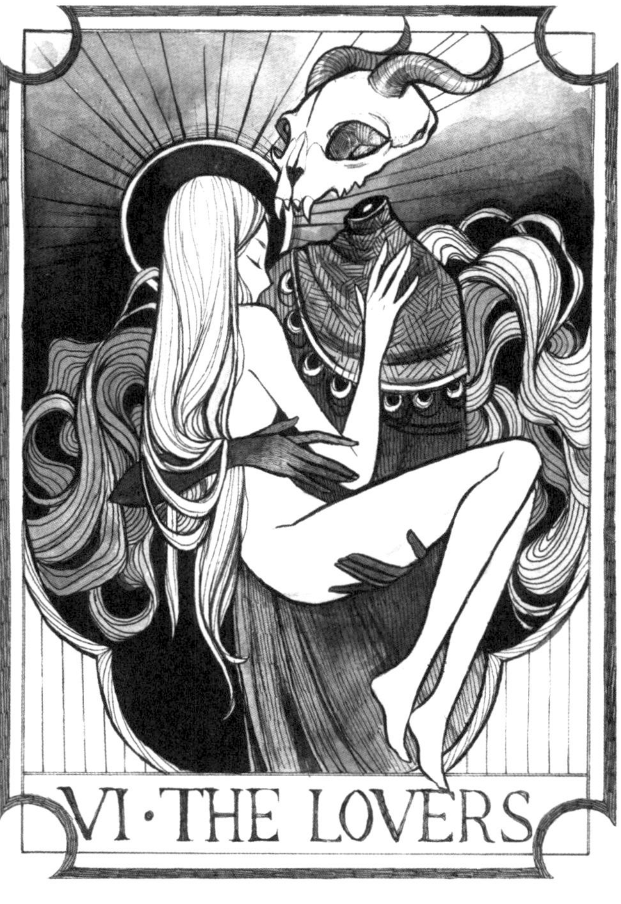

Attempting originality

I have always been of the opinion that creativity can't exist in a vacuum, since almost everything has already been made in one way or another. Really, there's no use in trying to create something groundbreaking and completely new just for the sake of it. Instead, I try focusing on taking an existing subject and reframing it in a new way. Take a beloved concept, and look at it from a new perspective. I've made many pieces inspired by tarot card designs, which of course isn't a brand-new concept, but there are still countless ways to interpret them. Putting your own spin on existing ideas can generate fresh and unique takes.

Top left:
The Devil
Above:
VI. The Lovers

Opposite page:
What Hides Beneath

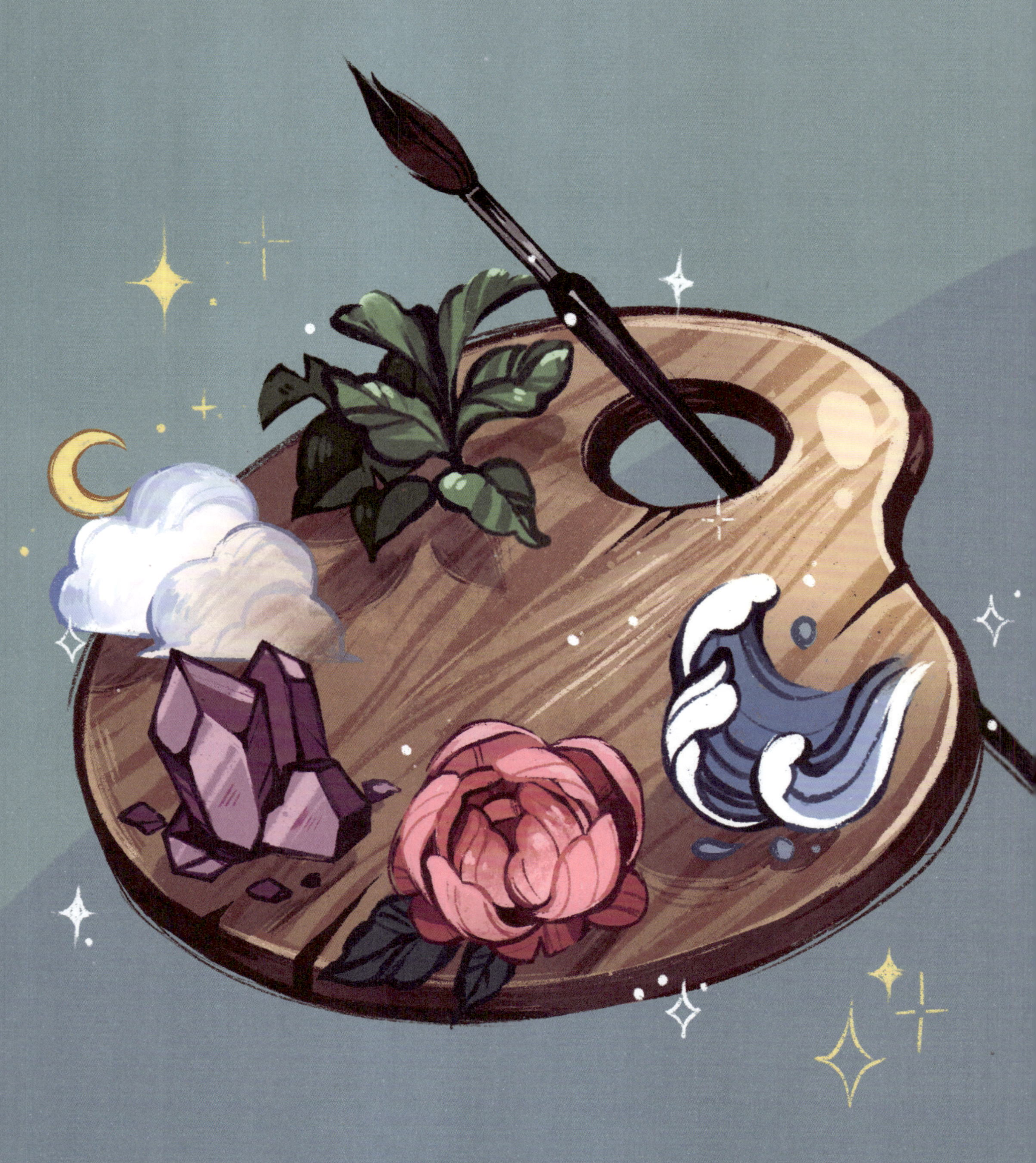

Creative Process

The starting point

As I wish to portray otherworldly themes in my art, I start the creative process by immersing myself in fiction. Books, movies, art, anything really. Just seeing the way other people find ways to augment reality inspires me to find ways to do it myself.

I especially love stories, since you have to picture the scenery for yourself rather than rely on visual imagery. At times, I find reality to be pretty mundane, and so I try to spend as much time as possible in the realms of fantasy and science fiction. I guess I prefer the reflection of life rather than life itself. Escapism at its finest!

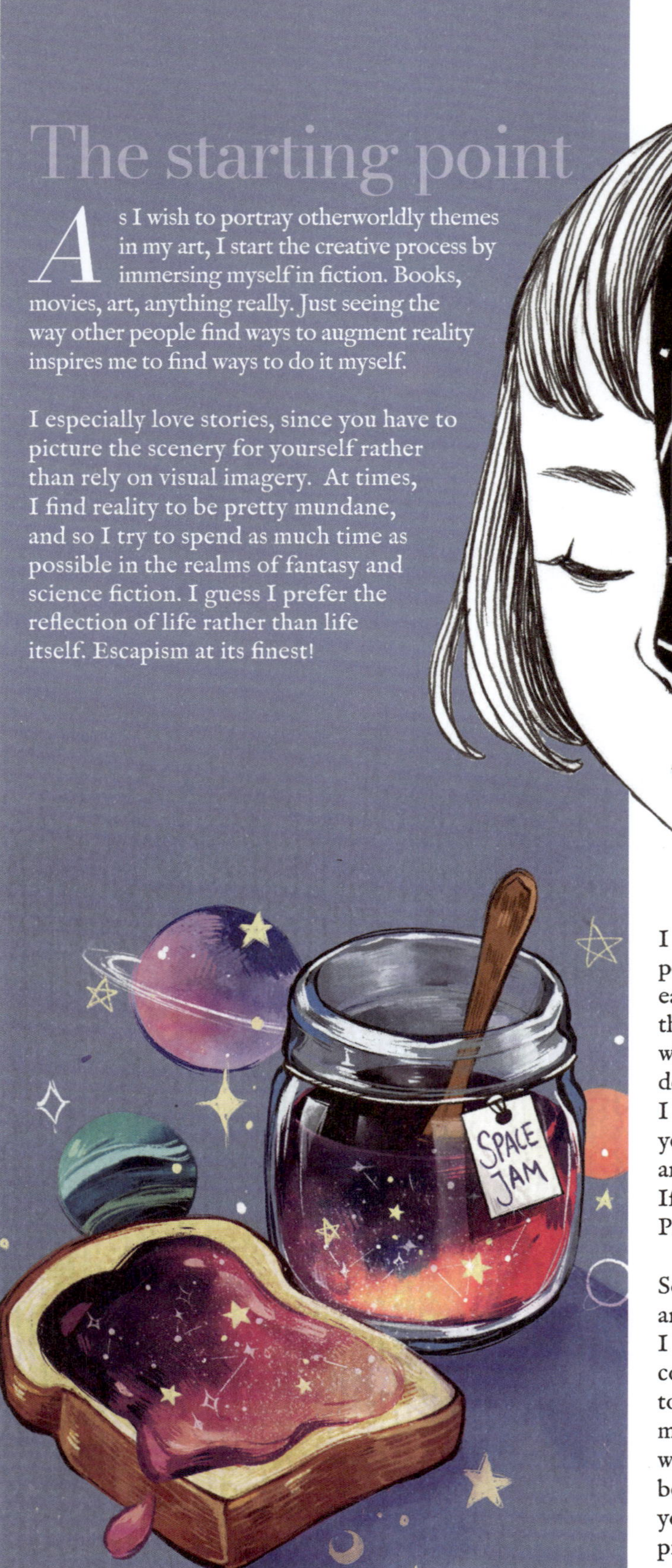

I begin an illustration with a visual story I want to portray. I usually write down random scribblings in the early hours of the morning, but I can't always decipher them the day after. Many of my ideas pop into my head while I fall asleep. Sometimes I decide not to write them down thinking I'll remember them the next day, but I never do. I often wonder what gems I've lost over the years. Once my ideas are written down, I sketch poses and layouts until everything starts to work in harmony. If I need additional inspiration and references, I browse Pinterest for some quick ideas.

Something I wish someone had told me as a younger artist is that ideas are cheap, and meant to be spent. I used to ponder over a concept for weeks, scared to commit it to paper because I didn't feel skilled enough to effectively execute it. However, I now find that the more I draw and "spend" my ideas, the more come my way. I encourage any budding artist to do the same, because even if the final results don't look as good as you'd hoped, you will have learned so much from the process. Creativity is to some extent a learned skillset, and you can vastly improve just by daring to explore.

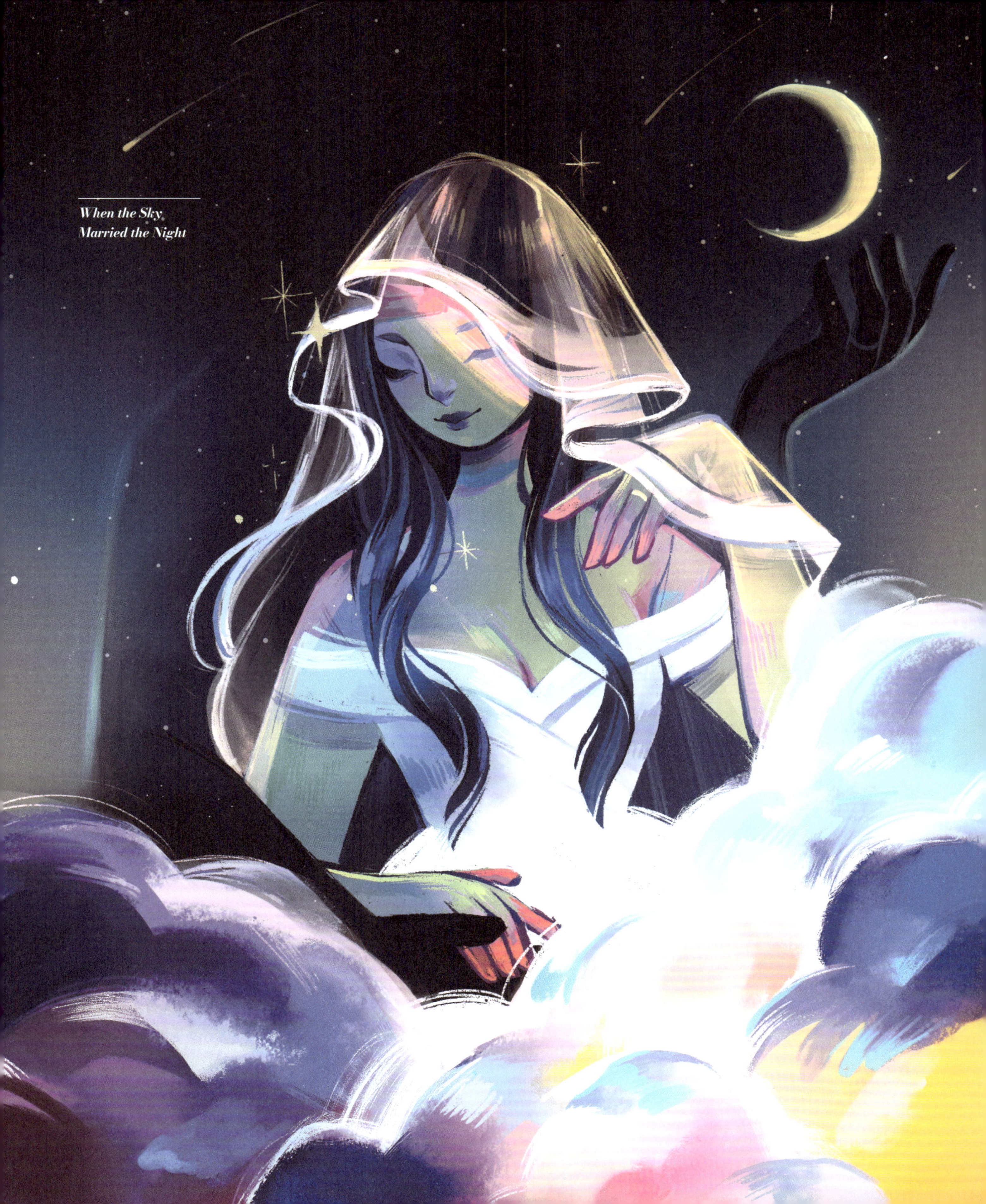
When the Sky
Married the Night

The benefits of being your own worst critic

One thing that keeps me practicing is the hope to minimize the friction between conception and execution. The images I want to draw always look slightly better inside my head, but the more I practice, the better I become at capturing my visions. Nothing is ever perfect and I always manage to find flaws, but I take what I have learned from each piece on to the next. As tedious as it is to be your own worst critic, I do believe it's healthy in small doses.

For example, if you were to experience a constant state of satisfaction with your artwork, you wouldn't feel the need to push forward and challenge your ways. Being critical of your work may not feel comfortable, but the dissatisfaction can be useful in helping to uncover the aspects of your creative practice you could improve. You have to be able to identify your mistakes in order to correct them!

Sometimes I find myself feeling excessively critical about my own work, which pushes me into a negative thought spiral of fearing I've suddenly lost my ability to make good art. But, in reality, it's due to my brain taking a leap toward becoming more analytical and better at evaluating what looks good, hence why I suddenly start to notice all the errors I had difficulty spotting before. Eventually, with practice, my art-making abilities align with the way I evaluate art, and that's a fabulous feeling! It feels like the real-life equivalent of leveling up.

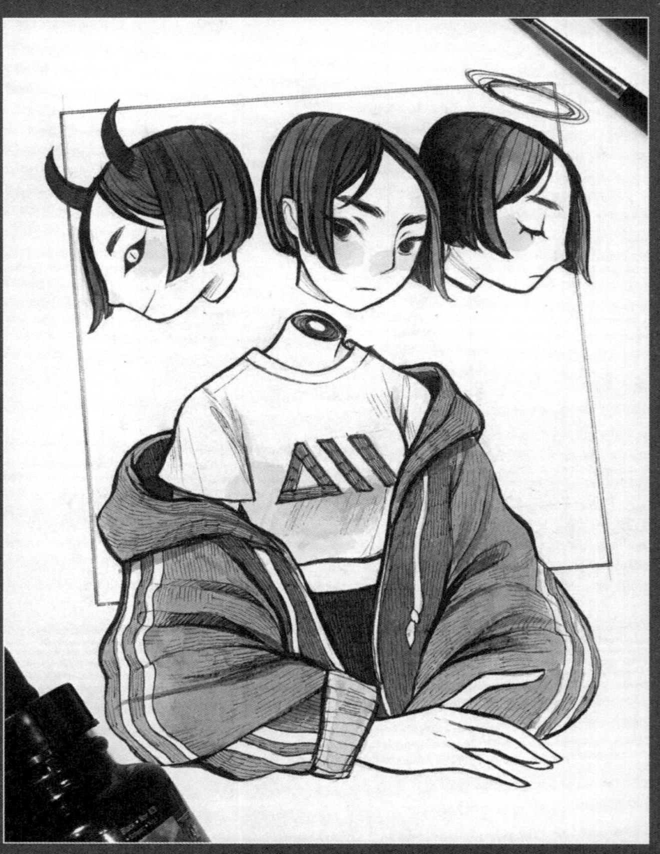

This page: ***Influences***
Created for Inktober 2019.

Opposite page: ***Summoning***
Created for Inktober 2018.

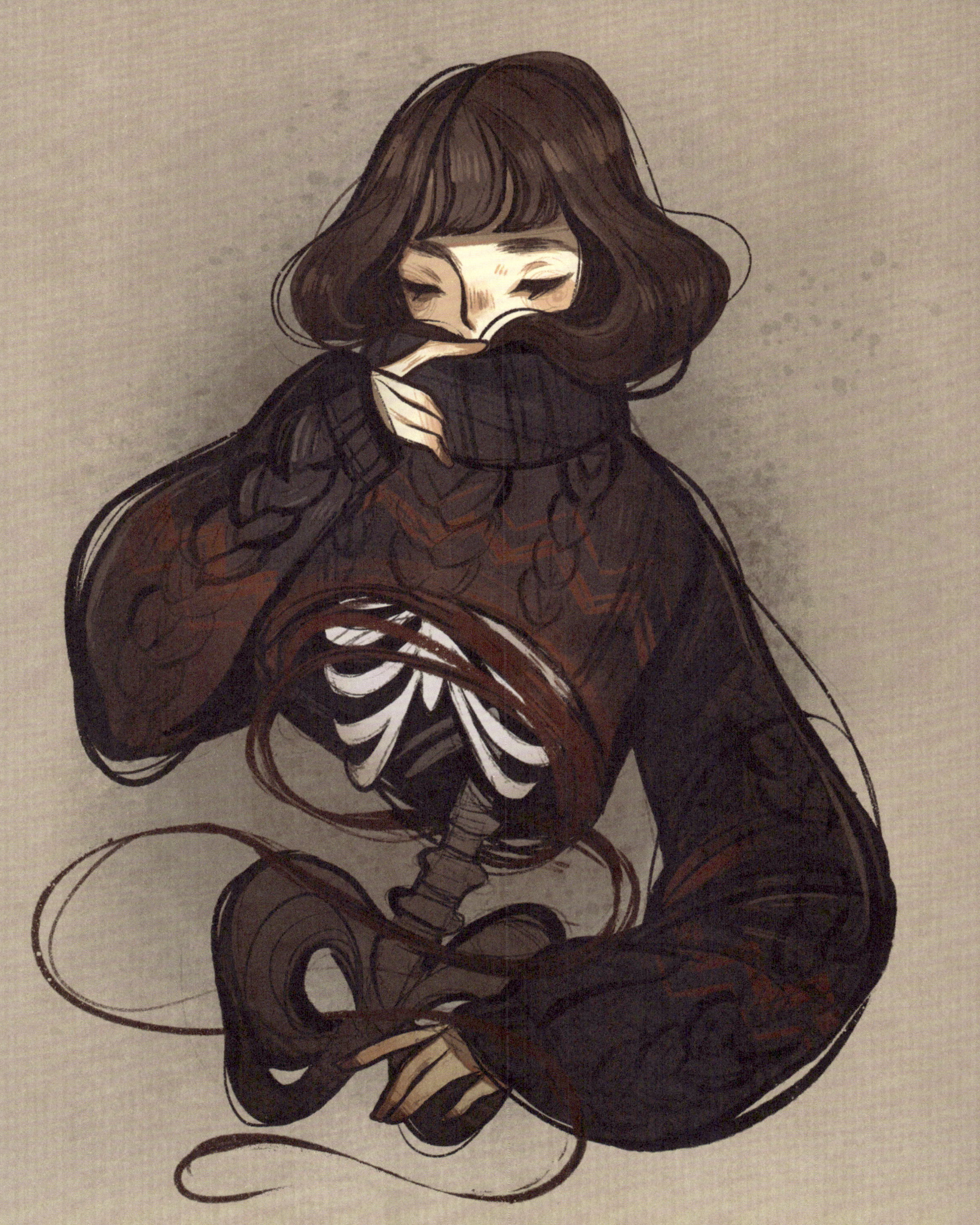

Study of a Pixie

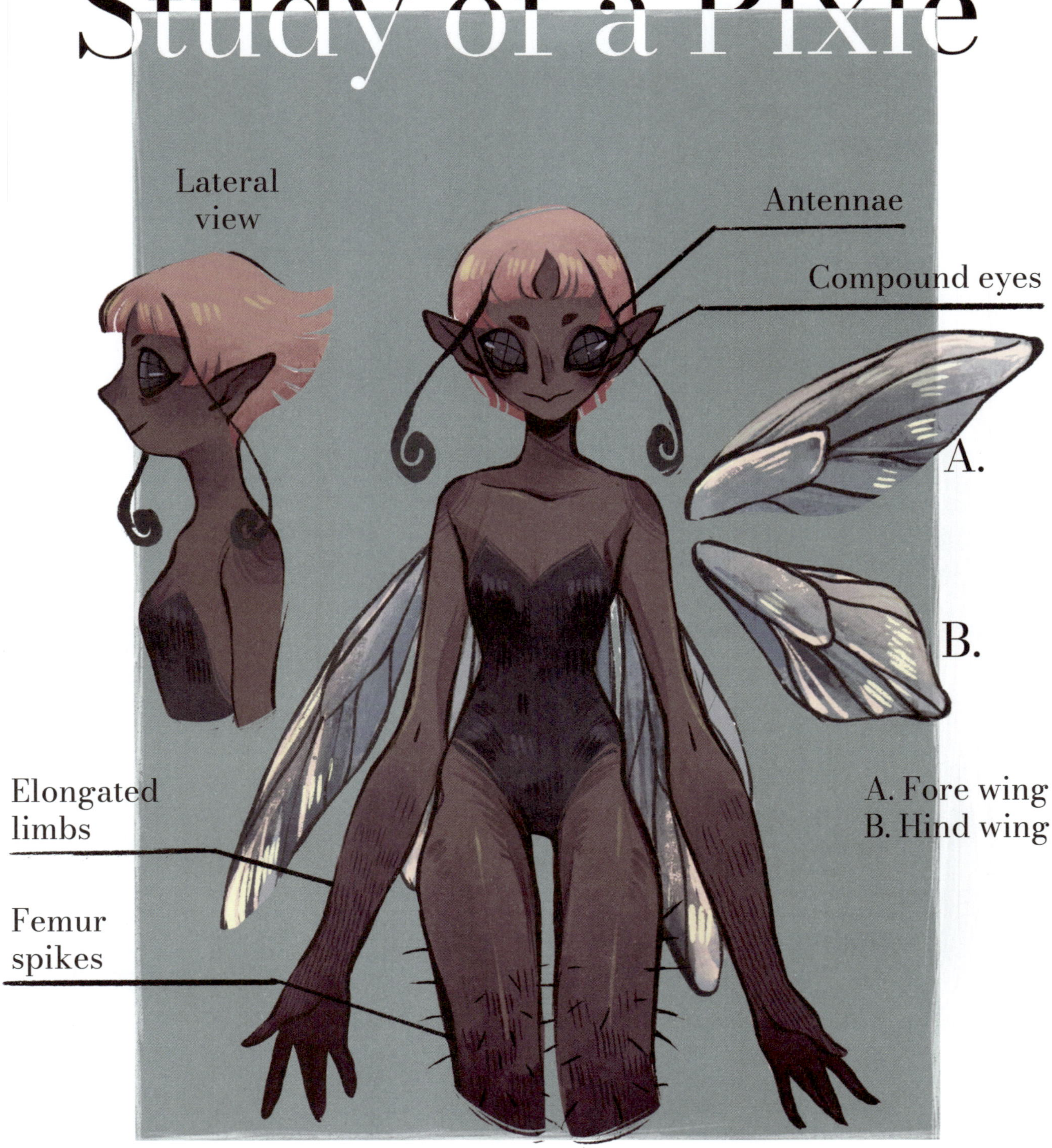

Lateral view

Antennae

Compound eyes

A.

B.

Elongated limbs

Femur spikes

A. Fore wing
B. Hind wing

Pixies are tiny humanoid creatures with mischievous dispositions. Notorious pranksters, their favorite pastimes are leading travelers astray and frightening young children.

Tackling art block

When I feel void of inspiration and completely drained on the creativity front, I try to let go of the pressure of creating something new and instead focus my energy on drawing things I'm comfortable with. Basically, I just keep the engines running until I've refueled!

During those times I might spend the day drawing hands or flowers – elements I've drawn so many times I can almost work on autopilot. I find that it helps to go back to basics in order to regain control and confidence in myself and my abilities. It's easy to get stuck inside your own head during art blocks and become overwhelmed by the feeling that you're not good enough, so I find it helps to just draw the things I like and stay within my comfort zone.

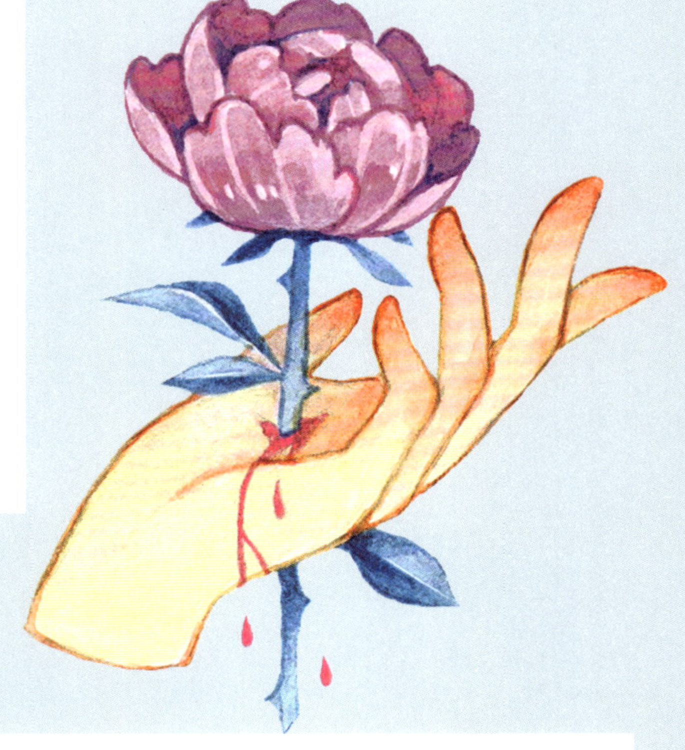

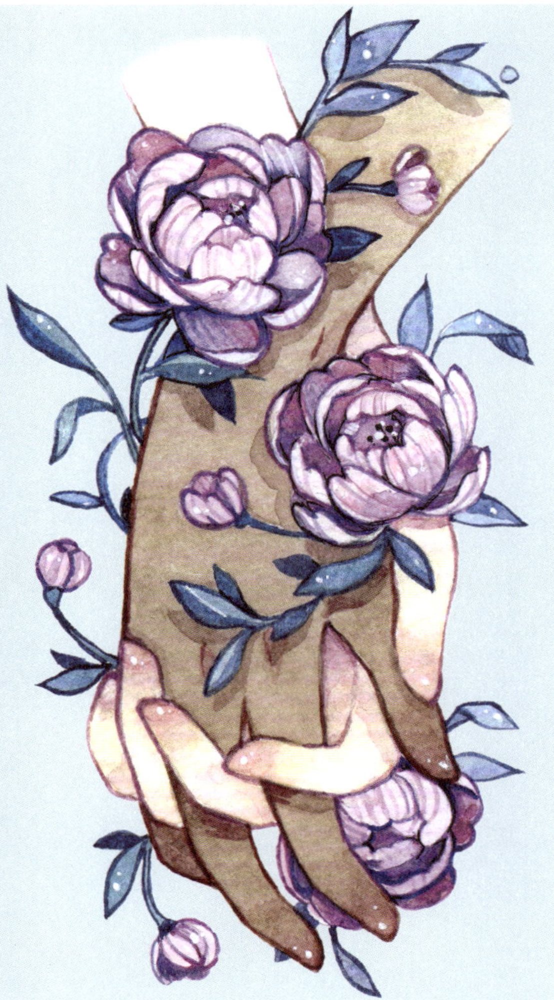

We know that in order to improve as much as possible, it's useful to challenge ourselves and attempt new things, but what can be lost in the process is the enjoyment. So, it's great to take a vacation from self-improvement and just indulge in some alternative fixations every now and then.

I do experience moments where I am just so fed up with drawing that I can't look at a piece of paper without wanting to tear it apart, and during those days it's best to just let it go. Creating art is an expression, and it's inevitably going to be emotionally taxing on any artist to some extent. Instead, I spend my time performing a completely unrelated hobby, such as hiking or cooking. It's healthy to engage in activities that empty the mind, because often that's when the most random and creative ideas emerge.

Alternatively, I might just pour myself a glass of red wine, slump into the sofa for several hours, and try to figure out where my ability to draw went to hide! Follow your intuition and pay attention to what your body tells you that you need.

Overcoming the fear of sharing artwork

It's strange to think that I now make a living through sharing my artwork to a global audience, because I used to be extremely averse to the idea of other people seeing my work. I would experience an intense feeling of dread whenever anyone looked at my sketchbook, because it felt like an exposed expression of my soul. There's something deeply personal about an artist's sketchbook; it's like a visual diary.

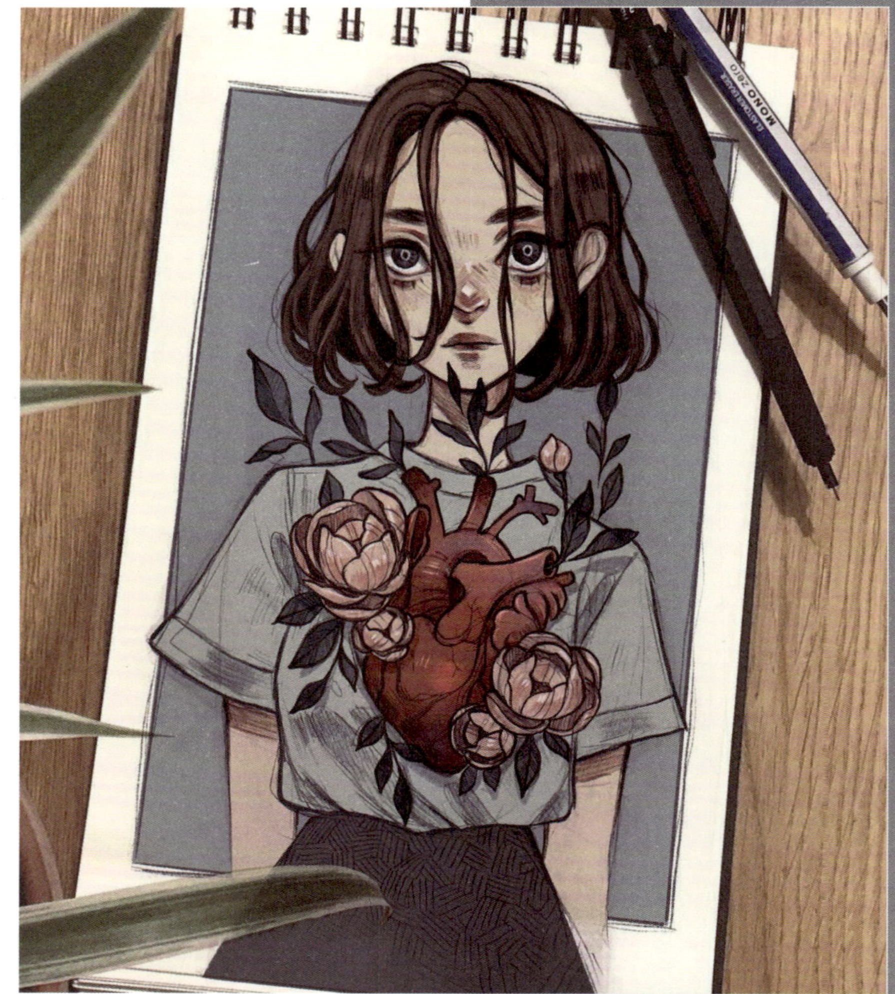

I became more comfortable with the idea of sharing my work once I became active on Instagram – it's just so much easier to showcase your creations online to an anonymous crowd rather than in person with friends and family. It's also easier to take on criticism when you can hide behind a screen. I still really dislike having my artwork observed when I'm there in person; there's just something about having to bear witness to a person looking through a physical manifestation of your soul that makes my skin crawl.

It was actually my partner who suggested that I start sharing my work online, and he's been a huge source of encouragement over the years. I don't think I would have found this path if it wasn't for him (thanks, Isac!)

I was really shocked at the level of support and kindness I received when I started posting my art online, as I initially found the world of internet art communities quite intimidating. I'm sure you can relate to the feeling of being totally overwhelmed when you browse through the internet and encounter all the massively talented people who exist out there. It can be pretty disheartening to realize that there's always going to be someone who outperforms you in some way. But hey, that's just life! It's filled to the brim with excellent artists, but you don't have to be the best in order to be great. Art looks good in all skill levels, and it has much more to do with being able to express creativity genuinely rather than expertise alone.

Opposite page: Digital illustrations.

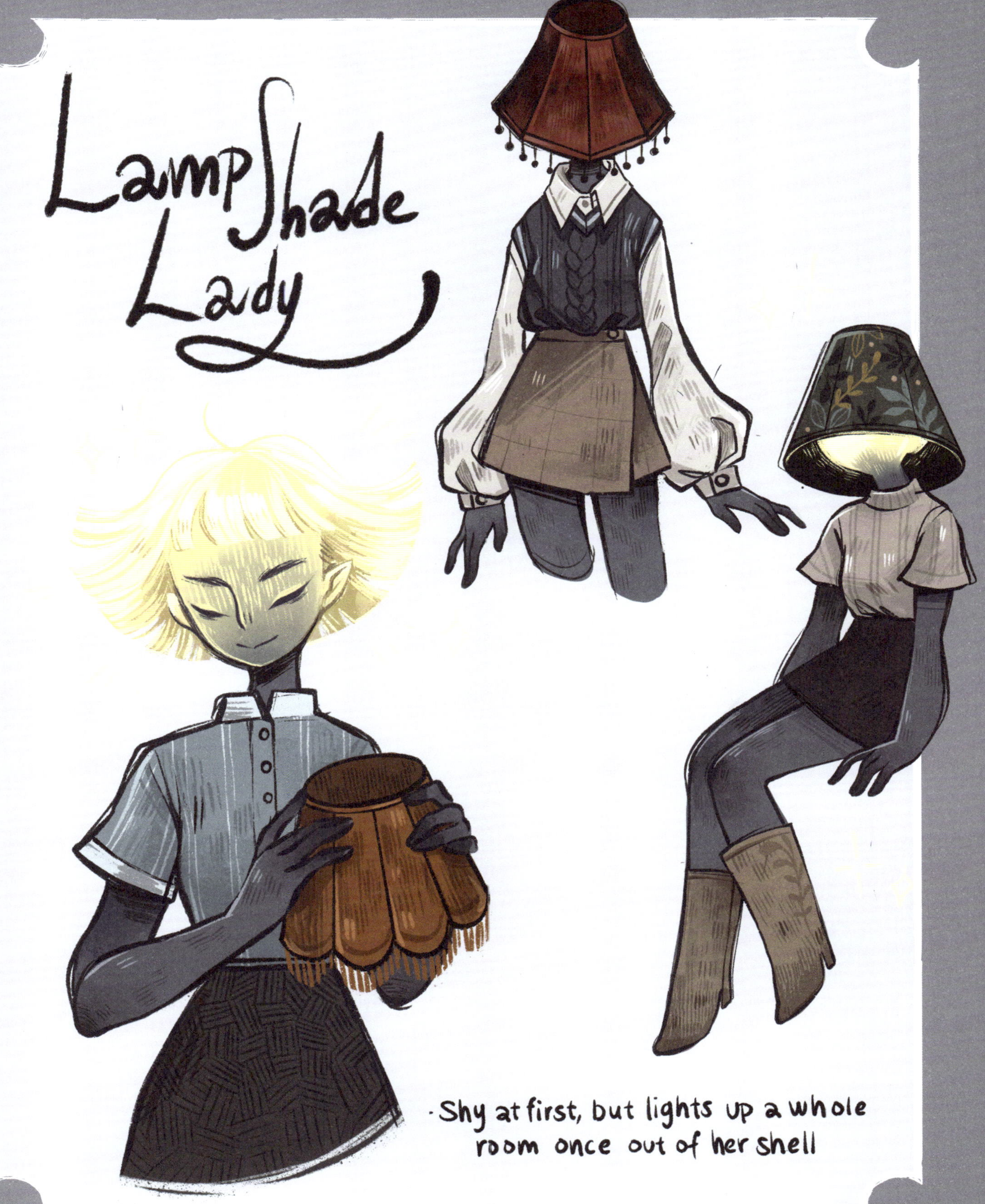

Lamp Shade
Lady
·Shy at first, but lights up a whole
room once out of her shell

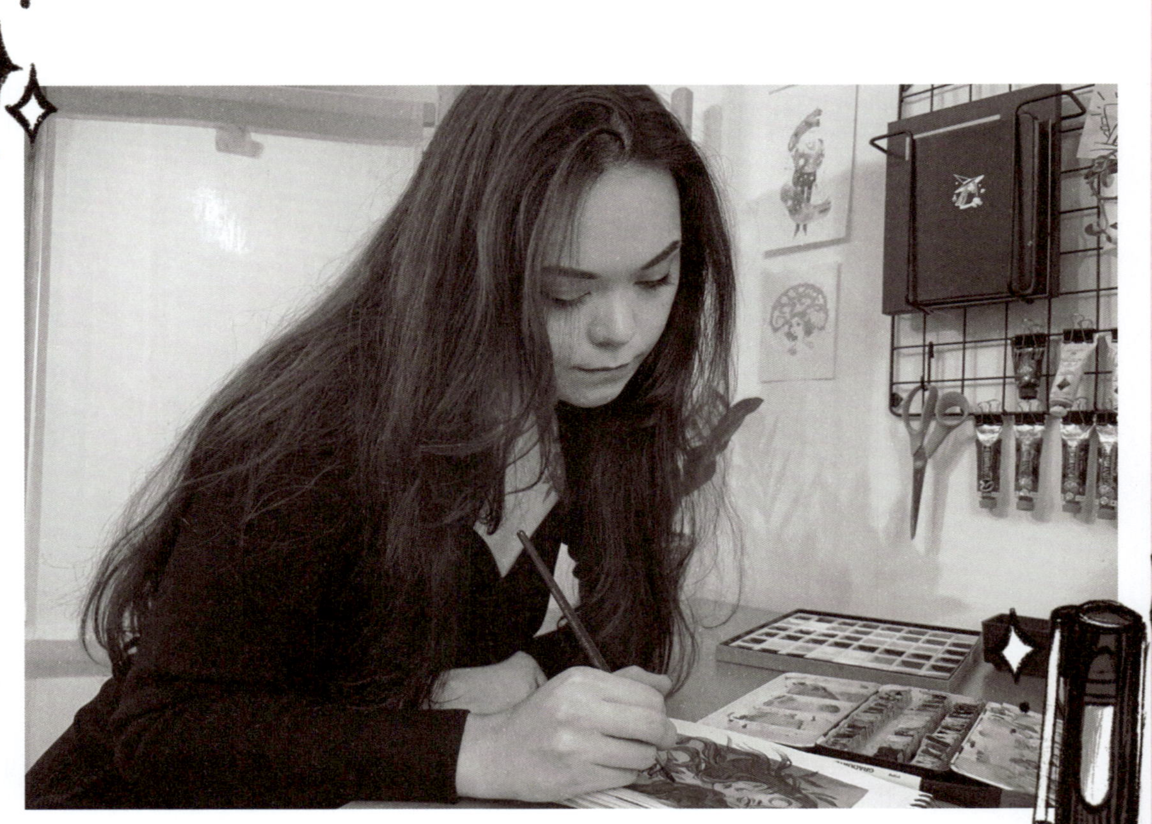

Working as an artist

Navigating the world of work as an artist can be pretty confusing, since there is no clear-cut path to success. I remember being very confused about my future prospects within this industry because there are no guidelines to follow, and instead you're urged to experiment and forge your own path. That's a really hard thing to do when you have just recently graduated and you have absolutely no idea what you're doing.

You might also receive some well-intended but unhelpful comments from family and friends letting you know how difficult it will be to make a living out of it. And they're partially right, it might be difficult. But if you know in your heart that it's what you want to do, then I have no doubt you'll succeed! A very common misconception is that you need to be extraordinarily talented in order to survive as a freelance artist – which is something I've believed for the majority of my life. I have come to realize that having a career in art is dependent on lots of different factors, and not just skill level alone. These factors include your ability to market and promote yourself, a unique stylistic language, or finding a niche and specializing in it. Due to social media it's become possible to find your own community and to connect directly with an audience, and there will always be someone who enjoys your work.

Ultimately, I believe that the main component of maintaining a moderately successful art career is to simply love what you do and allowing that passion for your work to shine through your creations. It might also help to become comfortable with the idea of not being wealthy, and recognize that this is perhaps not a career path you should follow if monetary gain is your end goal. That's not to say that it's impossible, but there are definitely more lucrative career options.

Oh, if only I could have found a passion for juridical law instead of art, all my financial woes would disappear!

At work in my studio.

No artist's journey will look the same as another's, and there are options to explore:

If you like creating your own works and connecting with an audience, perhaps working as a self-employed artist and opening a web shop where you sell prints and other merchandise might be a more suitable route to take.

Alternatively, if you'd rather have a sociable working environment and collaborate with other like-minded people, perhaps an office job at a studio might be a better fit. If you wish to work in a studio, it's a good idea to enroll in a school dedicated to that field, not only due to the skills you'll learn but also from the connections it'll bring.

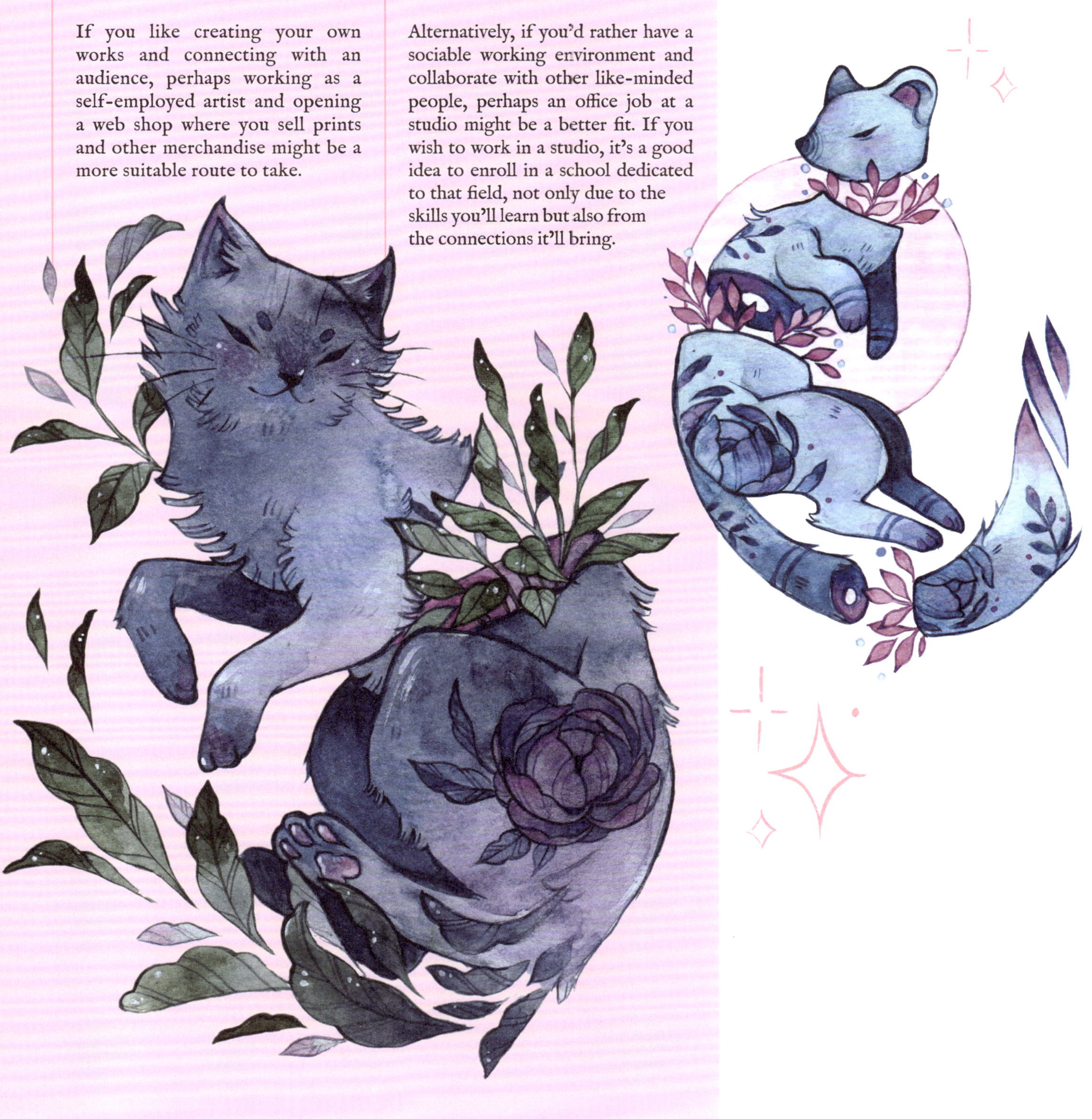

> Regardless of the route you take, it's always important to build an effective portfolio

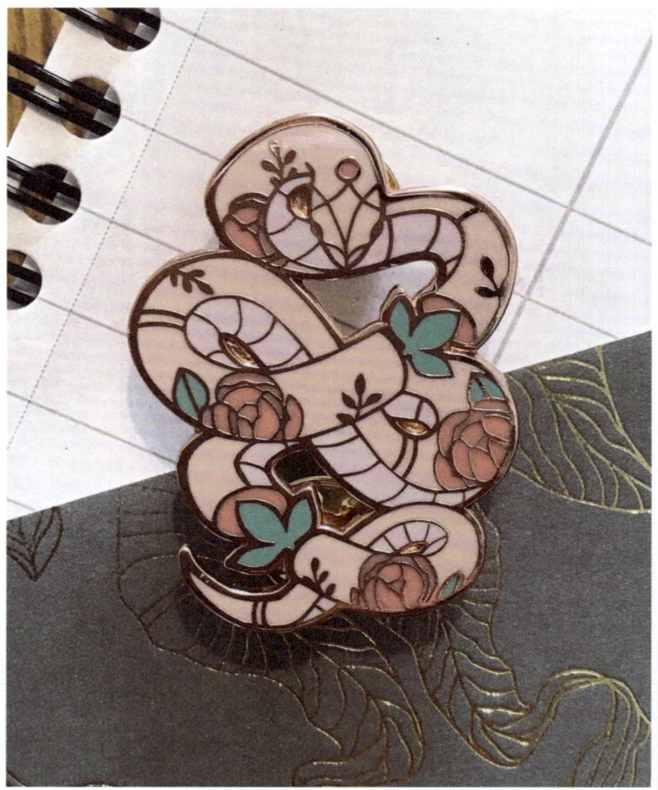

I predominantly make a living through freelance work, where I design everything from children's toys, characters for games, to commissioned art pieces. I also maintain an online store where I sell prints, original paintings, and other fun things! I really enjoy taking on work from companies where I try to bring their vision to life, but it's also a great feeling when someone purchases a piece of art I've made. It can be a good idea to complement your art-related work with a part-time job, since it can be hard to make a living when you're first starting out and a part-time job can take the pressure off. I worked as a night receptionist for a few years, which was an ideal position for me because it was often very quiet. This meant I could pull out my sketchbook and draw between my duties.

Regardless of the route you take, it's always important to build an effective portfolio. The contents within should be cohesive and work well as a collection. For example, avoid placing a study of an apple made in graphite next to a digital painting of a skyscraper, because it'll jumble the narrative. It can also be beneficial to tailor your portfolio to the job you're applying for; if it's a position with a heavy focus on graphic design, it's a good idea to showcase as much of your art that fits within that mold as possible.

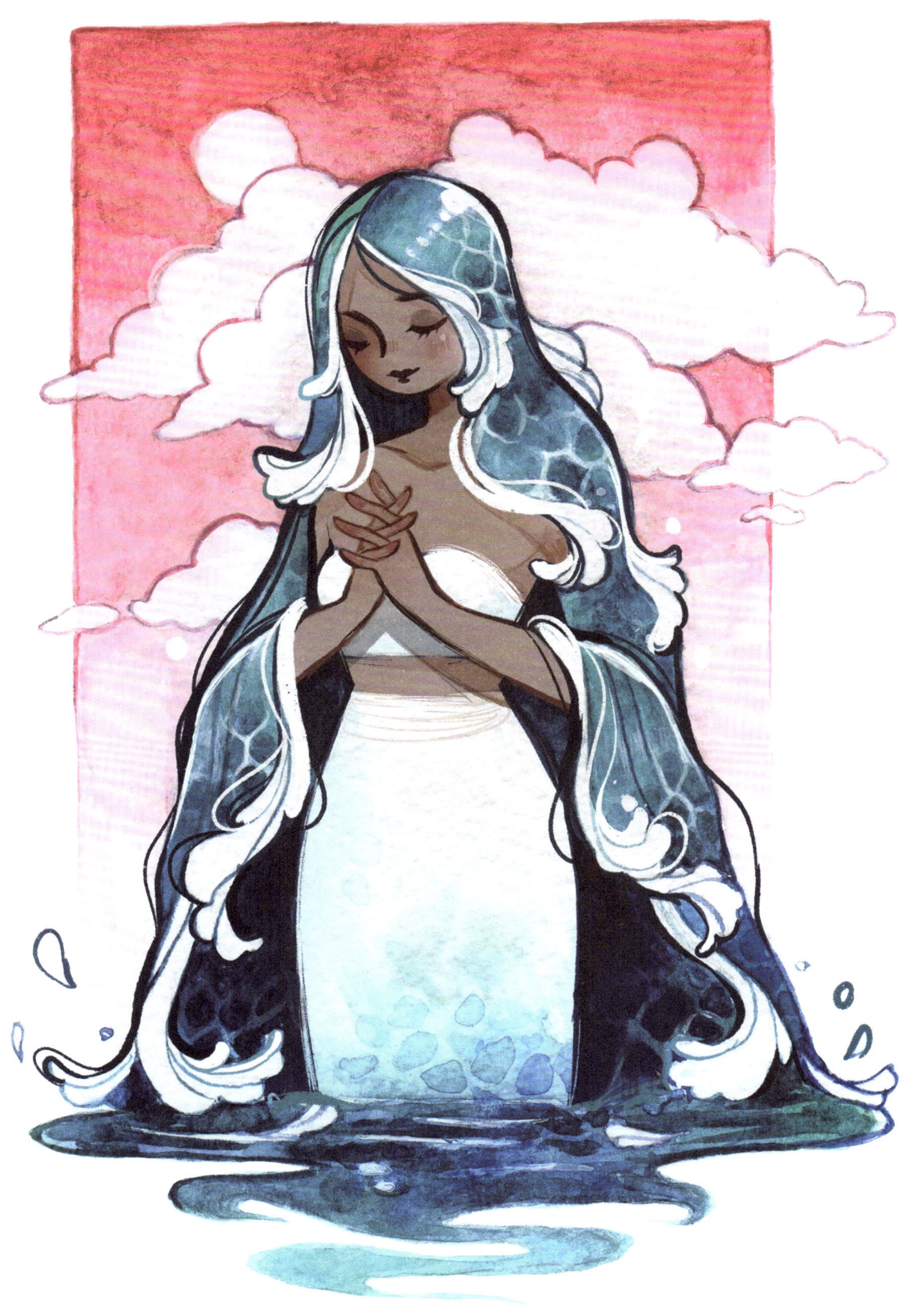

How to build an audience

I think it's a shame that today's art education curriculum doesn't put a bigger emphasis on how to use the internet as a marketing tool – it's an amazing way to reach out to an audience on your own terms and has provided so many artists the opportunity to succeed. Me, for example!

The obvious advice is to start posting regularly, as often as once a day if you feel motivated enough. It's good to stay as active as possible during that first period, and familiarize yourself with the platform. It doesn't have to be anything elaborate or finished – some work-in-progress pieces or a page out of your sketchbook will work well.

You don't have to be a fully realized artist in order to get started, in fact it's really nice to be able to follow an artist from their beginning stages and watch as they progress. You'll spend years practicing, and so if you avoid posting your art because you don't feel good enough you might never get started! This is, after all, a lifelong path, and you will always find new things to improve on. Letting others watch as you learn and grow is a great way of connecting with an audience, and you may be able to inspire and encourage others who are at a similar stage in their own development. If you feel comfortable, you could also continue on to create tutorials for others and share your knowledge.

I highly recommend engaging with others within the art community, and connecting to the people who are making similar art to you! Comment and offer feedback, and just make yourself a known presence. After all, we are all artists who are working toward similar goals. It's really easy to get lost amidst all the other talented individuals out there, so finding your people and being active is key! A great way to do this is to engage in various art trends and to visit your favorite art-related social media hashtags.

However, if your goal is to focus on improving your skills, it might be better to avoid social media and concentrate solely on practice, as you might hinder your progress if you prioritize your art looking presentable over trying out new things. You could paint yourself into a box if you always strive to create something just for the sake of appeasing the social media algorithm. It's good to draw things that are just intended to hone your skills or to try out new things, even if the result isn't attractive. Ultimately you learn more from trying out something new and not quite succeeding, rather than drawing something you already know will work. Be comfortable with the idea of creating unappealing and ugly art, because this is where most of the learning happens.

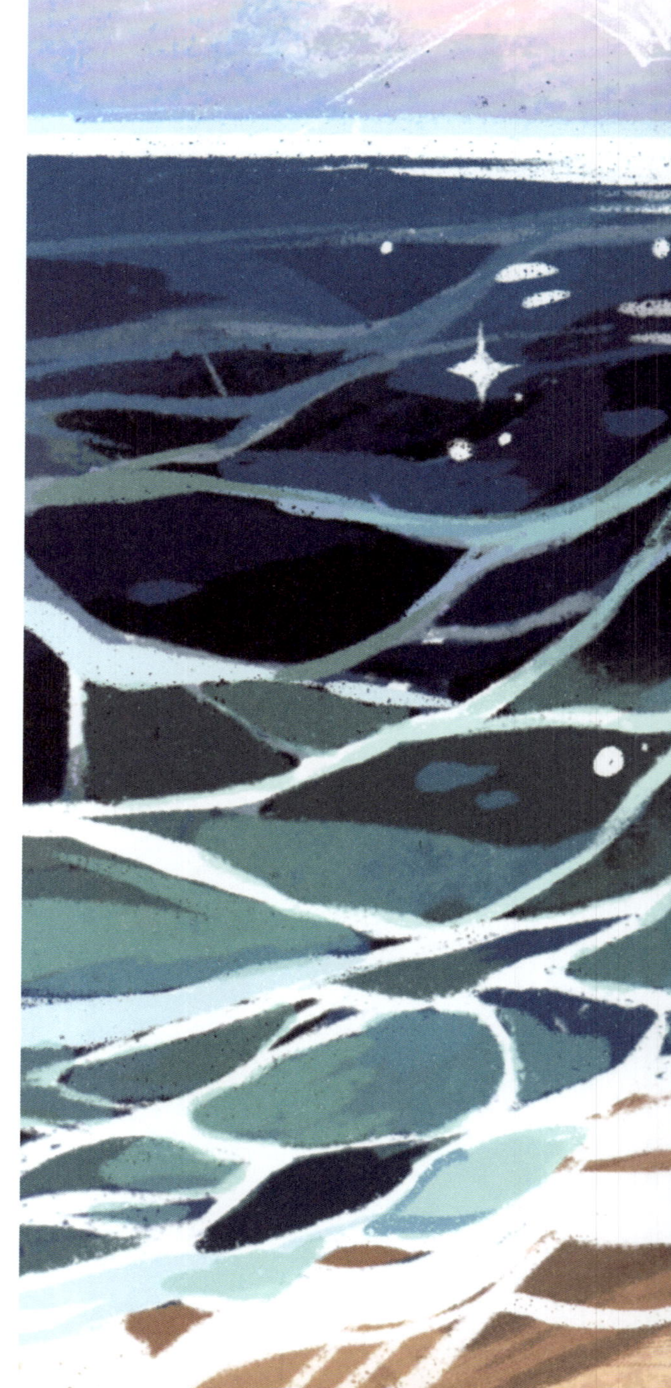

Ocean

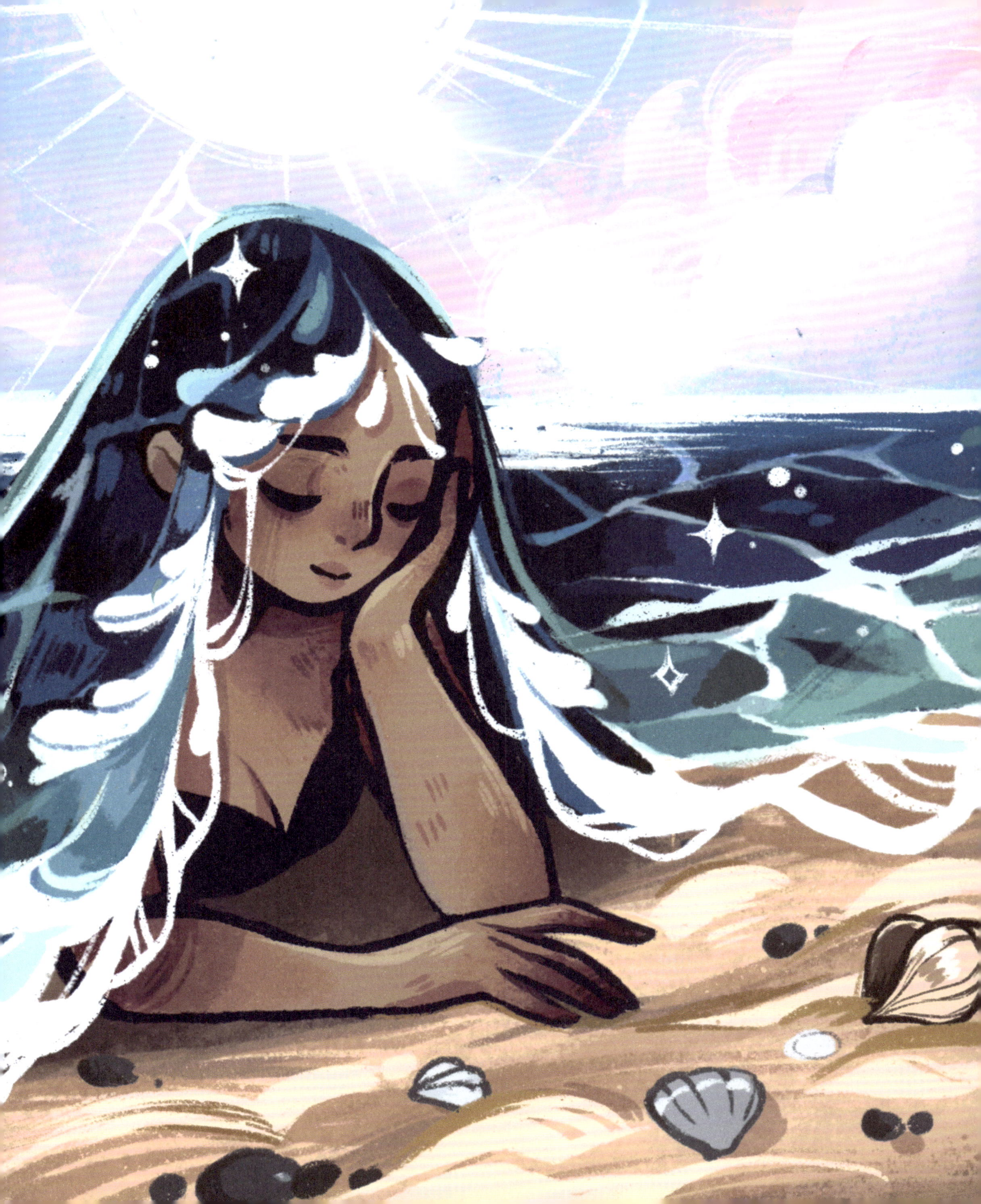

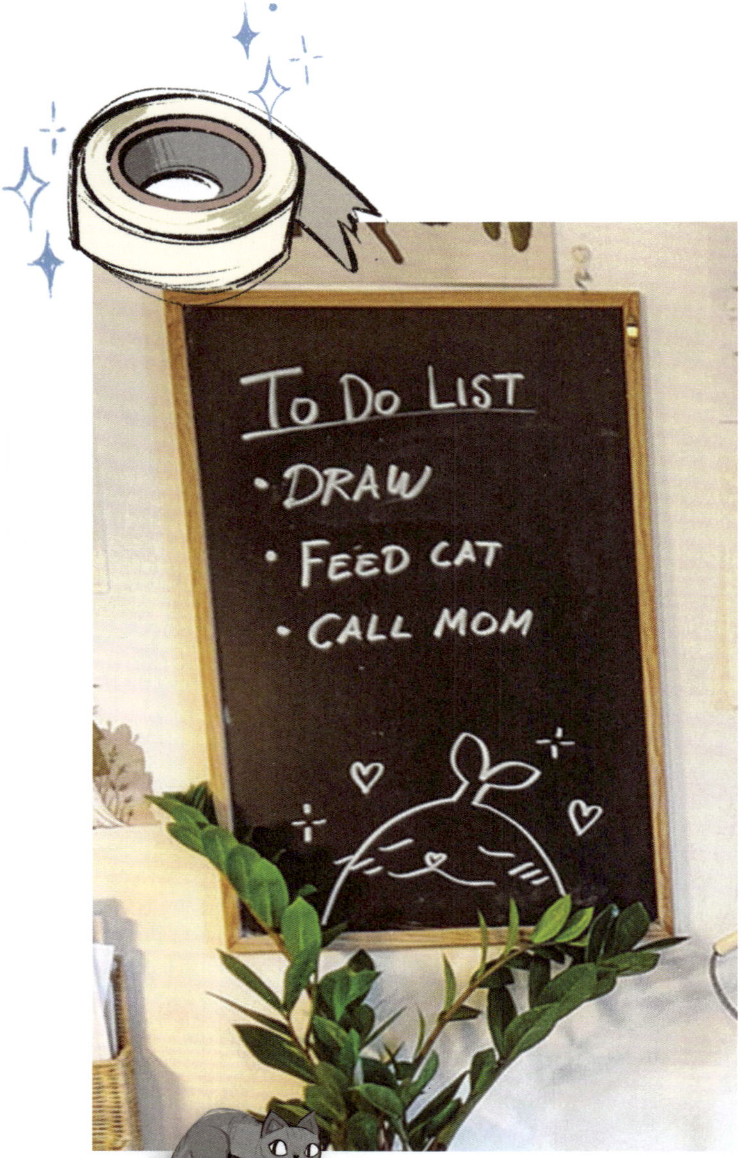

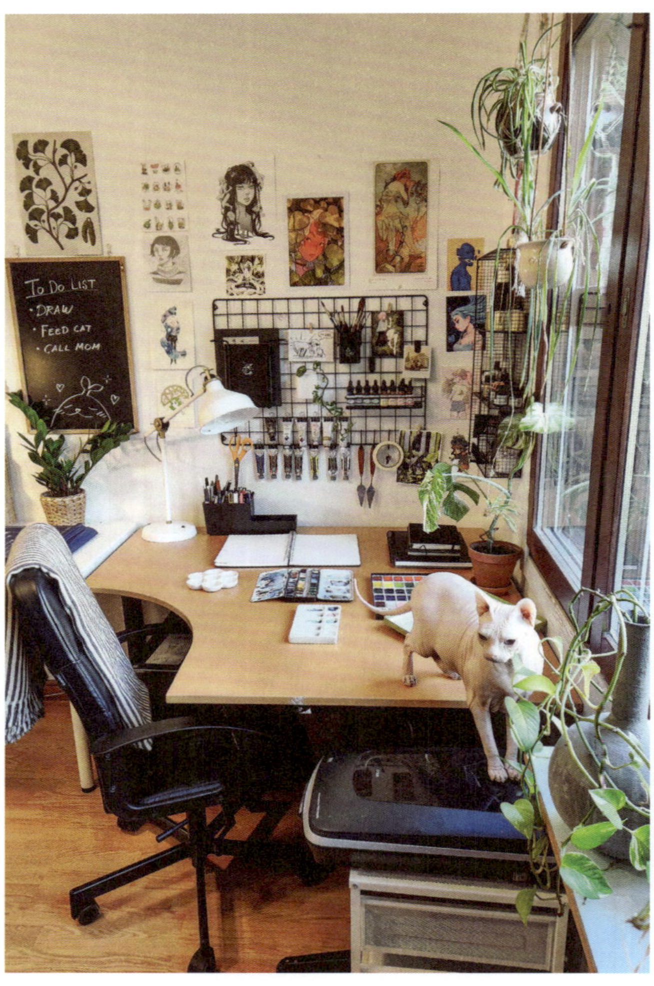

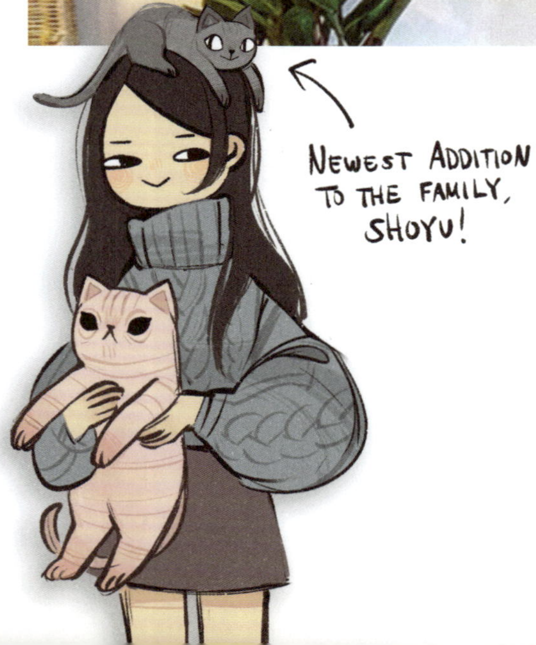

NEWEST ADDITION TO THE FAMILY, SHOYU!

Workspace

I work from home, and have a home office that I share with my partner, Isac. He works as a 2D artist at a game studio. He likes to think that his side of the office is a bit smaller because he doesn't use it as much, but we both know that the real reason I get the bigger half is because I have more followers on Instagram!

As you can see, my workspace comprises of several desk spaces set up for use with different media. I have a dedicated work station for when I work in traditional media, complete with gouache and watercolor paints, pens, pencils, and sketchbooks. It's located under a window to make the most of the light, and all the materials I need are within an arm's reach.

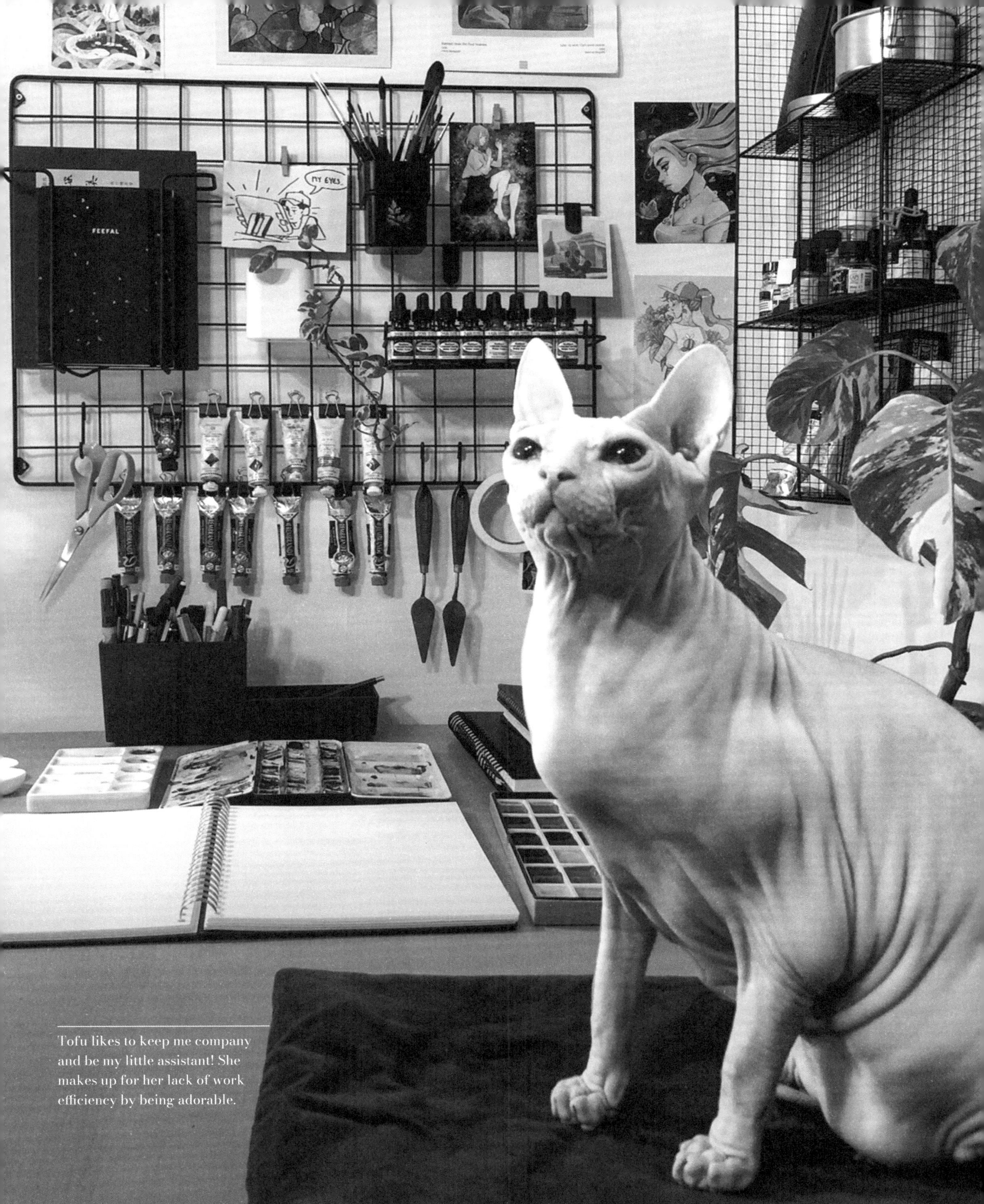

Tofu likes to keep me company and be my little assistant! She makes up for her lack of work efficiency by being adorable.

Tools & materials

Watercolors

My favorite brand of watercolors is Daniel Smith, but they have a high price tag, so are often out of my budget to use regularly. Most of the colors in my palette are Winsor & Newton, from their student and professional lines. When I'm looking for really intense colors, I like to use watercolor inks. My favorites are Dr. Ph. Martin's inks.

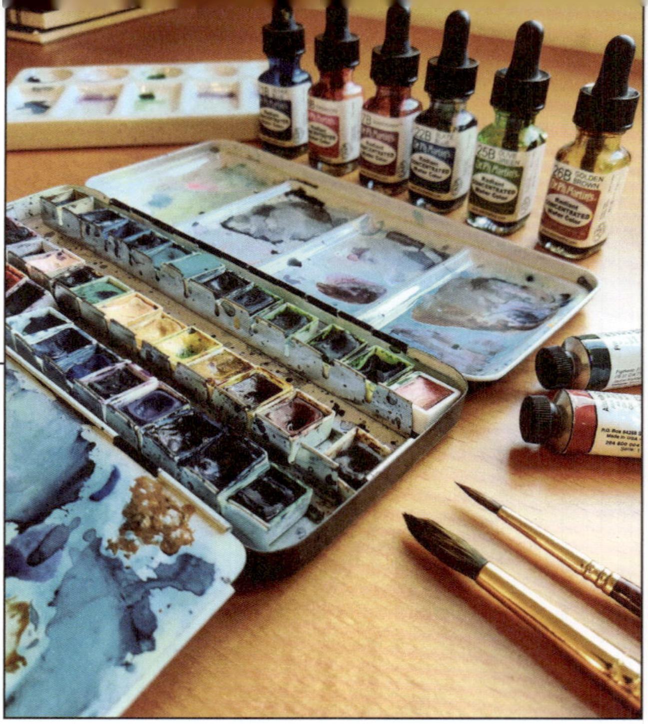

Ink and fineliner pens

I keep a wide variety of different sized fineliners, thin ones for neat details and thicker ones for bold lines. As for liquid drawing ink, any type of black acrylic ink will do for me!

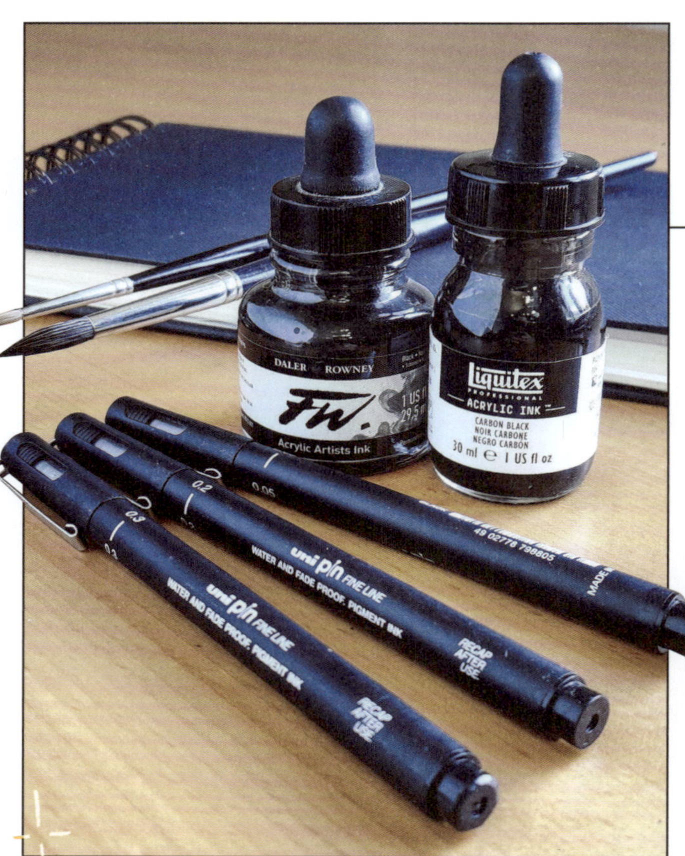

Digital art

When working digitally, I use Procreate on my iPad Pro. It's a really convenient tool, as it can be carried with you anywhere! As for brushes, I mainly stick to the ones that come preinstalled. My favorites are the "Dry ink brush" and the "6B pencil."

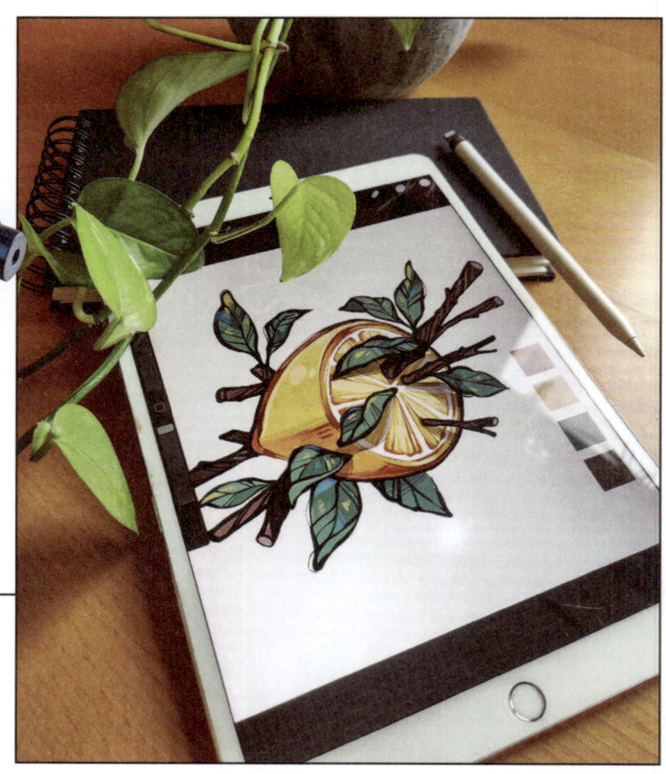

Gouache

My favorite gouache brand is Winsor & Newton, mainly because their paints are easy to find and come in a lot of different colors. As for brushes, I tend to prefer those with synthetic bristles that carry a denser feel, since I want to be able to create precise brushstrokes.

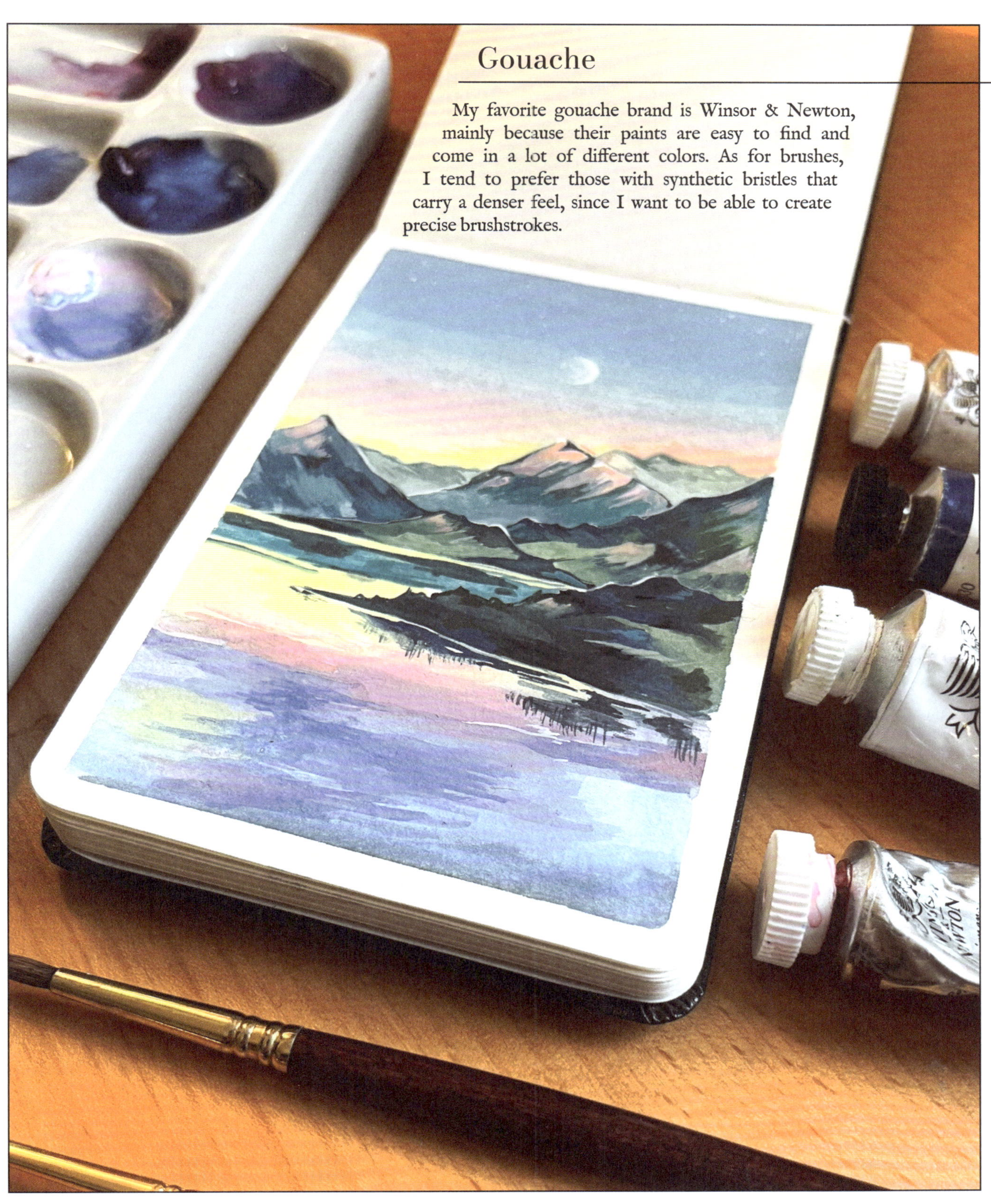

Black ink

I really enjoy working with fineliner pens and ink due to the simplicity of working in monochrome. I don't need to worry about which color palette to choose, or make any big preparations in order to get started. It's also really easy to acquire the materials – fineliners and a bottle of black ink can be picked up from any art shop or office supplies store.

I have an inherent interest in contrast, whether it be visual contrast in color and texture, or in context, such as opposing themes (black/white, life/death, day/night). I believe that is why I'm so fond of working with ink – the contrast created by the black pigment sitting on white paper represents the things I find most beautiful in life. I believe that arranging something next to its opposing element always makes for a lovely visual impact.

When working with black ink, you reside in a monotone realm where you have to find ways to be creative and add depth and life without the use of color. Pattern techniques and texture such as hatching and line thickness control become your best friend.

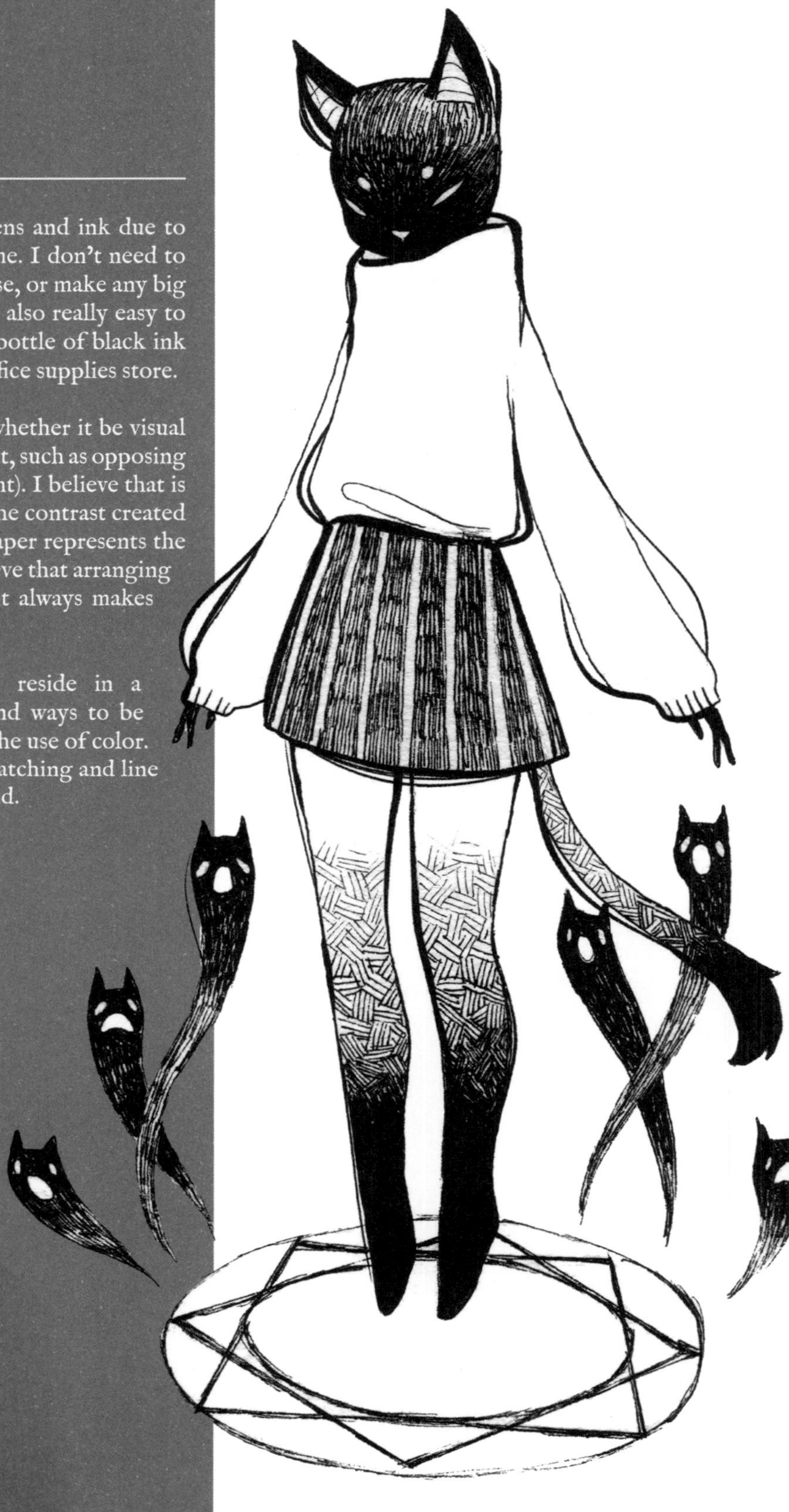

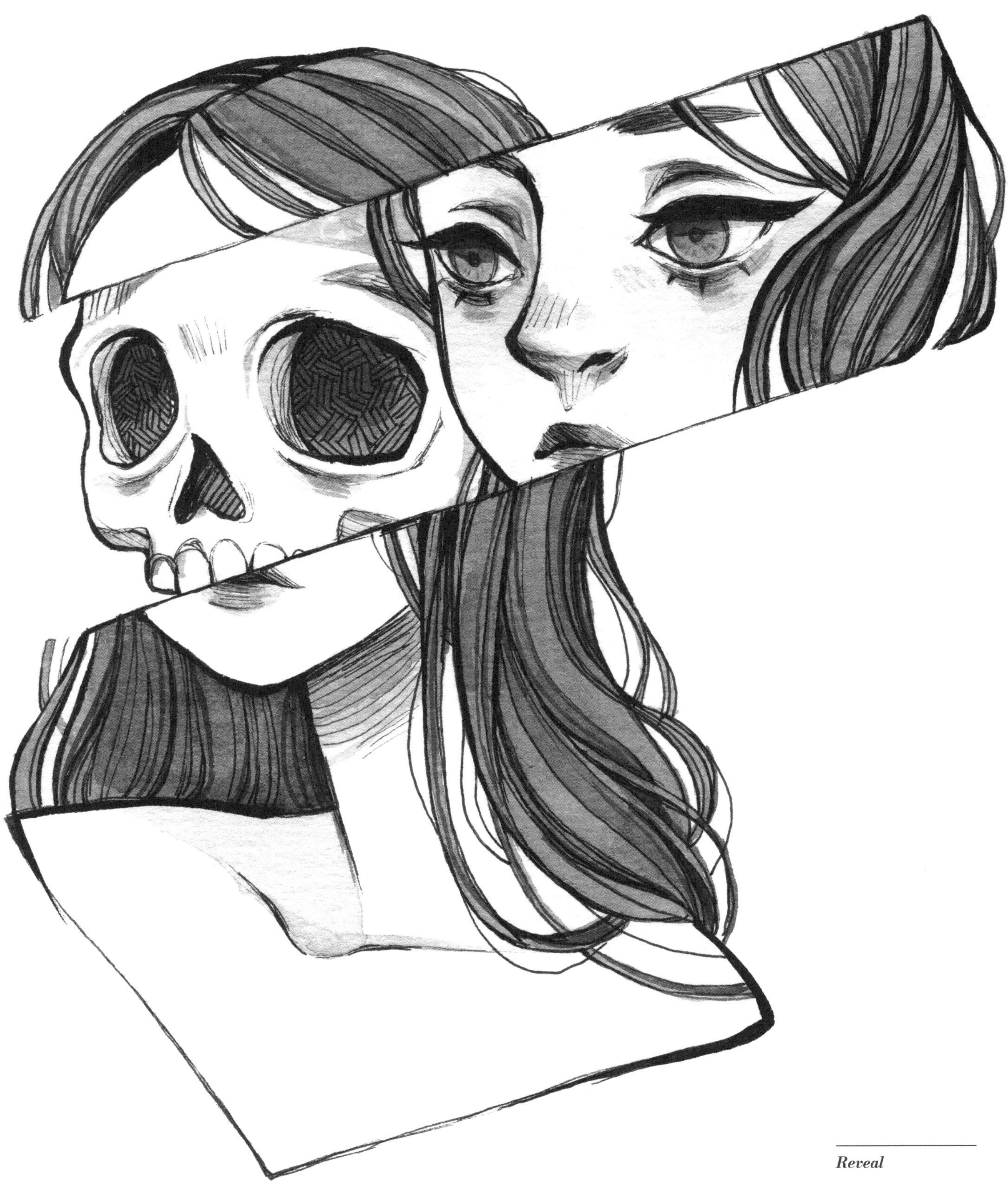

Reveal

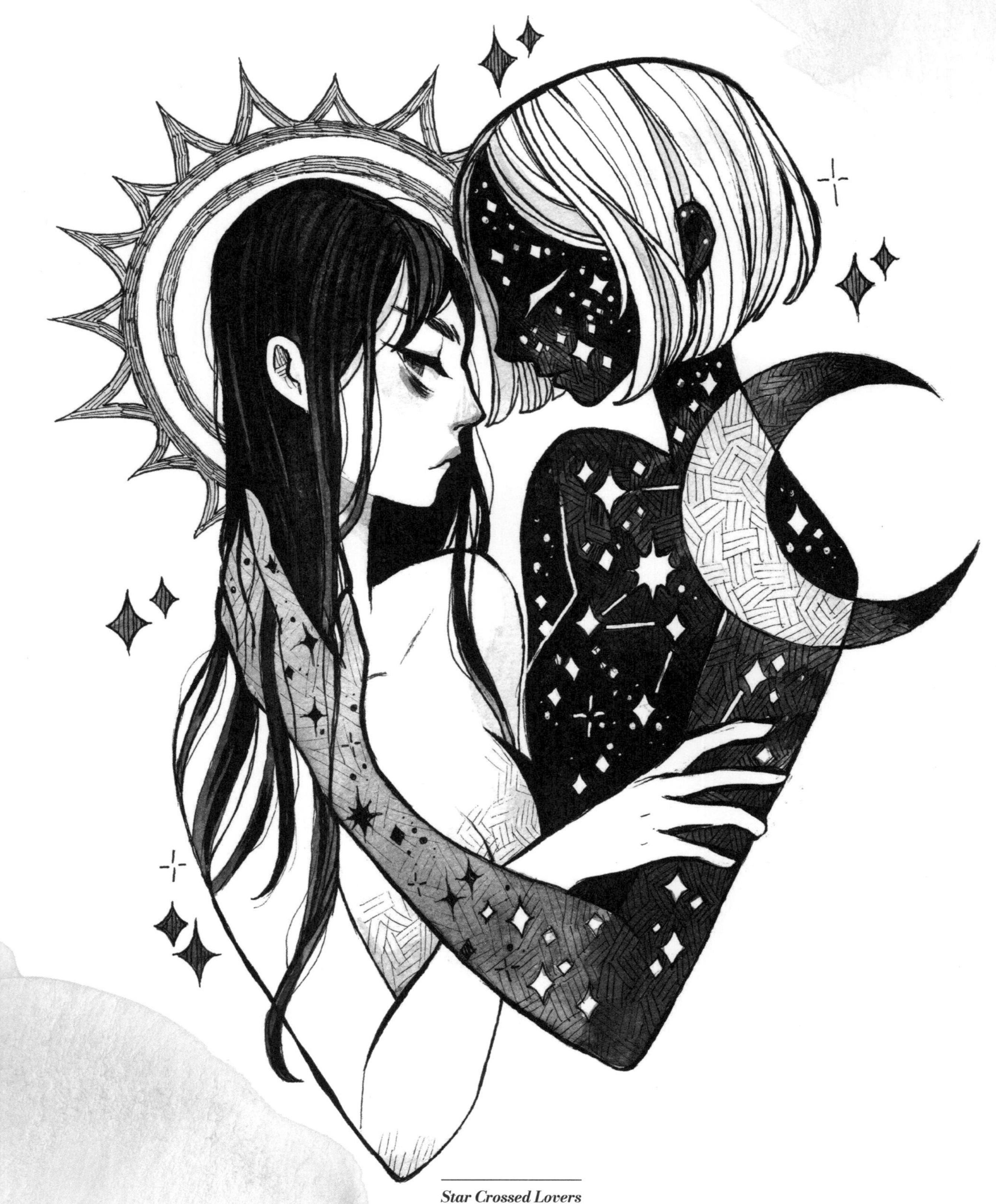

Star Crossed Lovers

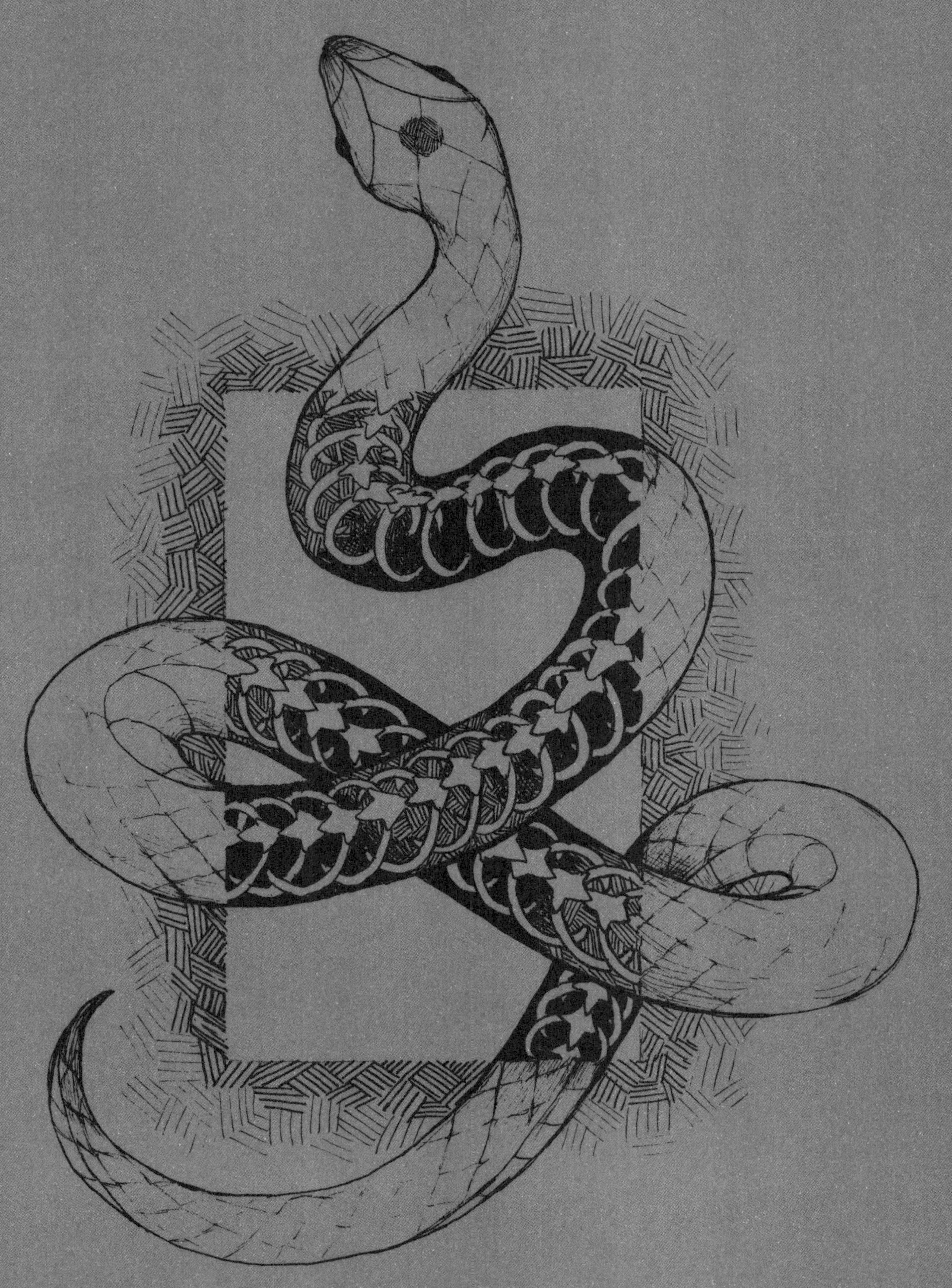

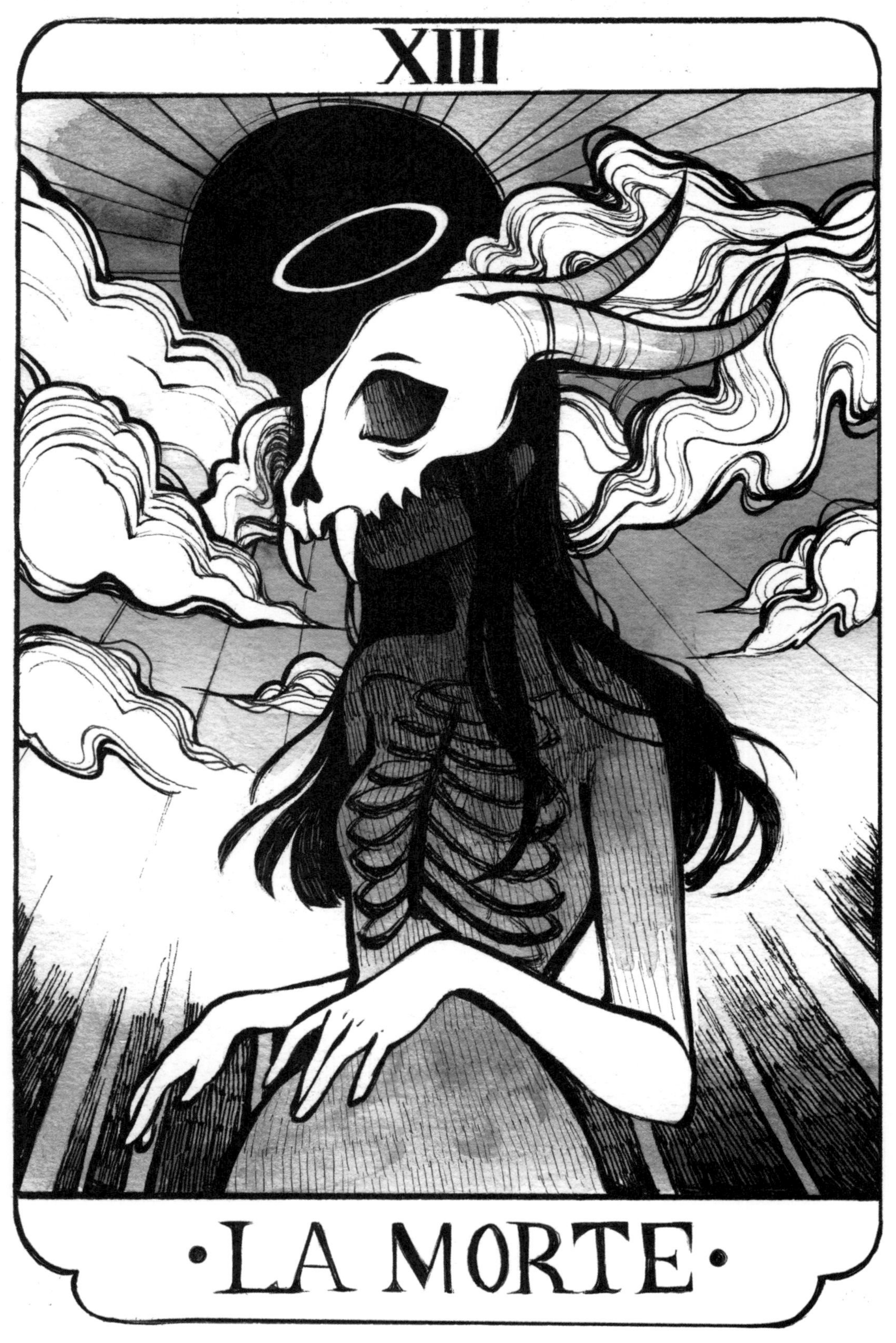

This page:
La Morte

Opposite page:
Ace of Hearts

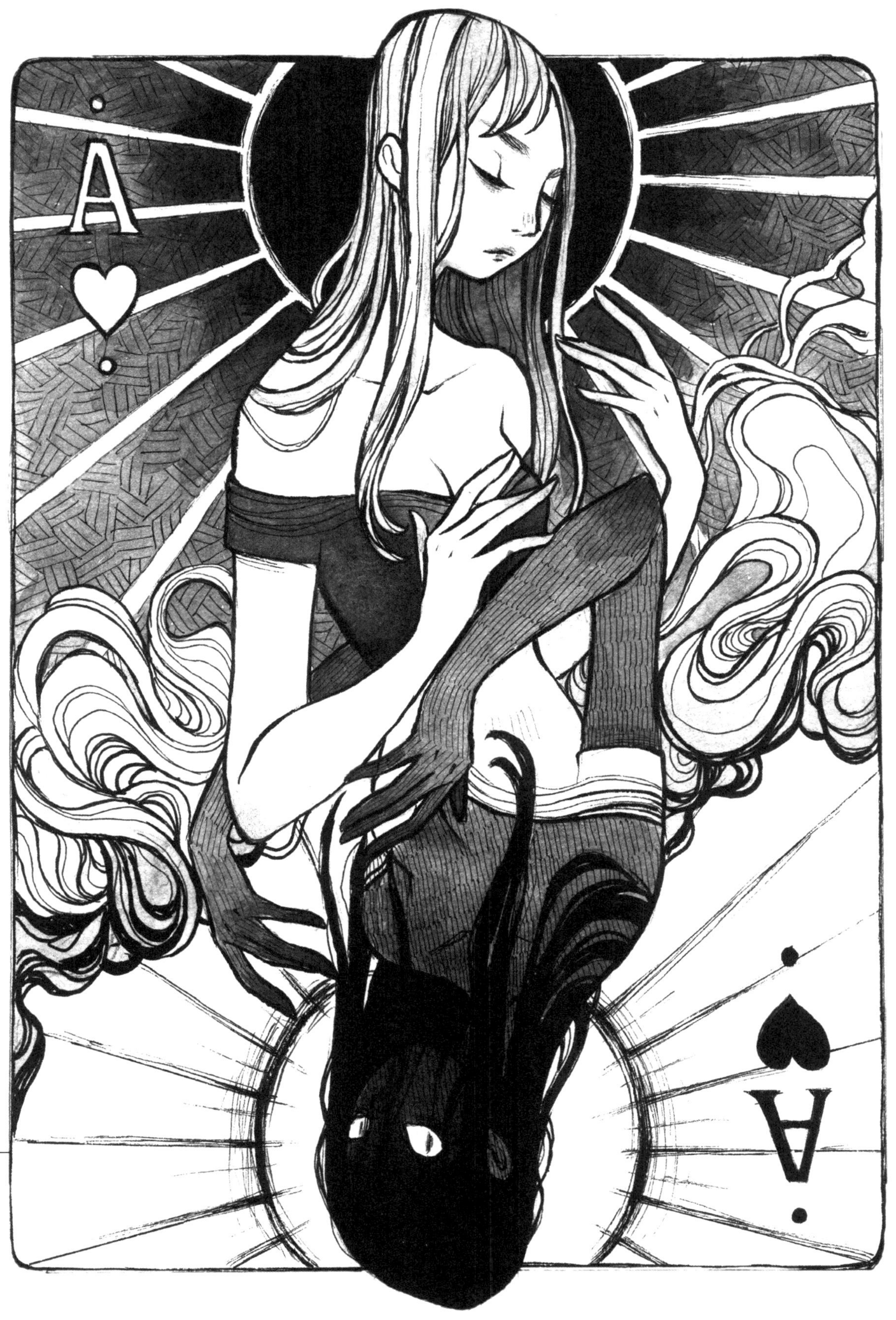
A
A

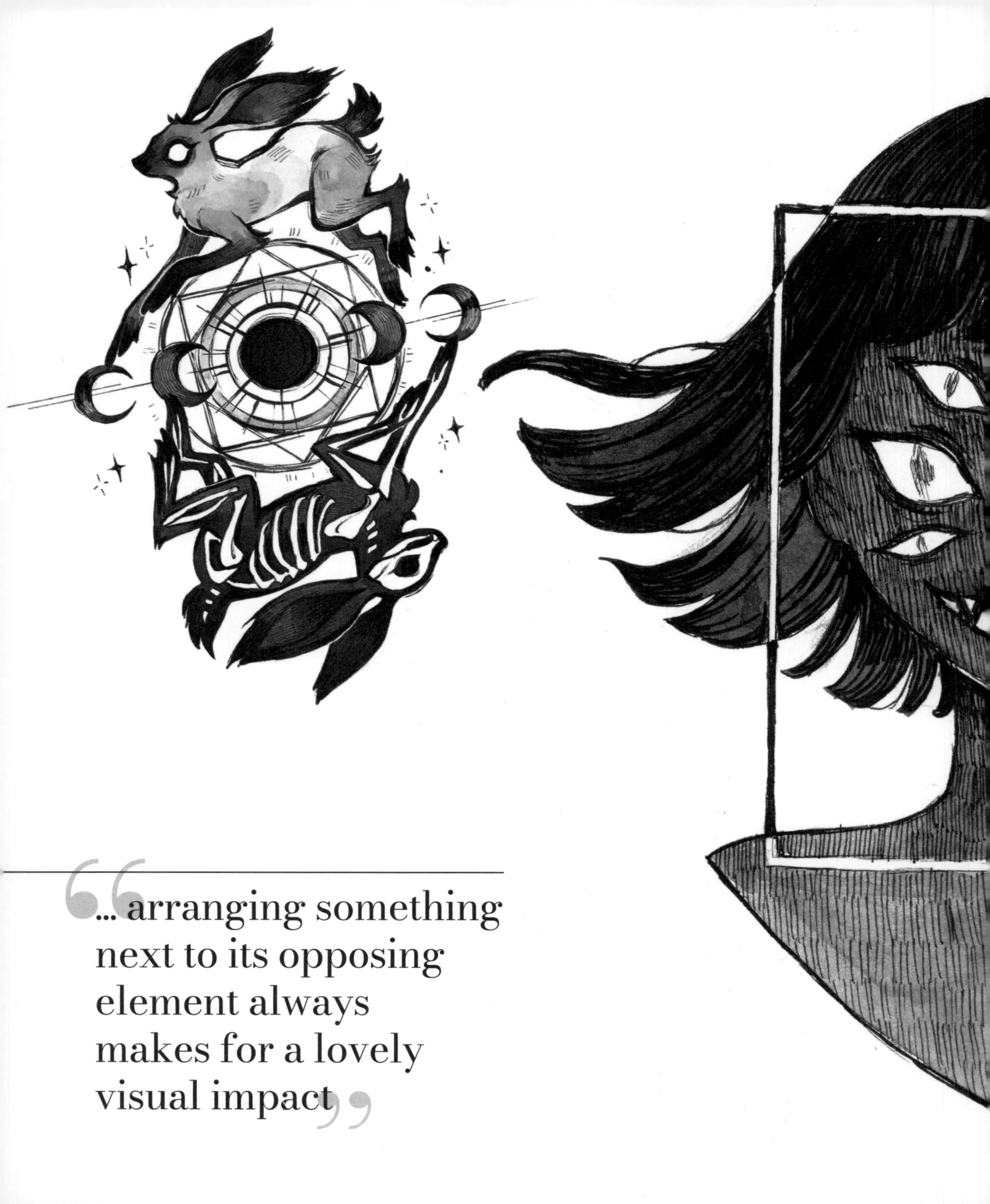

> ... arranging something next to its opposing element always makes for a lovely visual impact

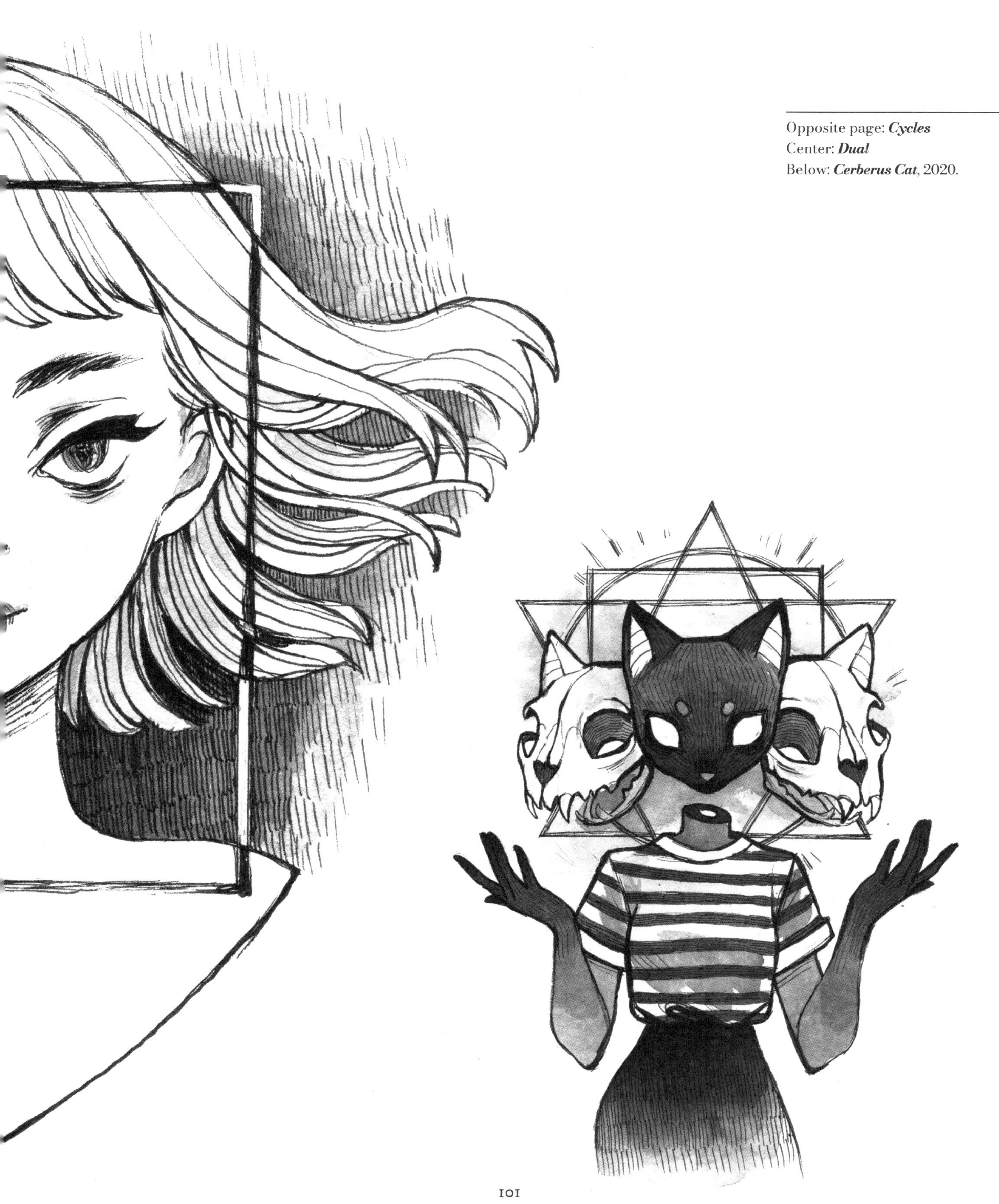

Opposite page: ***Cycles***
Center: ***Dual***
Below: ***Cerberus Cat***, 2020.

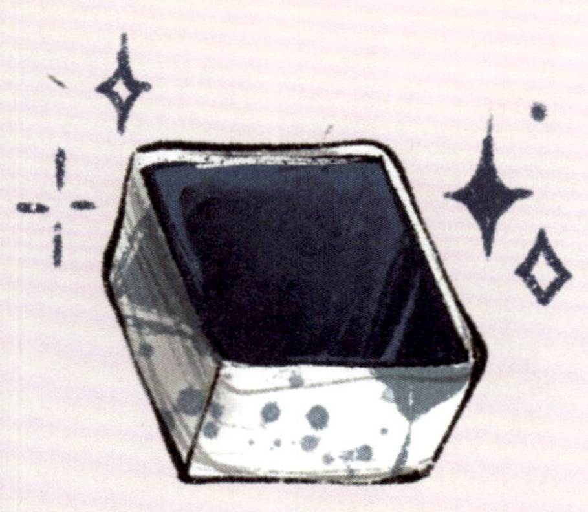

Watercolor paint

I love painting with watercolors because they're such a wild card – they really have a life of their own! The pigments react in a variety of ways depending on multiple factors, such as the granulation of the pigment, the opacity, how much water is used with them, and many others.

Watercolor is a very exciting medium, but can also be incredibly frustrating if you're unfamiliar with using it. I bought my first watercolor paint set, a Winsor & Newton Cotman kit, at age sixteen. I was an avid DeviantArt user and had been a big fan of the artist Koyamori for a while, who makes absolutely mind-blowing illustrations using the medium. My art style was very different from hers, but she made the pigments look so lovely and so I felt inspired to try them out myself.

Transitioning from drawing with pens and occasionally painting in acrylic to painting with watercolor was daunting at first because watercolors are so unique in their properties. Nonetheless, I'm really glad I persevered through the awkward phases because it's now one of my absolute favorite mediums to use. It's messy, unreliable, and colorful, but with the right brushes it can also be used in a very precise manner.

Another aspect that I really enjoy is that painting with watercolor forces you to slow down and calm down, as you have to wait for the paint to dry before adding another layer. If you try to rush the painting process and add more pigment before the surface has properly dried, it'll make a blurry spectacle and ruin any idea of precision you had in mind. The amount of line art I've ruined by not being patient enough is no joke, and I still have a hard time playing the waiting game sometimes!

Watercolors are also great in terms of practicality – they're super-portable and a single large tube pretty much lasts you a lifetime. Unlike many other types of paint, watercolors can be kept in dry form and mixed again with water to reactivate the pigments, so you never have to waste any paint.

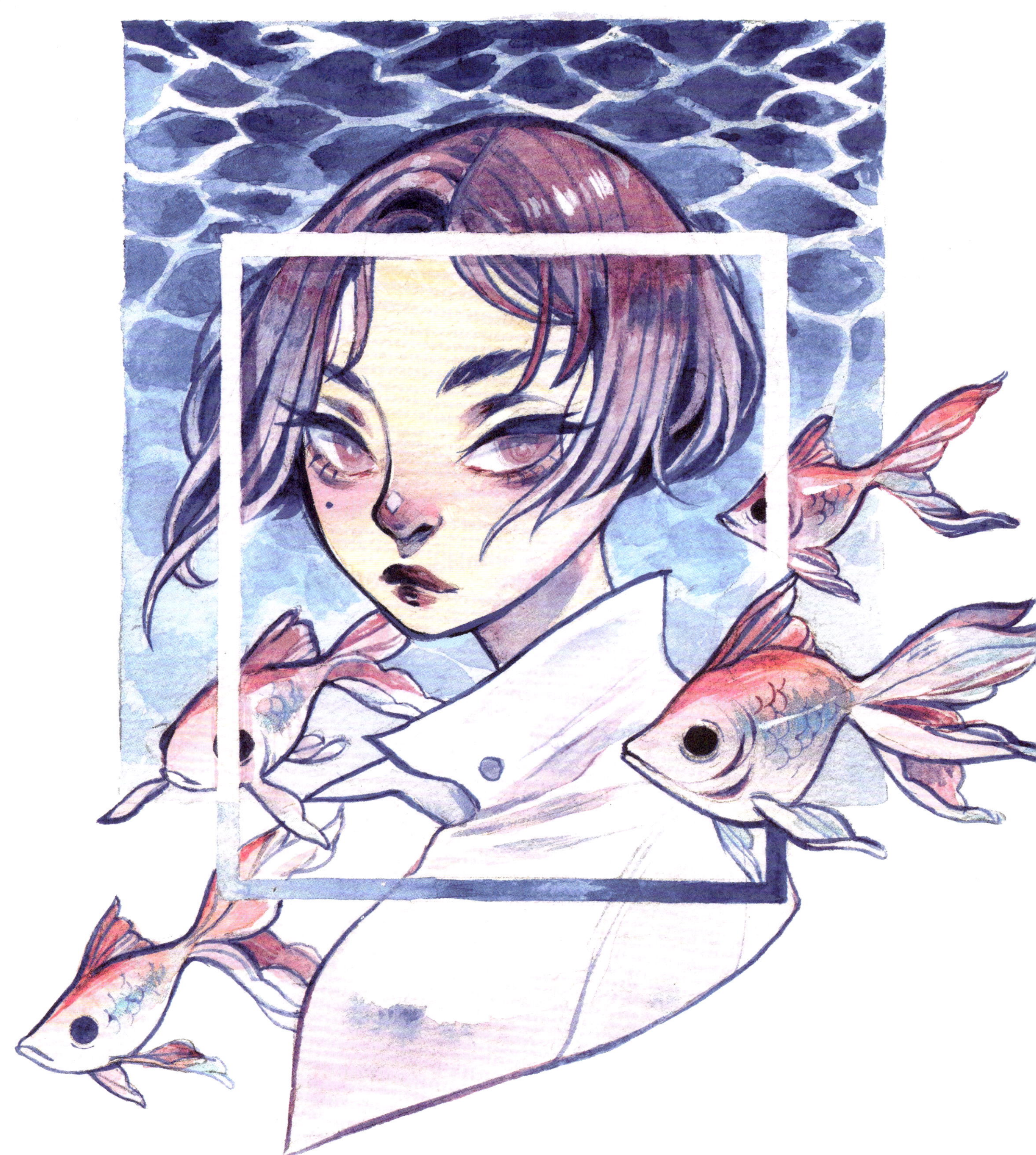

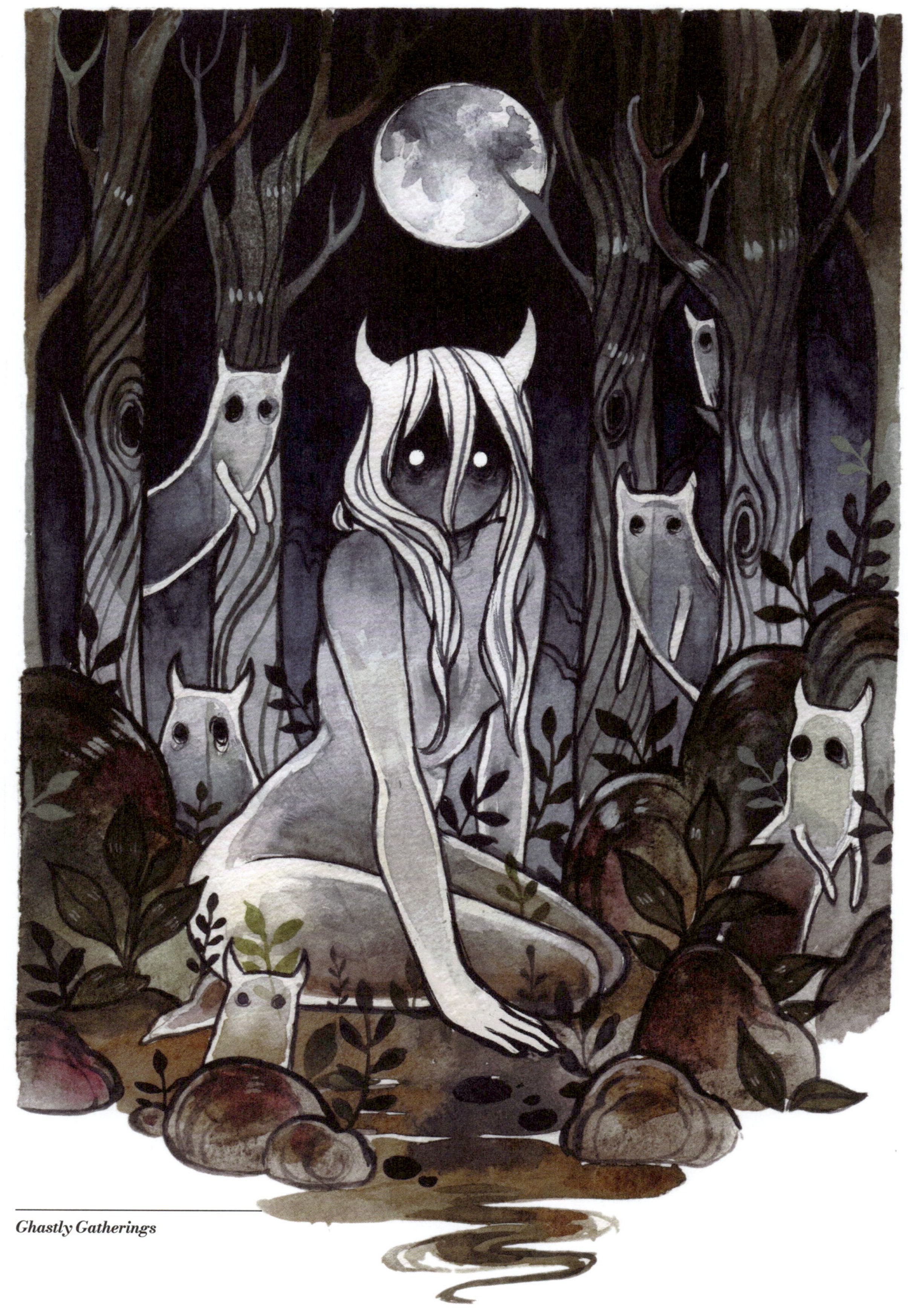

Ghastly Gatherings

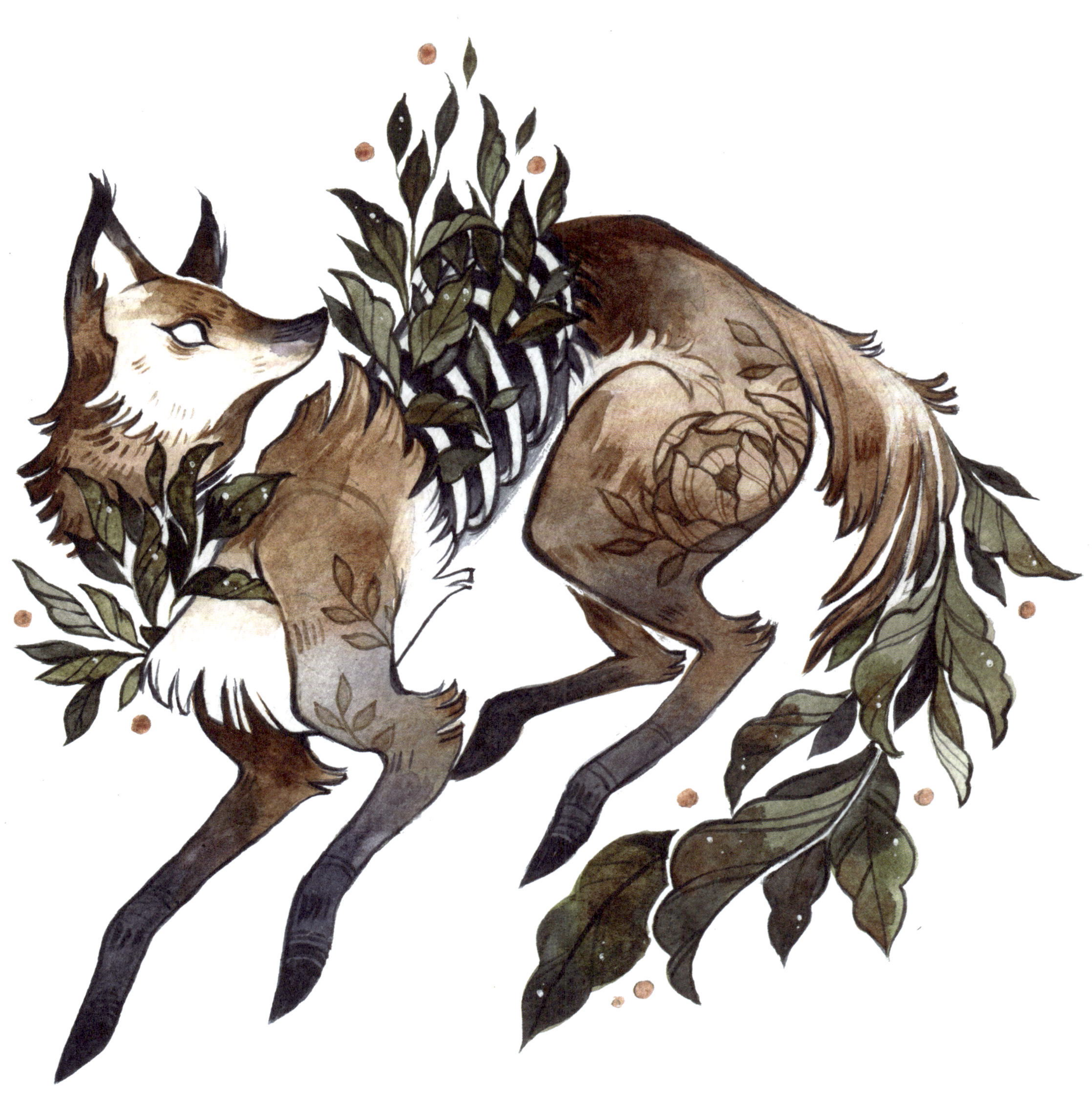

Floral Fox I'm very inspired by the cycle of life, how everything ends and begins anew... from flora to fauna, then back to flora once more.

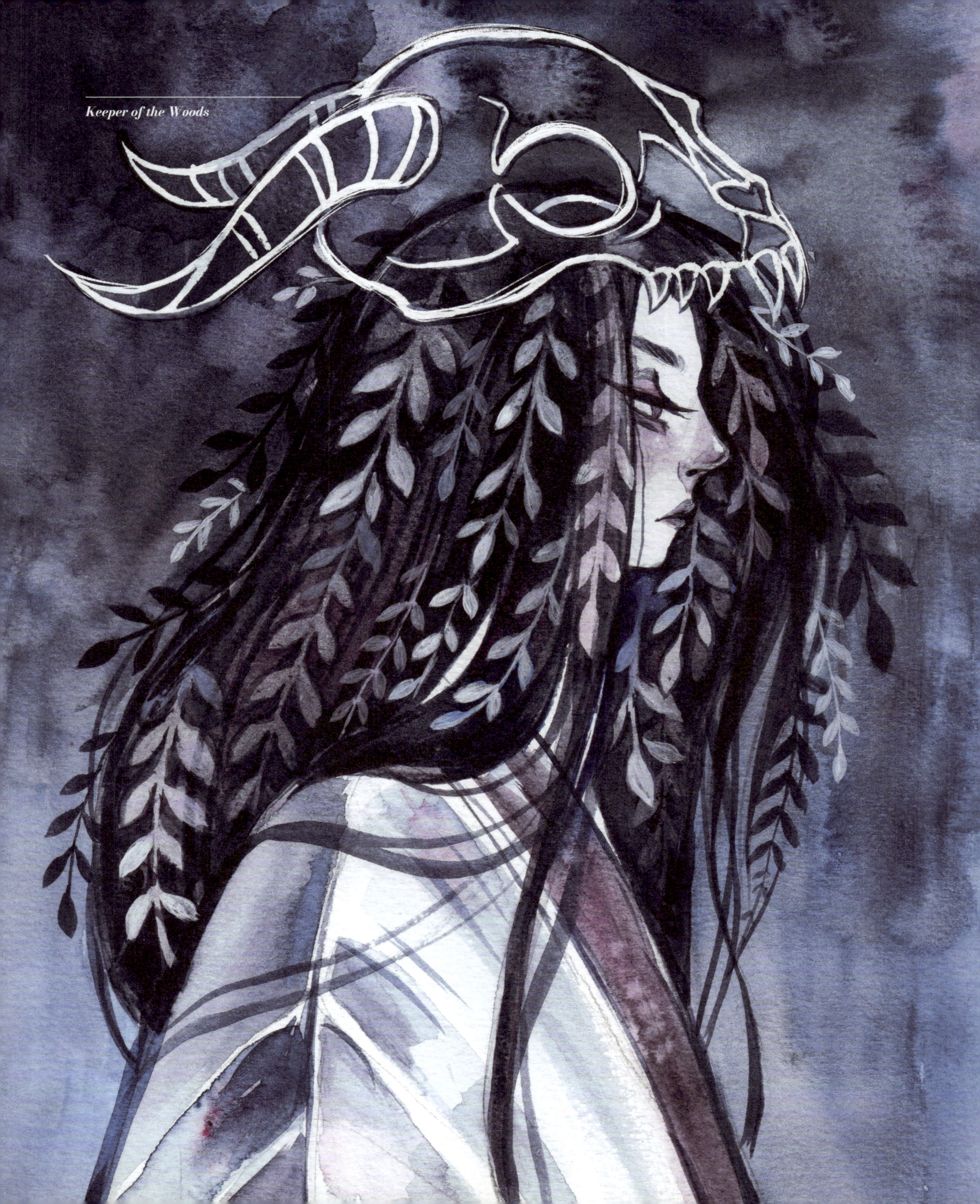
Keeper of the Woods

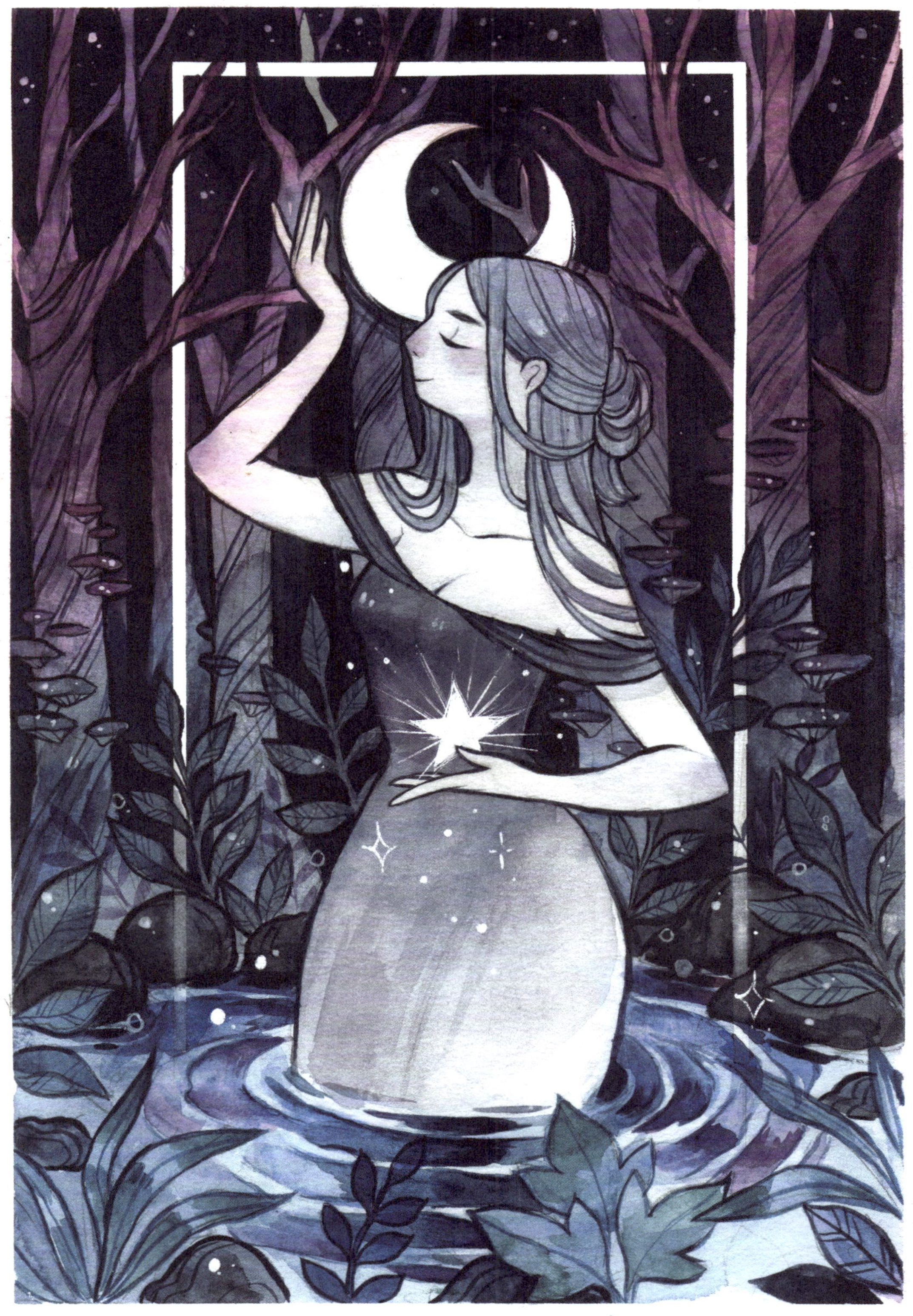

Mother Moon

Floral Snake

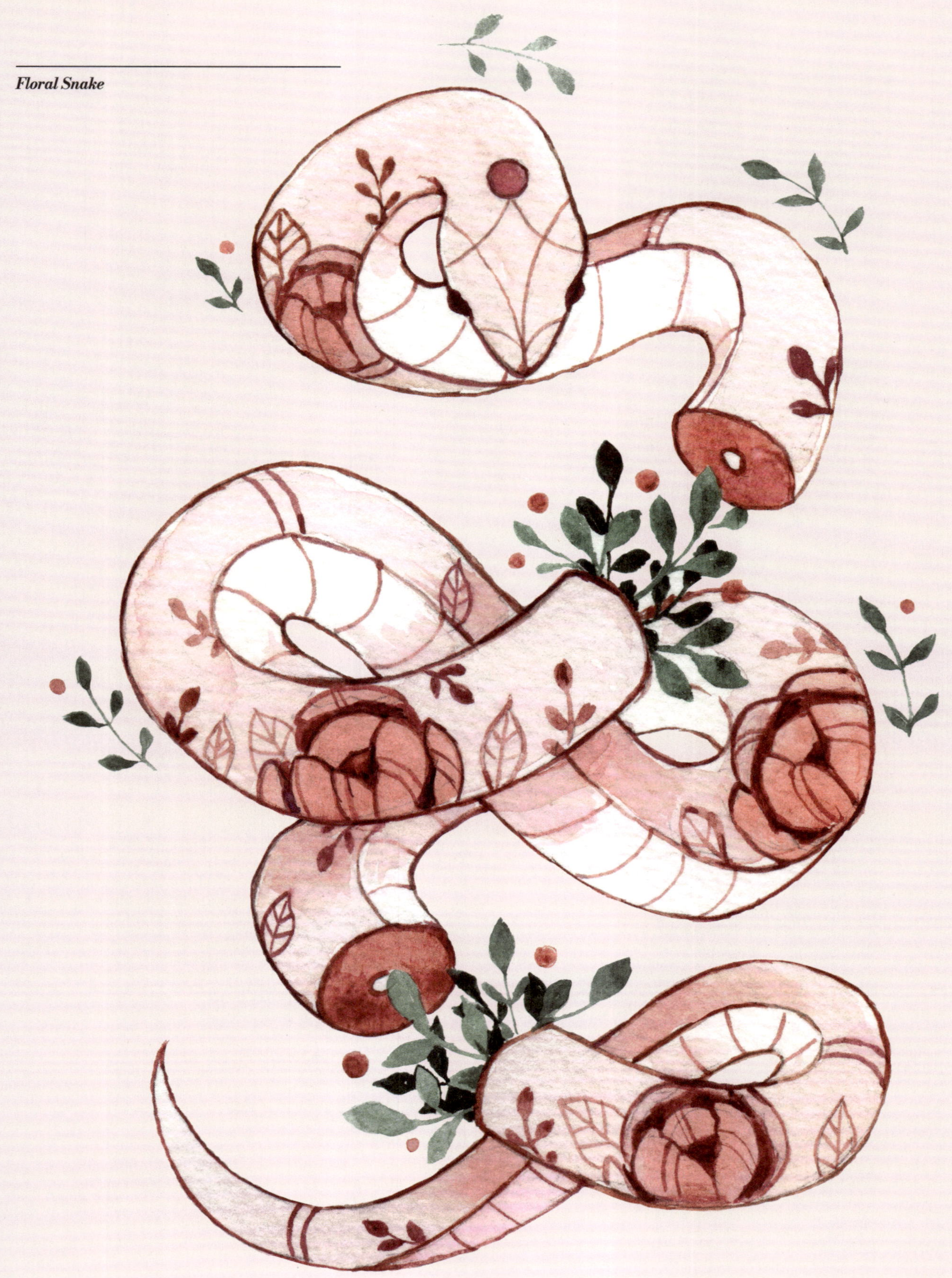

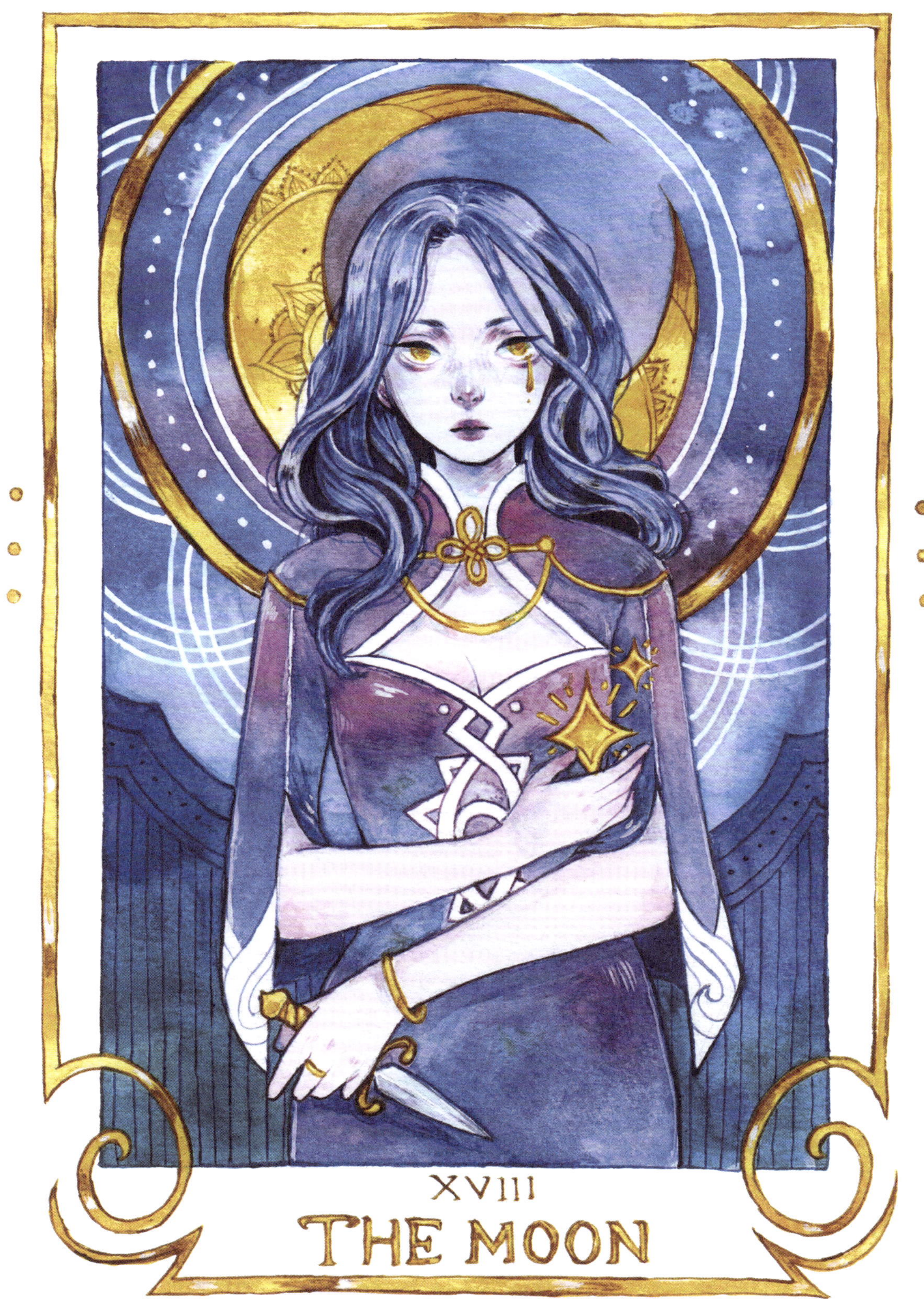
XVIII
THE MOON

Digital tools

I don't know where to begin the discussion of digital art. How do I accurately express the amount I've struggled with this medium? I'm sure you're aware that the general consensus for the past fifteen years or so has been that digital art is the future, and that if you wish for longevity within this field, it's in your best interest to get a grasp on it. Seeing as I've been way more comfortable with traditional mediums the vast majority of my life, this felt like a huge slap in the face.

I remember getting my first Wacom tablet at age thirteen. It was really outdated and I couldn't for the life of me figure out how to make it work. I asked for a more updated version as a birthday present when I turned sixteen, thinking I'd finally be able to master the techniques once I had a better tool, but unfortunately, I still struggled. I even invested in a used Cintiq, because I thought the transition would be easier if I could draw directly onto the screen, and that still didn't work.

The main reason I had such an aversion to it is because of the endless amounts of corrections you're allowed, and that you could spend as much as time as you want rendering the same thing over and over again. This doesn't sound like a bad thing, but I like that traditional medium has limitations and a natural finishing point where you know you have to stop and move on to the next piece to avoid overworking it. Digitally, I would spend countless hours sketching out the same thing over and over, before finally giving up in frustration.

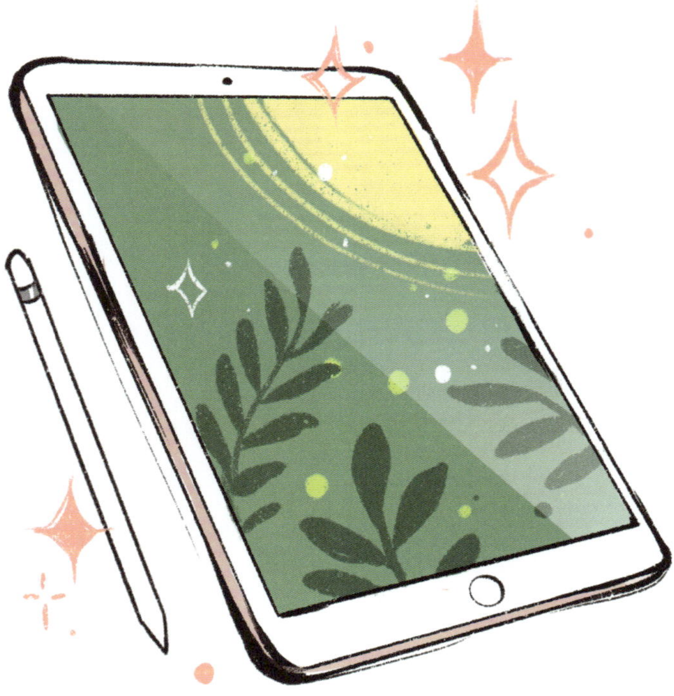

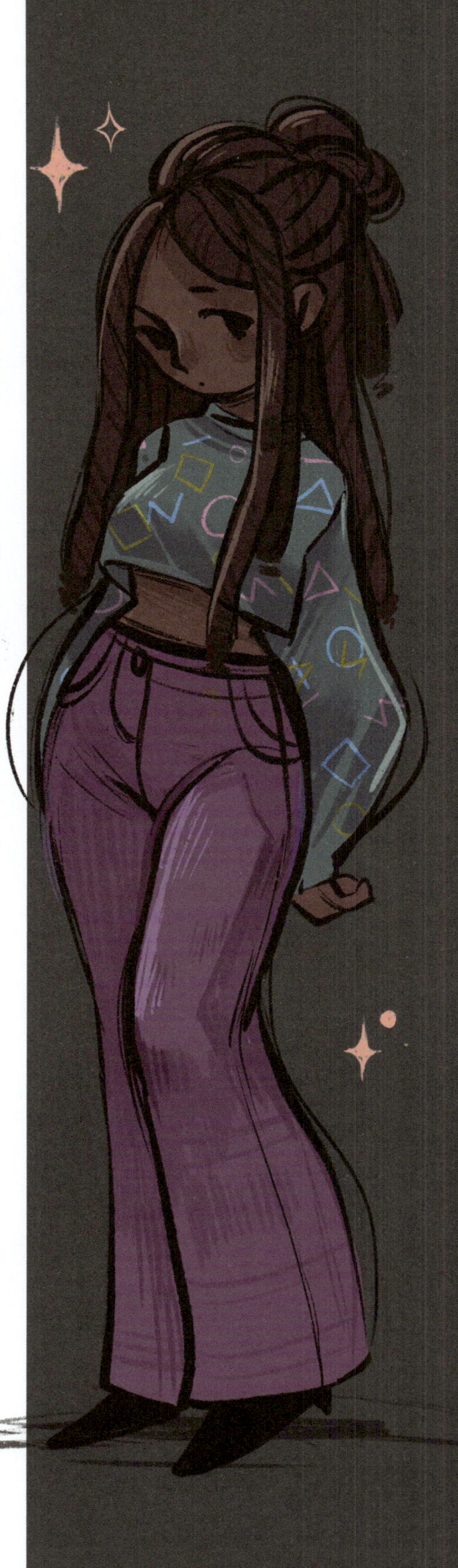

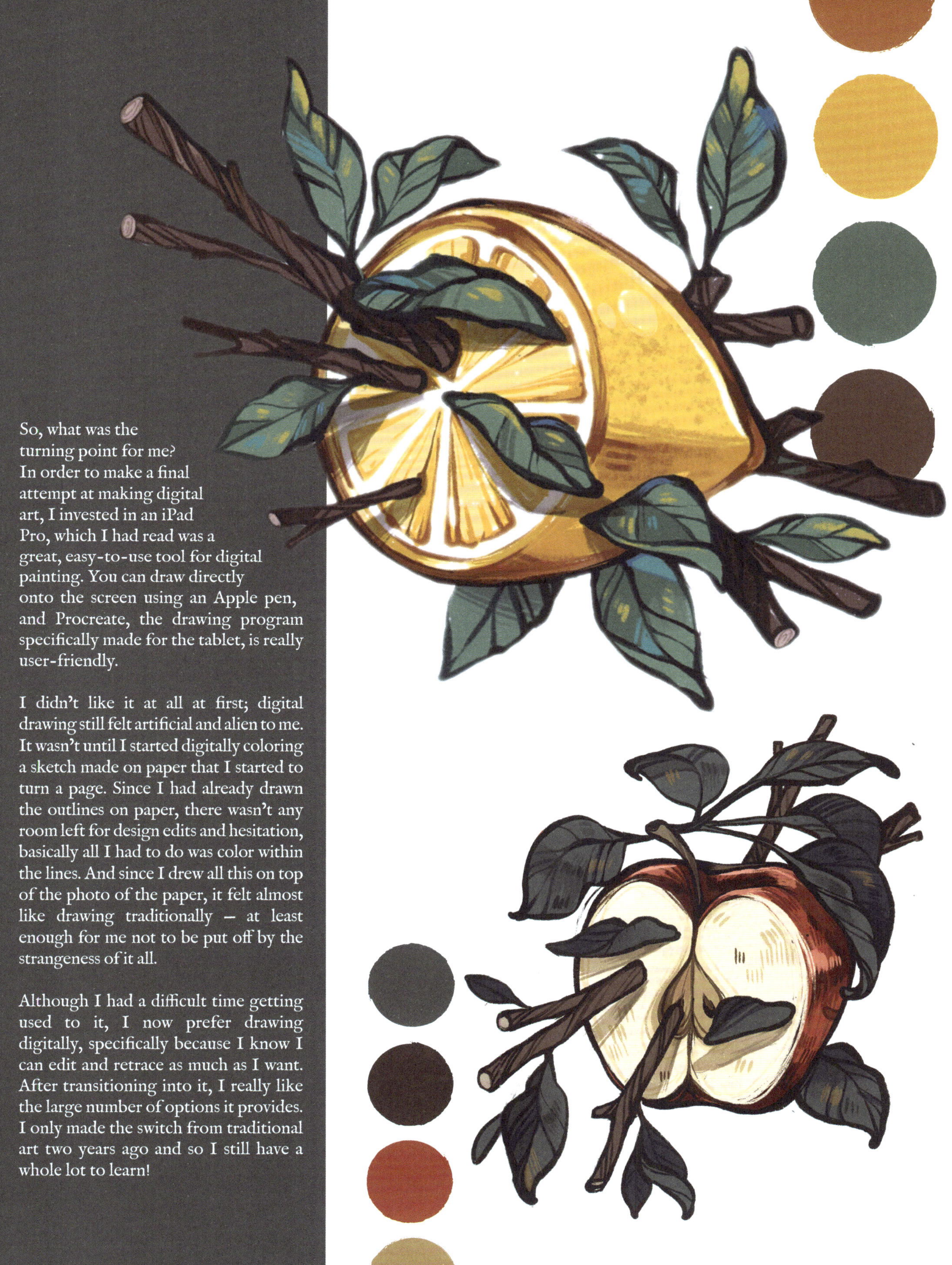

So, what was the turning point for me? In order to make a final attempt at making digital art, I invested in an iPad Pro, which I had read was a great, easy-to-use tool for digital painting. You can draw directly onto the screen using an Apple pen, and Procreate, the drawing program specifically made for the tablet, is really user-friendly.

I didn't like it at all at first; digital drawing still felt artificial and alien to me. It wasn't until I started digitally coloring a sketch made on paper that I started to turn a page. Since I had already drawn the outlines on paper, there wasn't any room left for design edits and hesitation, basically all I had to do was color within the lines. And since I drew all this on top of the photo of the paper, it felt almost like drawing traditionally – at least enough for me not to be put off by the strangeness of it all.

Although I had a difficult time getting used to it, I now prefer drawing digitally, specifically because I know I can edit and retrace as much as I want. After transitioning into it, I really like the large number of options it provides. I only made the switch from traditional art two years ago and so I still have a whole lot to learn!

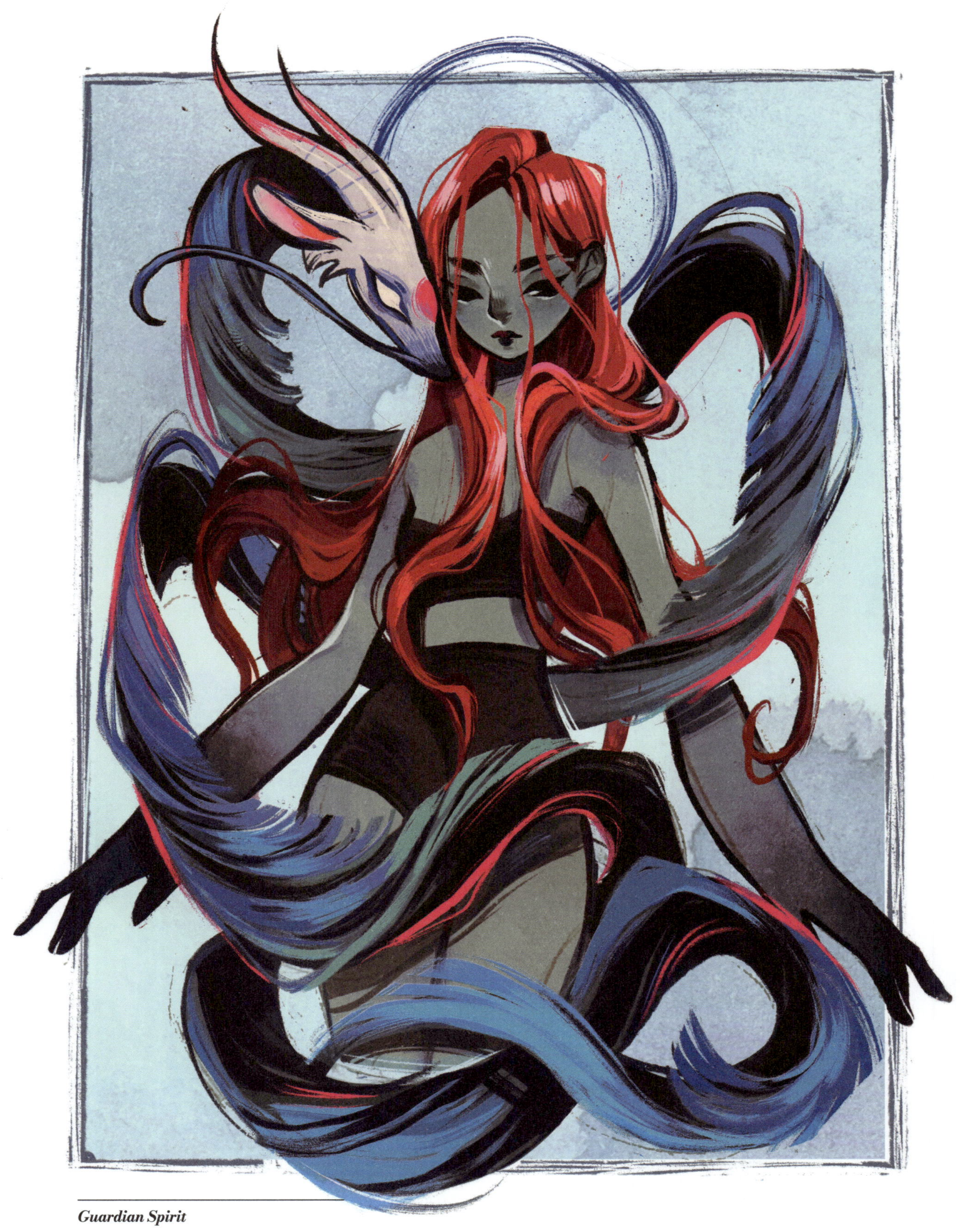

Guardian Spirit

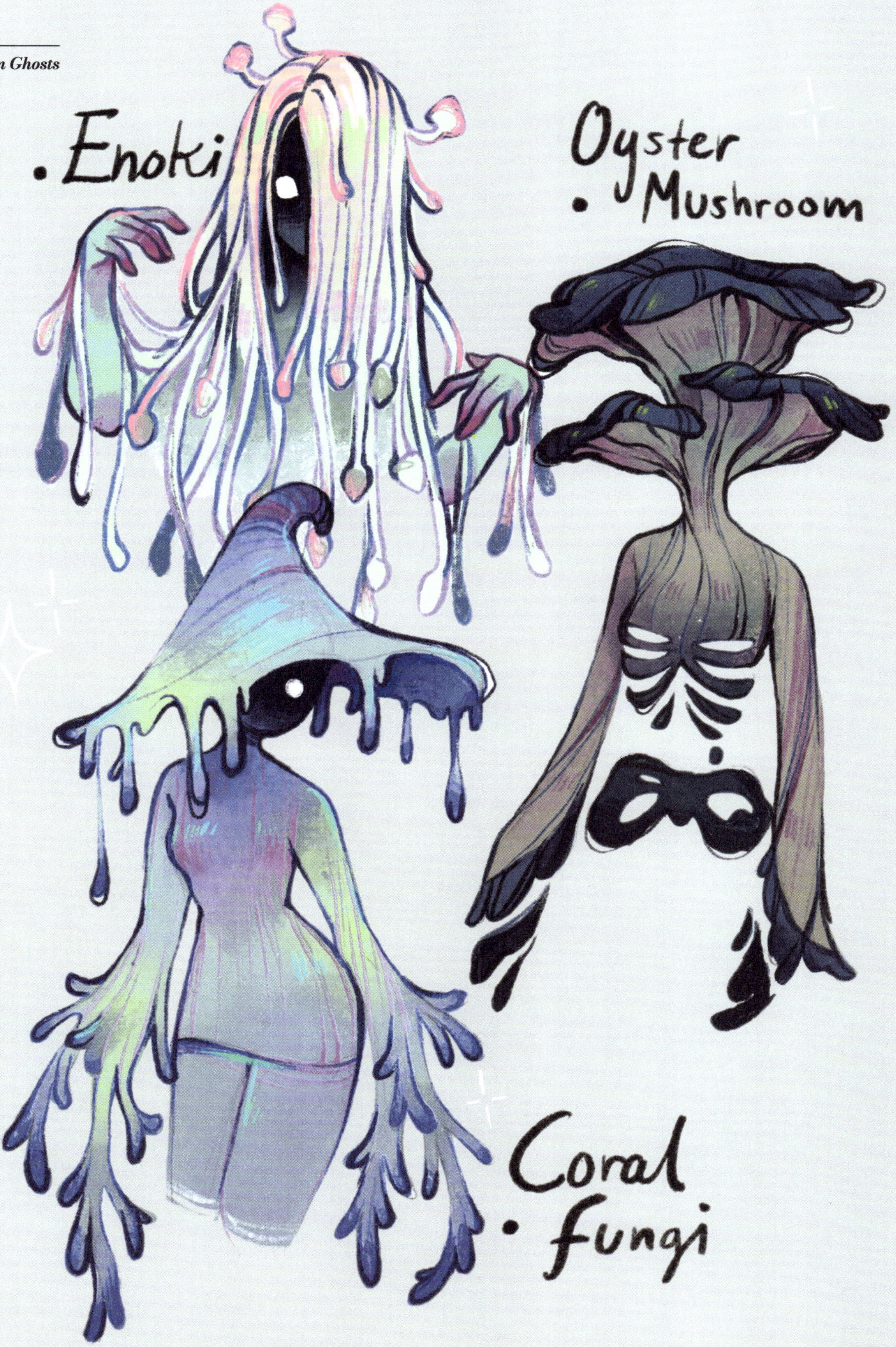

. Enoki
Oyster
. Mushroom
Coral
. fungi

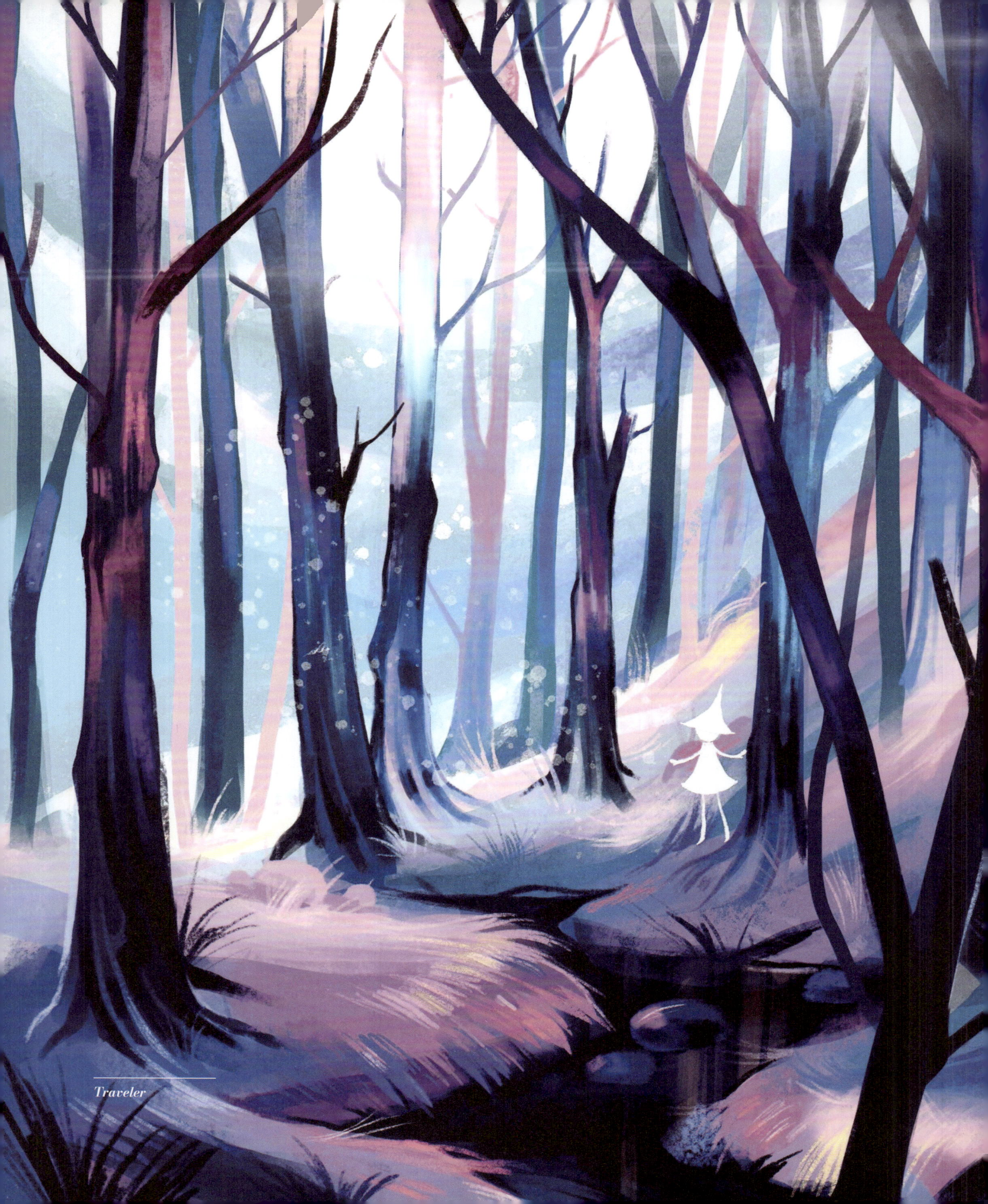

Traveler

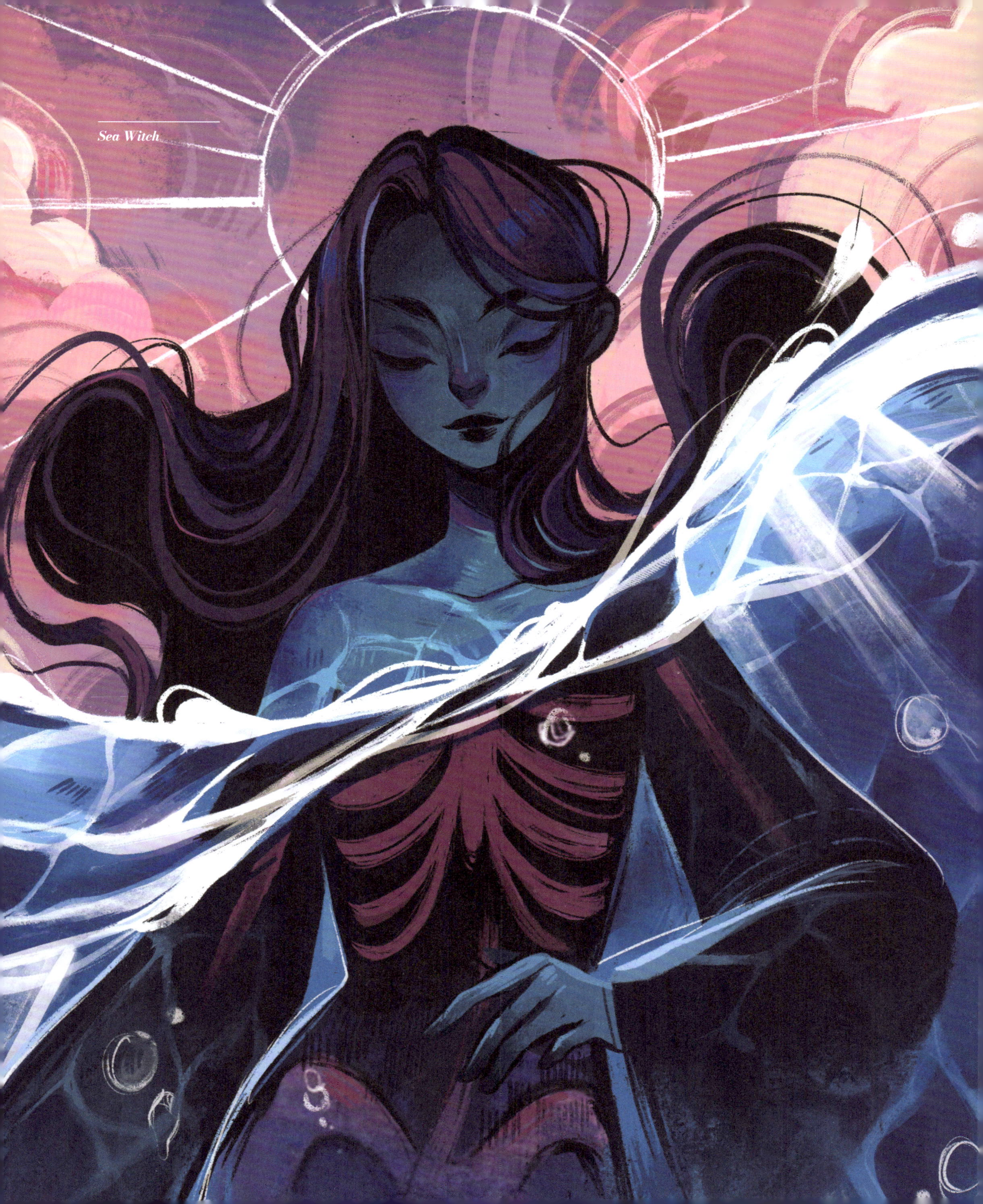

Sea Witch

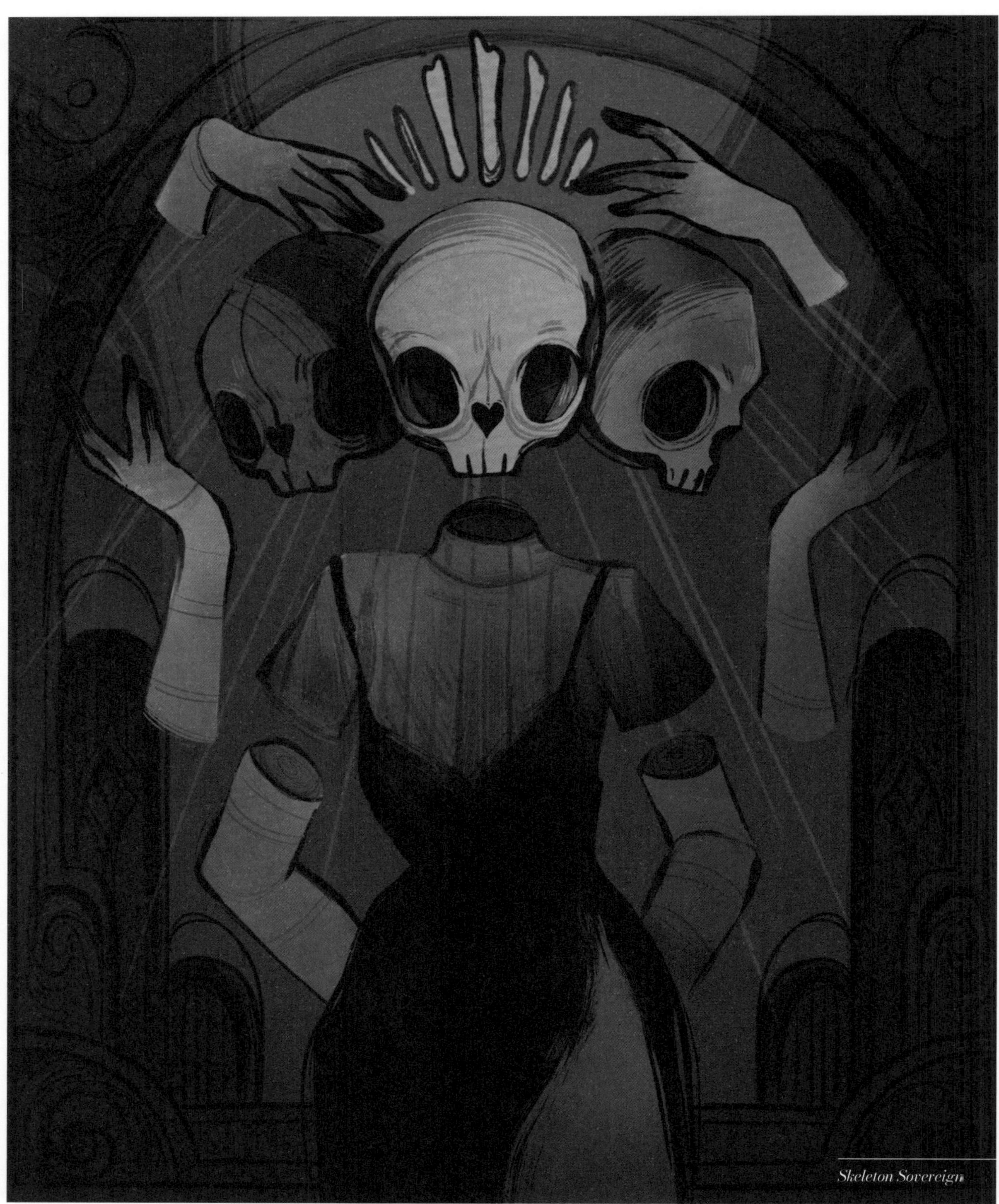

Skeleton Sovereign

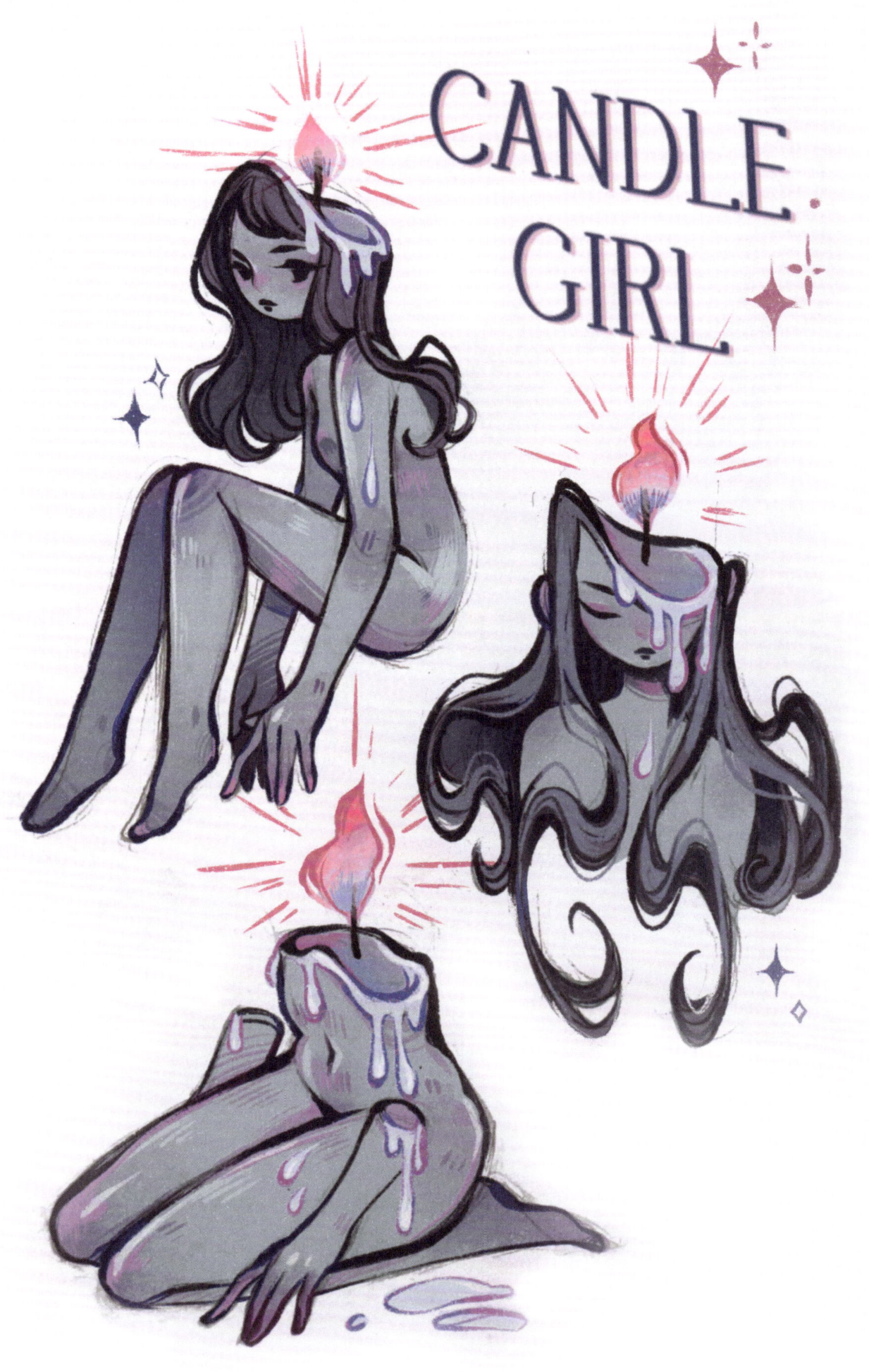
CANDLE
GIRL

Gouache paint

I used to think of gouache paint as essentially just opaque watercolor, and so I initially found it very difficult to work with because I kept trying to use it in the same way I would use watercolor paints. It wasn't until I started to appreciate gouache's unique qualities that I started to enjoy working with it. Gouache can produce bold and graphic results, while watercolors can create flowy and translucent effects. Gouache can be diluted and used in a similar way to watercolor, but in my opinion that doesn't get the most from the medium.

A quick gouache tip is that the colors tend to look different once dry, so it can be useful to create swatches of the paints you're planning on using on a piece of scrap paper before using them on the final design, so you'll know exactly what to expect.

Gouache has never really been my preferred medium, it's more like a cool cousin I only see about twice a year at family reunions. We might not see each other very often but it's always a blast when we do.

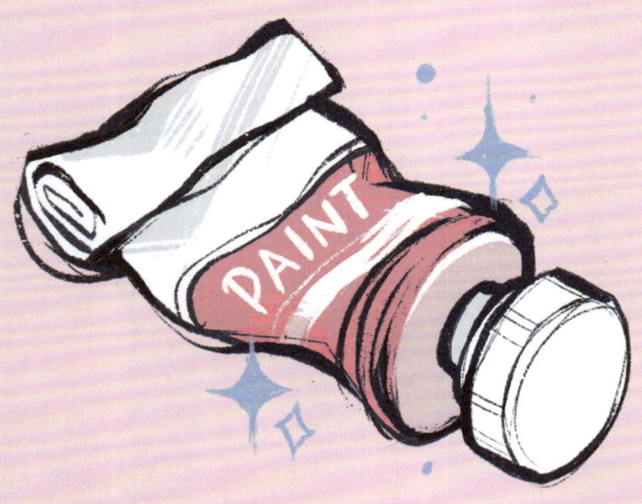

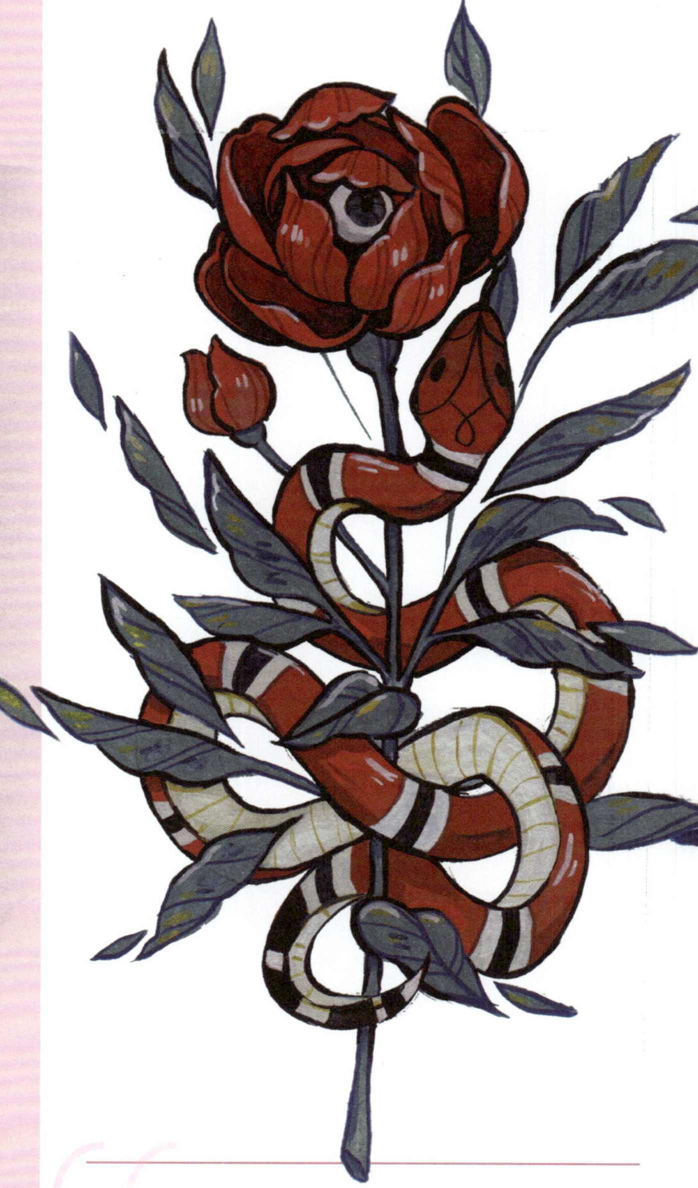

"... colors tend to look different once dry, so it can be useful to create swatches"

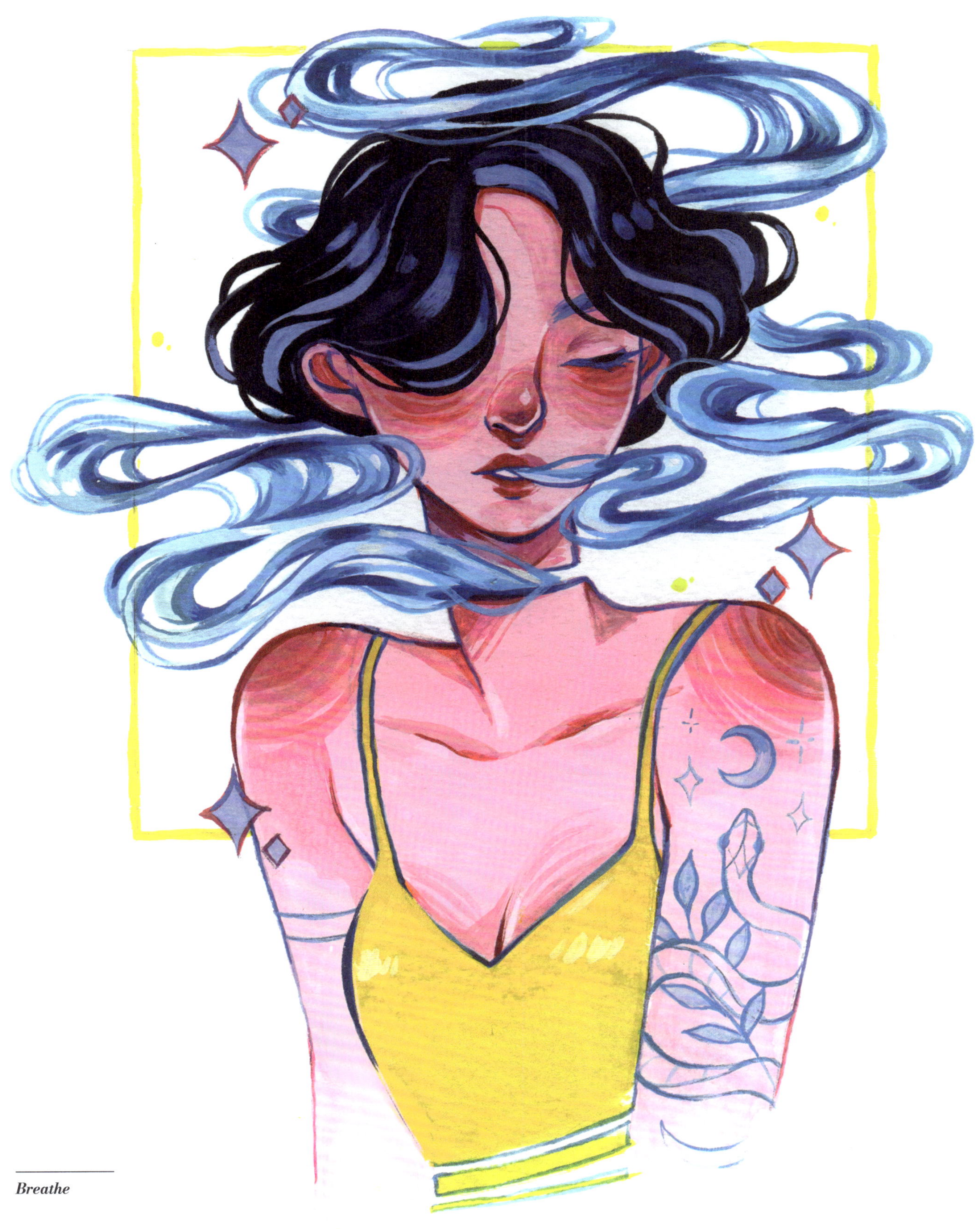

Breathe

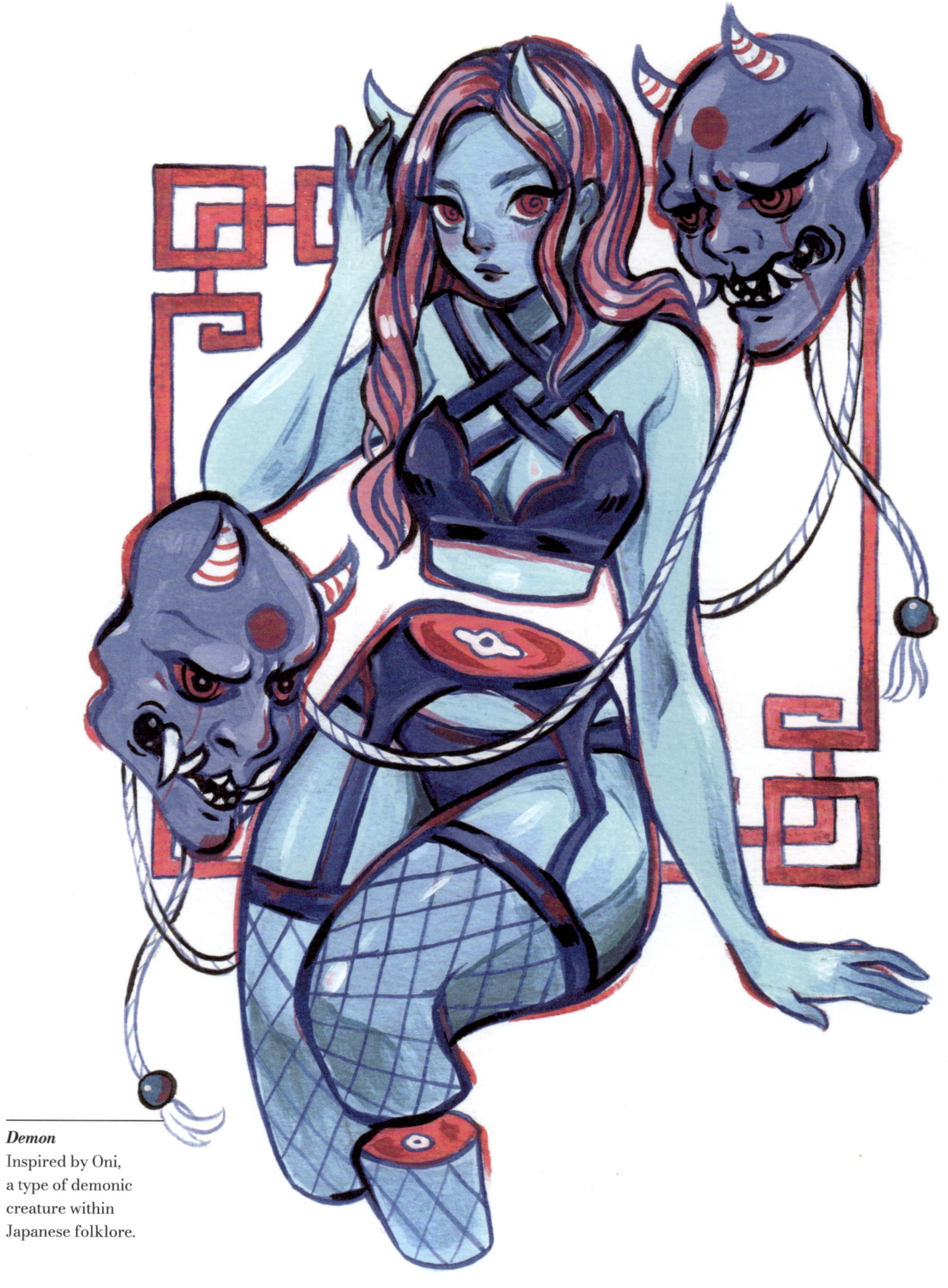

Demon
Inspired by Oni, a type of demonic creature within Japanese folklore.

Huldra

A huldra, or “skogsrå” is a creature from Scandinavian folklore. They're described as very beautiful. They have the tail of an ox and their backs are hollowed out like old trees.

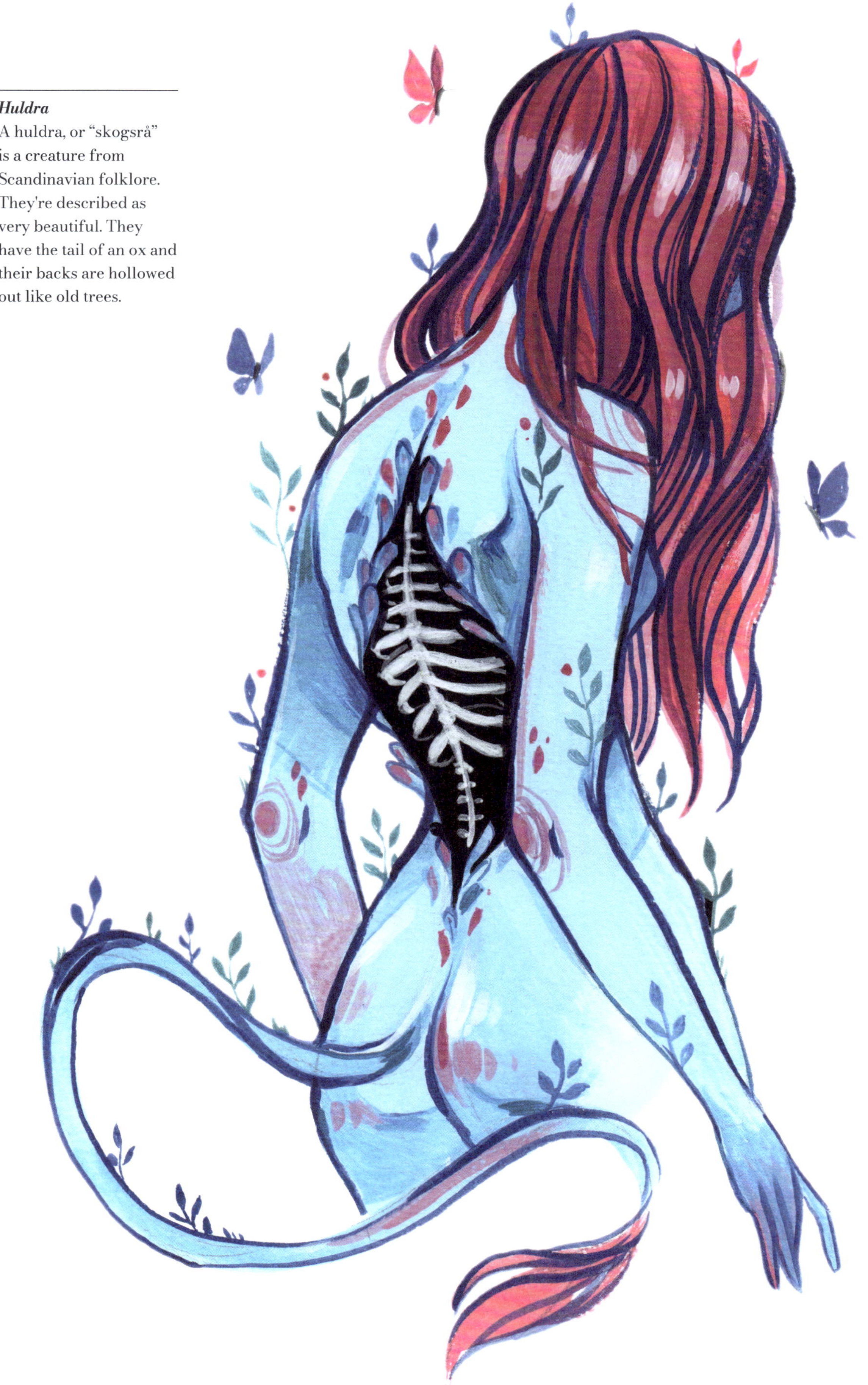

“It wasn’t until I started to appreciate gouache's unique qualities that I started to enjoy working with it”

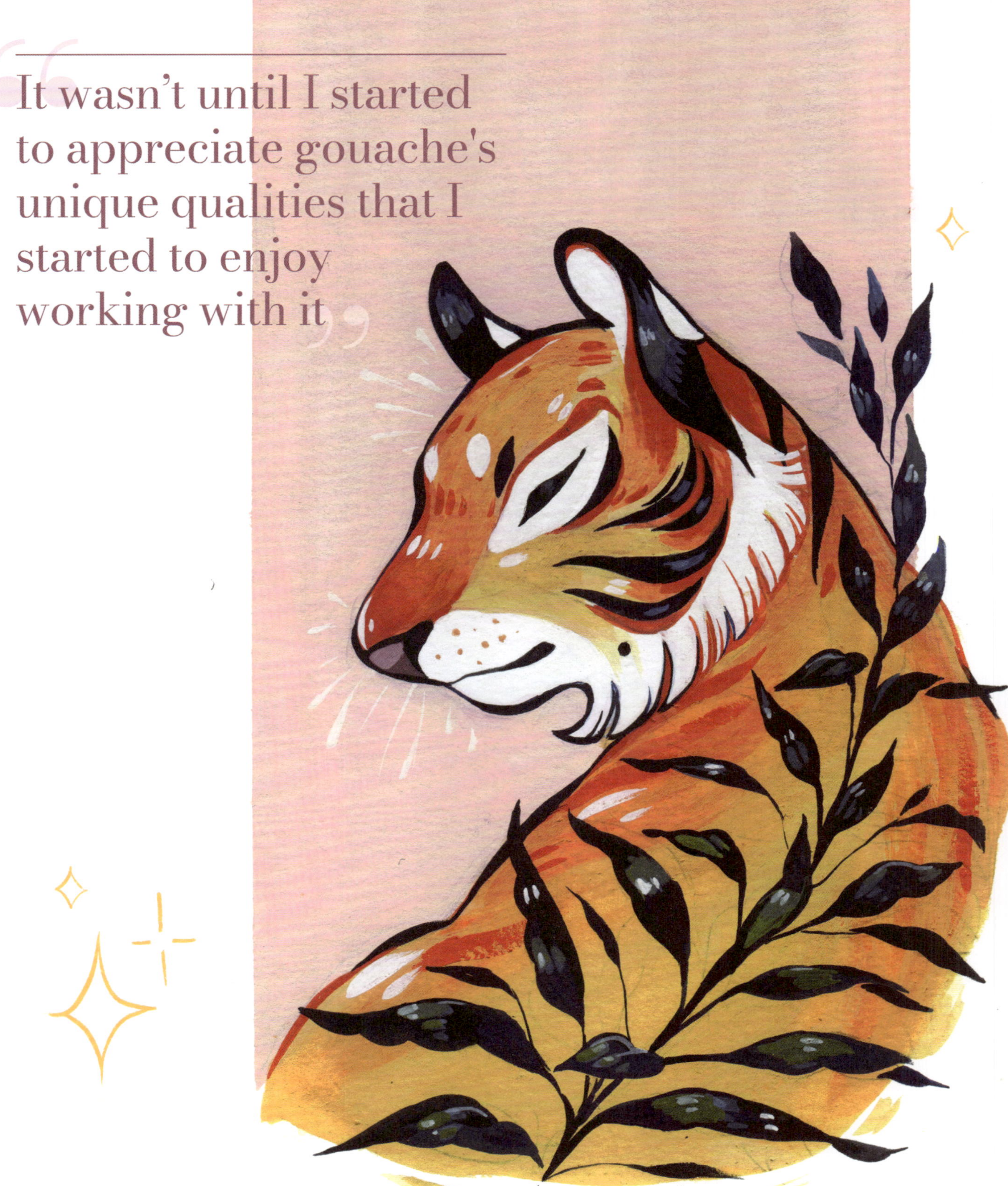

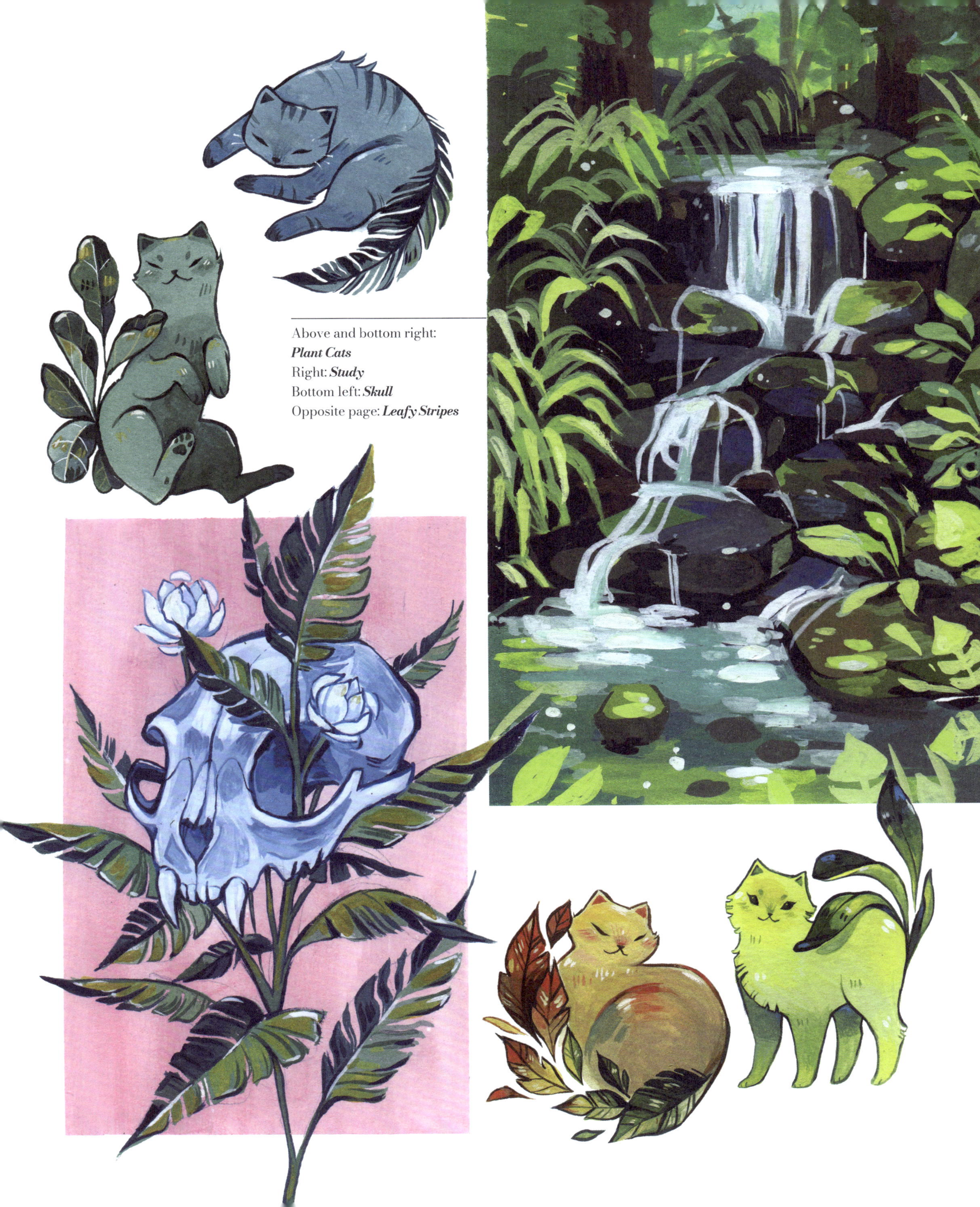

Above and bottom right: ***Plant Cats***
Right: ***Study***
Bottom left: ***Skull***
Opposite page: ***Leafy Stripes***

Ink techniques

Through this feature I demonstrate how I create a design in ink, cover a few basic tips regarding hatching, and share some of my favorite ways of using this medium. I am by no means an expert though, and there is much to learn about hatching and fineliners beyond what I've shown here, so feel free to explore for yourself!

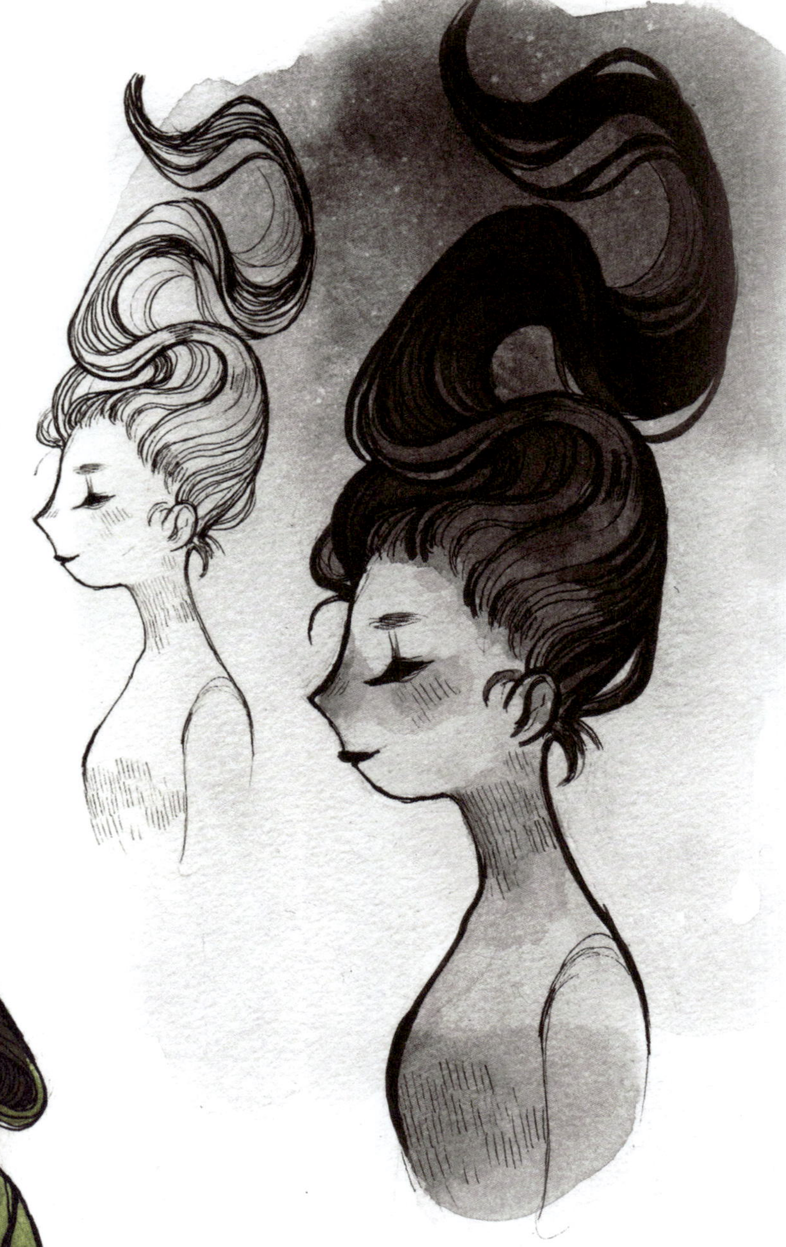

Bottled inks and fineliner pens

My favorite method when working with ink is to use a combination of fineliner pens and bottled ink. I love the texture that can be achieved with pen, and I find that adding a layer of diluted ink on the top of it helps the two ink techniques blend together harmoniously.

Though I usually stick to black ink, colored ink can also be fun to layer with! Depth can be built up in the application of colored inks in the same way as black ink, and a gradation of color can be seen even when using just one color.

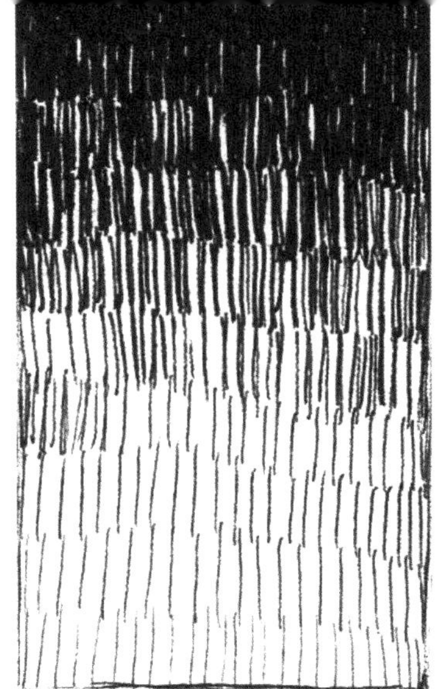

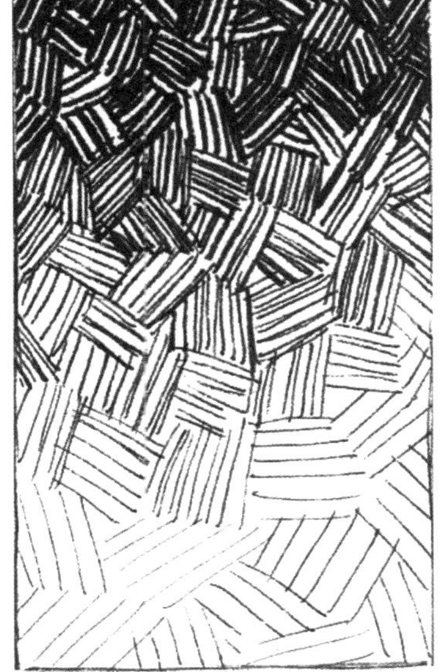

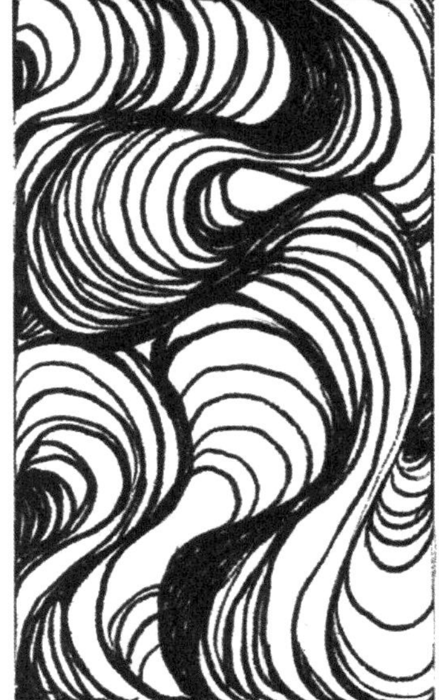

Hatching

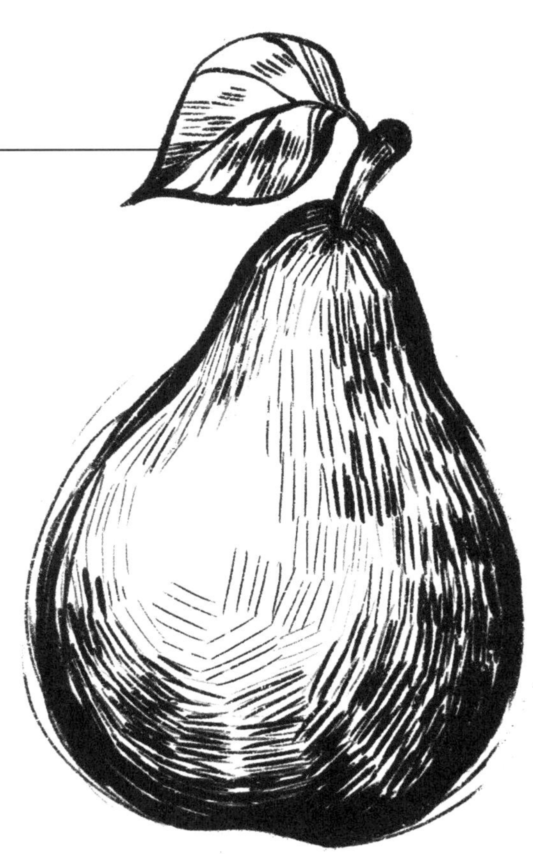

Above are some examples of patterns I like to use when drawing in ink. In the following tutorial, I use hatching purely as a means to add texture, but hatching techniques can also be used to add shading and contour edges.

I have shaded the pear opposite with a simple hatching technique. Many small parallel lines are applied to imply form and add depth to the pear. The overall dimensions of the drawing can be altered by how close or thick the parallel lines are. To get a sense of the form and lighting of the object, it is beneficial to draw hatching lines that follow the overall shape of the object.

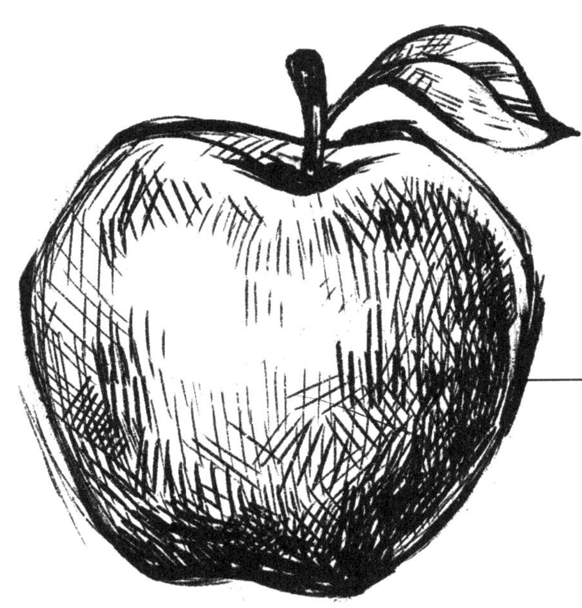

Cross-hatching

Here, I have drawn an apple using cross-hatching. As opposed to hatching that uses parallel lines, cross-hatching utilizes the crossing of lines to add depth, as implied by the name. The finish of cross-hatching is more sporadic and dynamic than that of hatching.

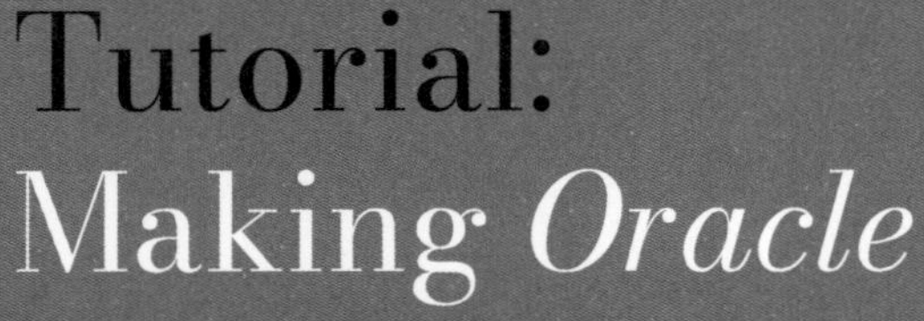

Tutorial: Making *Oracle*

When working with ink and fineliners, I like to put heavy emphasis on textures. Not only because I think it looks good, but also because I enjoy the process – there's just something relaxing and almost meditative about hatching and filling in lines. Sometimes I do get a little carried away and add a bit too much texture, but that's just part of the process.

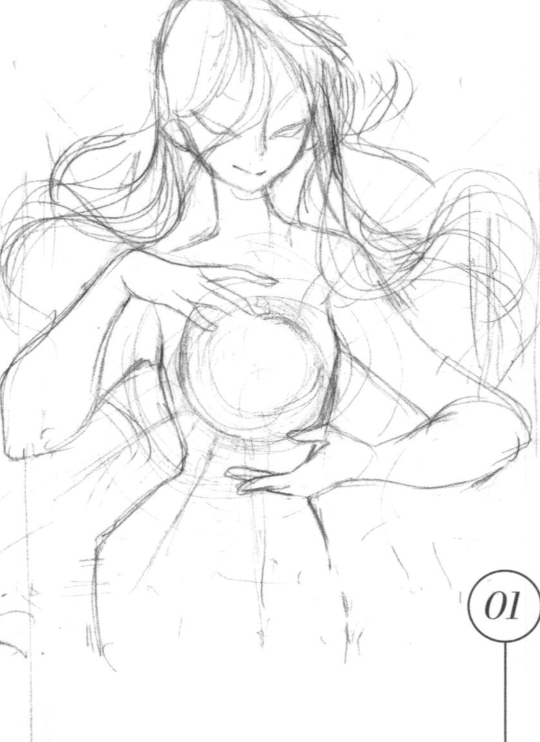

01 Loose sketch

I start by drawing a loose sketch of the illustration I have in mind directly onto the paper I'll be painting it on. I think sketching directly from the imagination gives your drawing a nice flow, which I've always found hard to emulate whenever I try to redraw an initial sketch.

02 Cleaning the sketch

Once I am satisfied with the overall composition and proportions of the design, I use a kneaded eraser to lighten and clean up the sketch. The kneaded eraser picks up excess graphite while leaving key details behind. Then, with more confident pencil strokes, I proceed to lay down the final design.

03 Adding definition

I want my character to be seen holding a light-emitting orb. To create beams of light that appear to shine evenly and symmetrically from the orb, I draw a dot in the center of the orb and use a ruler to draw out lines that would align with its core. It's a very simple and neat trick, and saves you a lot of time agonizing over uneven light rays!

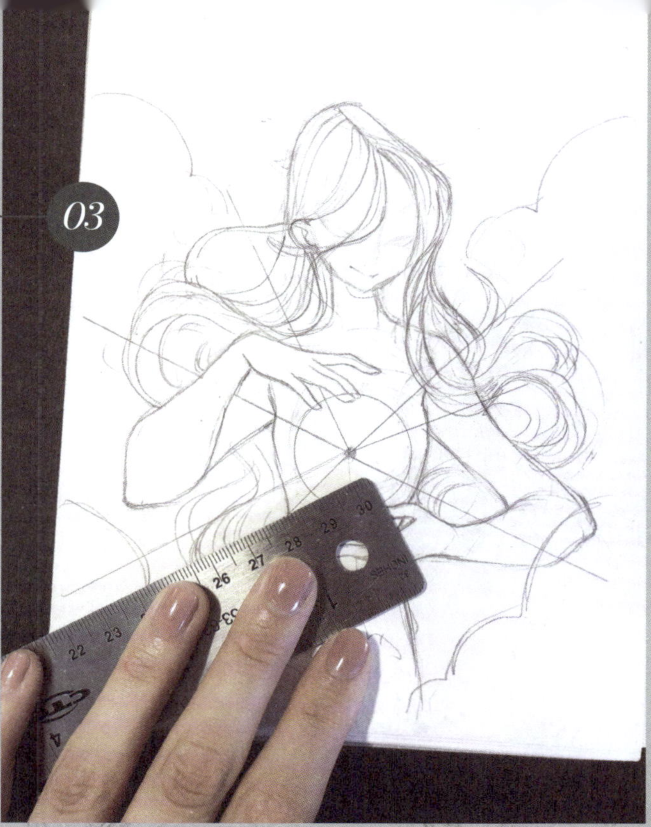

03

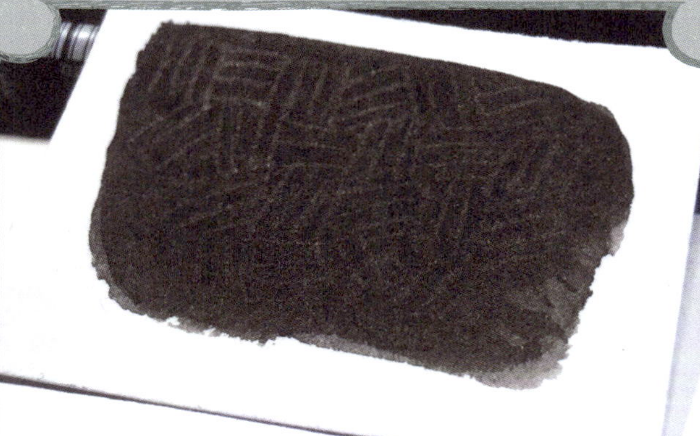

Fineliner reflections

If you start by painting with liquid ink and then use fineliner pens, rather than vice-versa, your pen work will reflect light at certain angles because the ink used in fineliners is slightly glossy. So, if you wish to avoid this effect, I recommend using fineliners first!

04

04 Inking linework

Next comes the dreaded part, drawing with ink! Ink is a permanent medium, so it can be a little daunting to apply. What I enjoy about using ink is that as the medium can't be removed, you have to learn to work with your mistakes. I like to use fineliner pens before introducing liquid ink, because acrylic ink has an effective matte finish that sits evenly on top of pen work.

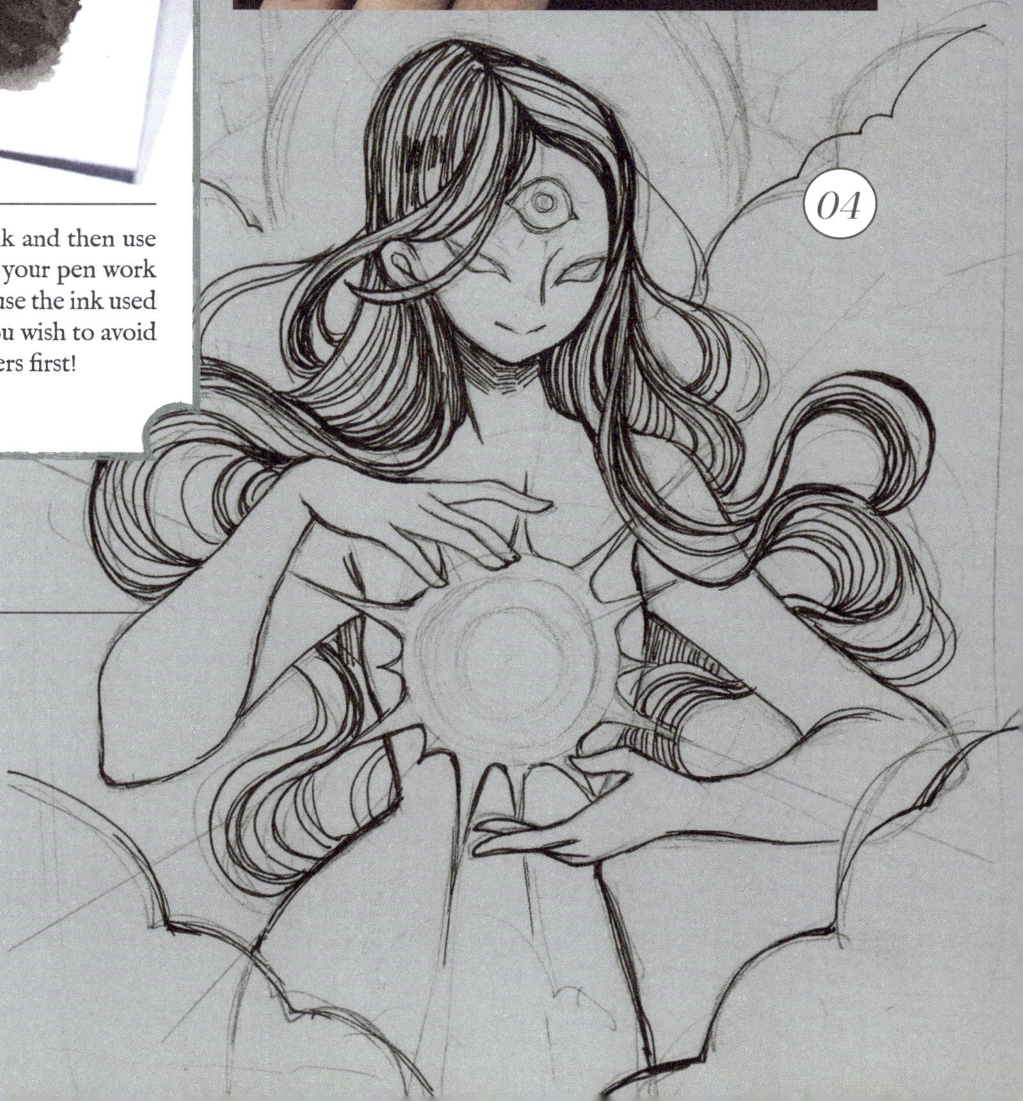

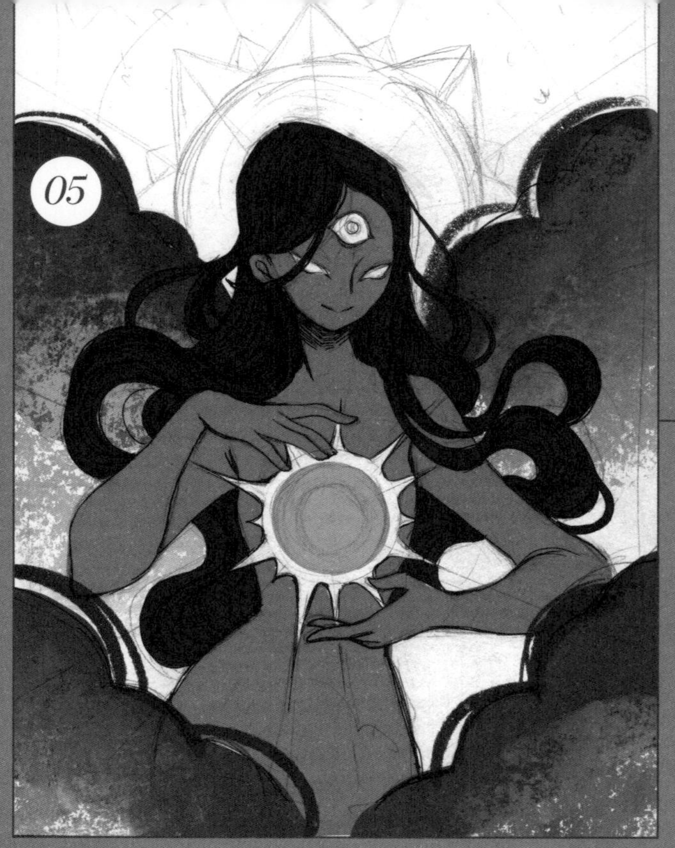

05 Digital mock-up

I'm unsure about which shades of gray to use, so I make a really quick digital mock-up to better visualize how the final piece will look. When working with a permanent medium such as ink, it's helpful to have a vague idea of how your colors and shades will align before starting the painting process. First, I scan my drawing, then I open it in Procreate, and finally I fill it with the shades I plan to use.

06 Initial hatching

Now that I have decided which shades of gray to use, I return to drawing with fineliner pens. I use hatching to introduce additional details to the hair and surrounding clouds. Hatching and cross-hatching are often used to apply shadow and dimension, but as I will layer this piece with ink washes later, I don't focus too closely on that aspect.

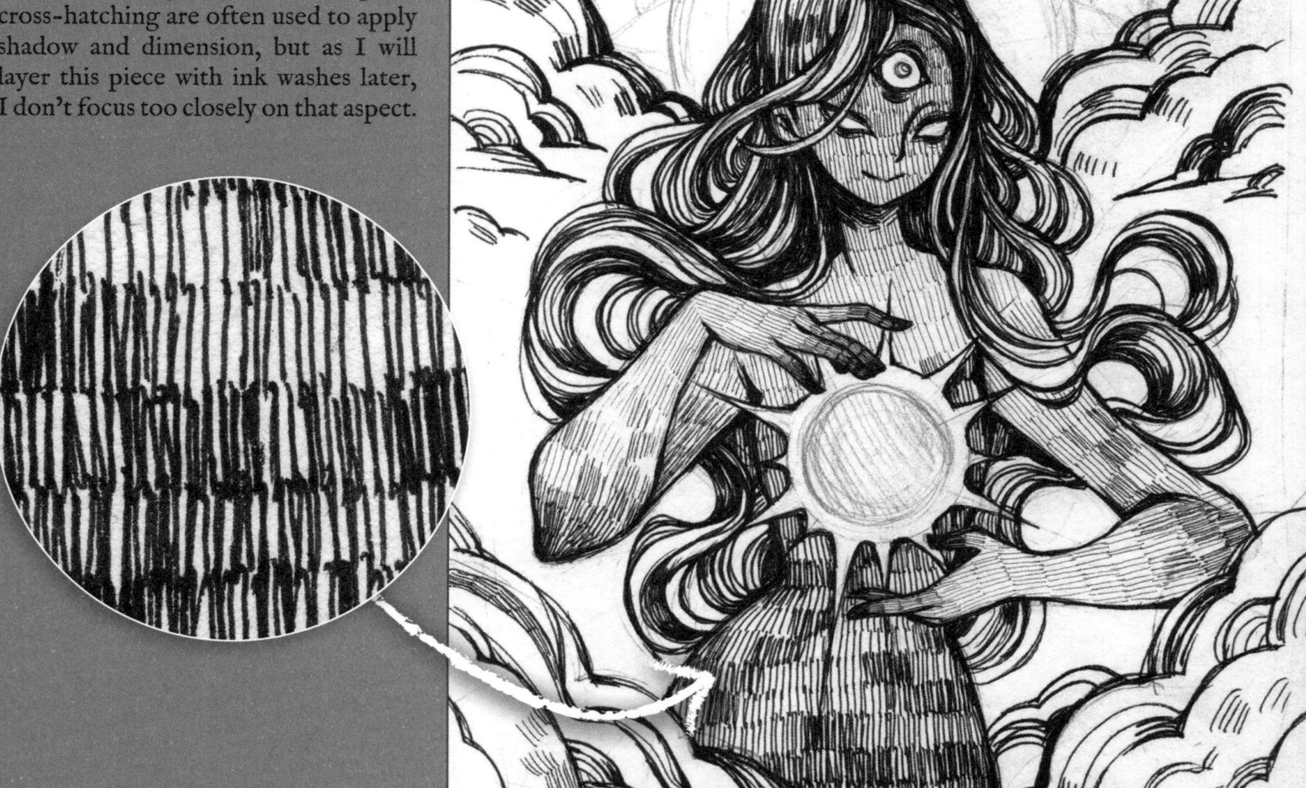

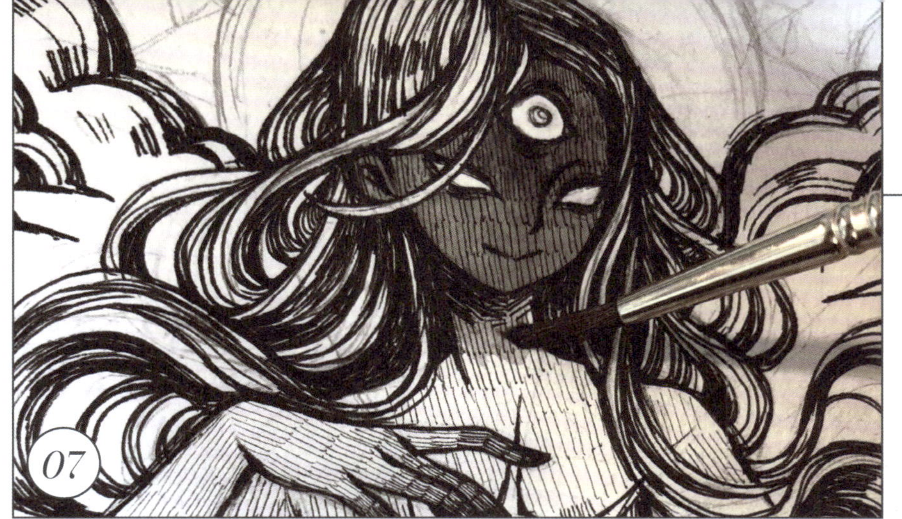

07 Ink wash

Next, I add a base layer of ink. I lay down a thin wash of diluted black acrylic ink at first. As the ink isn't water-soluble but sticks to the paper firmly, it's very easy to layer more ink on top.

08 Defining wash

I proceed by adding a second layer of ink, which adds some more dimension. I focus on the darkest inner parts and ends of her hair, her fingertips, and her elbows. I also add shadows to the surrounding clouds.

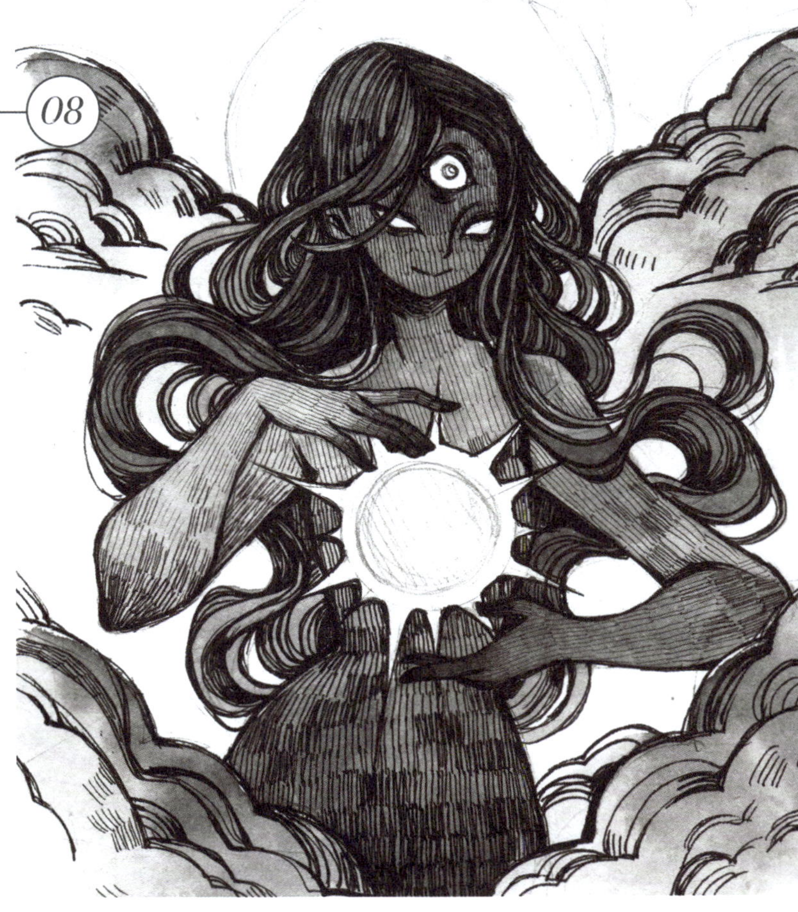

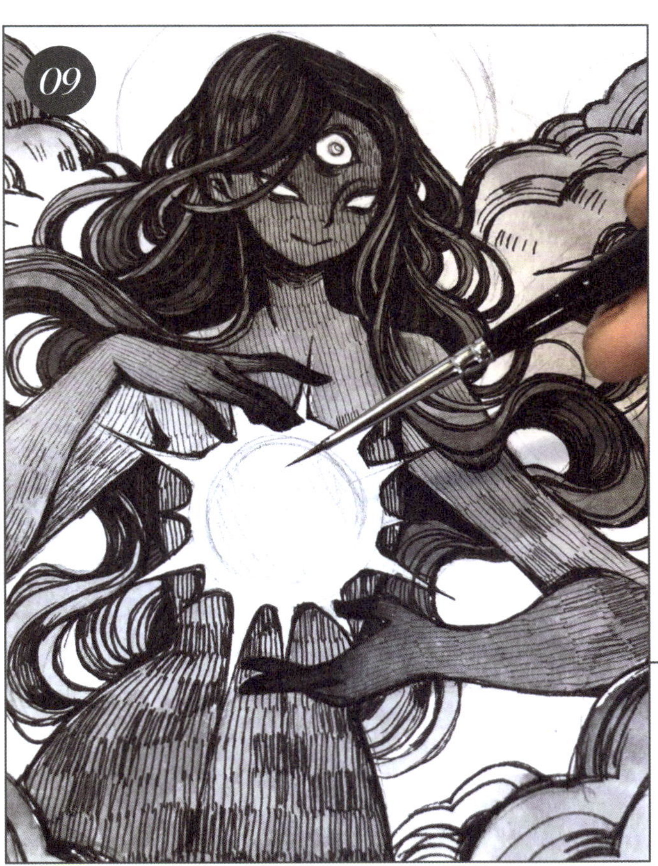

09 Lining

In addition to the linework made using pens, I also add some lining using the thin brush shown here. It's subtle, but I add thicker lines to the parts of her body that round out, such as her forearms, the back of her hand, and certain parts of her hair. This increases line weight where I want to add fluidity and makes the contours of the drawing more interesting.

10 Precision detailing

I want to add some detail to the orb and make the inner circle more even, so, after erasing the initial orb sketch, I use a circle stencil to draw a neater final version. It's a really nifty tool that I always keep at hand when drawing circles, since it can be difficult and a little time-consuming to draw a perfect circle by hand.

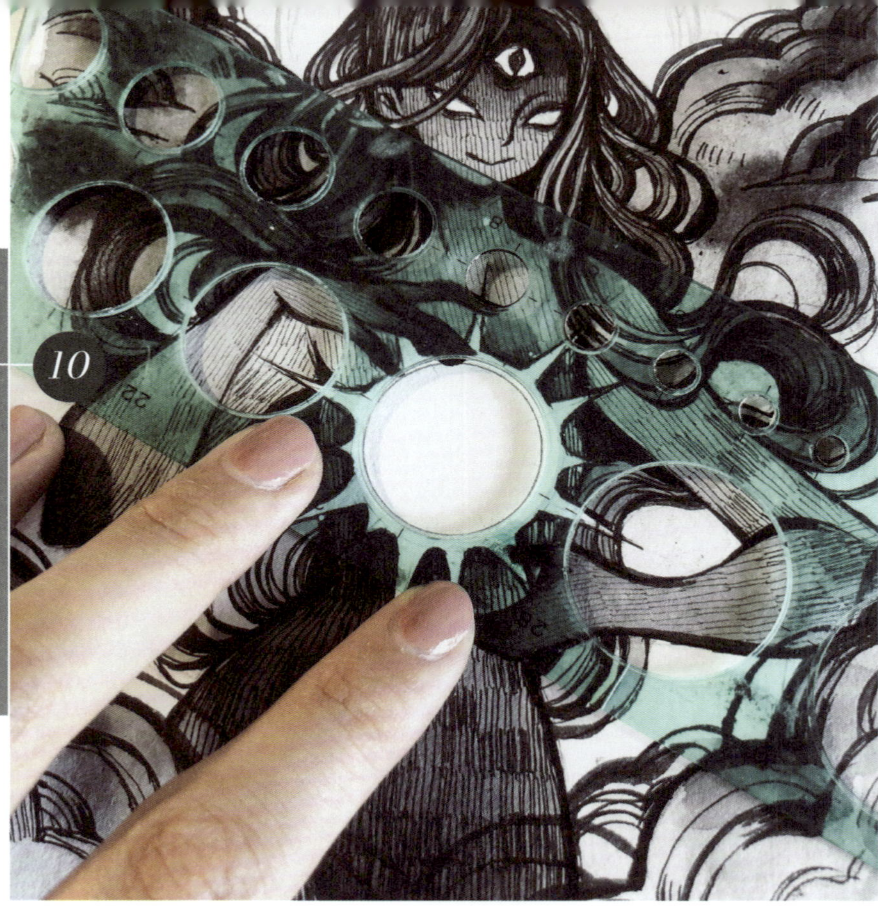

11 Making corrections

Although ink is a permanent medium, there is one handy trick for correcting light mistakes. By using a white gel pen (or any other white opaque medium), small ink blobs or marks can be blocked out. Using this method, I clean up the edges of the light orb.

12 Introducing a background

When I am satisfied with my drawing, I add a quick sunrise background to complete the piece. I experiment with various different background elements during the process of this drawing, but decide to go with something simpler since the rest of the piece is quite detailed. I use a ruler to create evenly spaced light ray lines that shine from the center of the semi-circle sun, which is the same technique I used when drawing the orb in step 03.

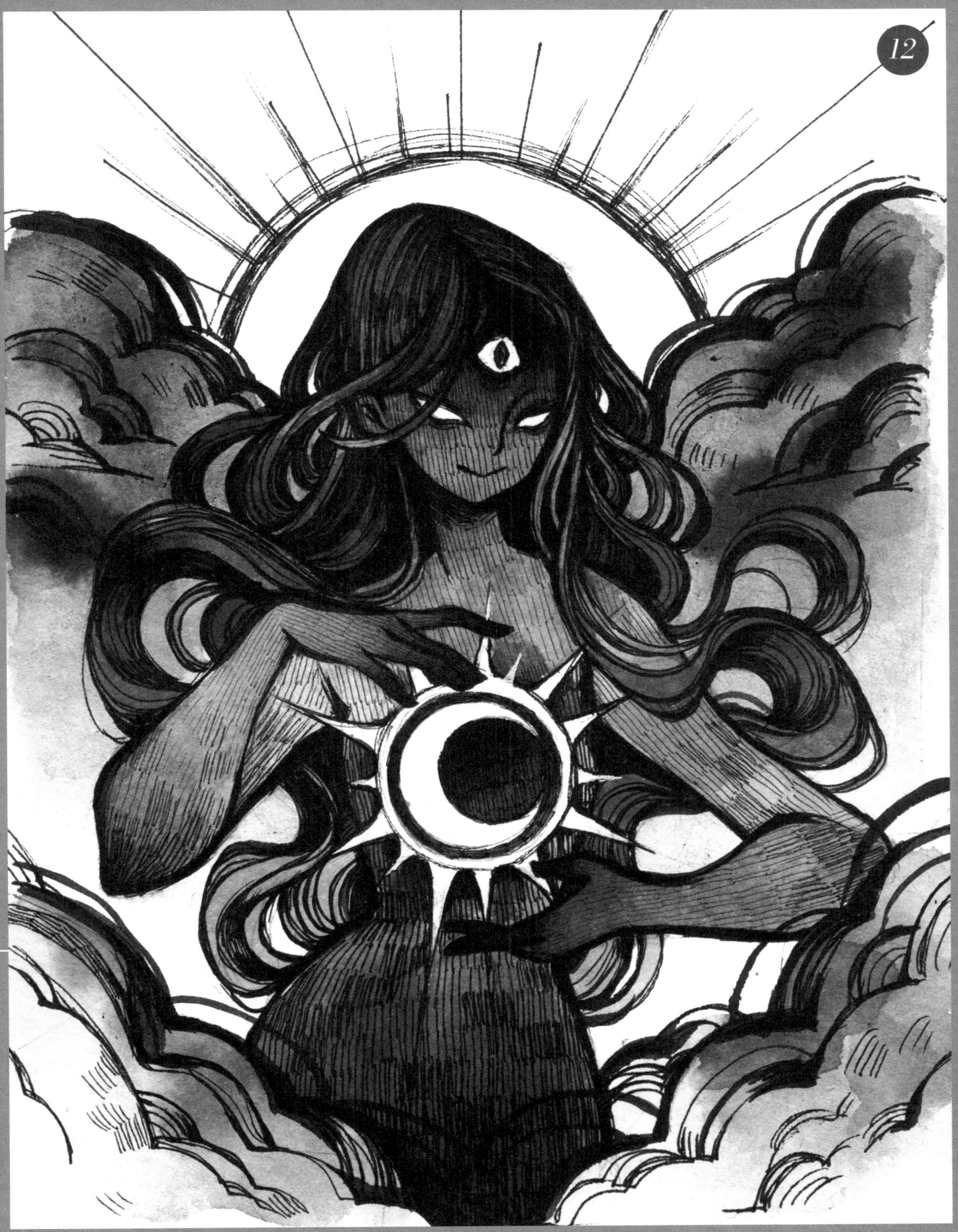
12

Tutorial: Designing *Dreams of Starry Skies and Steep Mountains*

In this tutorial, I demonstrate how I create an illustration that combines both traditional and digital media. I use watercolor paints with digital painting techniques to take advantage of the lovely texture of the watercolor paints and the intricate detail and precision that comes with working digitally.

I really enjoy using watercolor paints. They have been my favorite medium since I was a young teen. The way that the vivid pigments spread across white textured paper is just so dreamy! The only downside is that it's not a very forgiving medium, and you're somewhat limited in the number of mistakes you're allowed to make before the paper disintegrates.

Digital painting, however, is on the other end of the spectrum. Working on digital painting software allows you to alter and readjust your piece as much as you want, without having to adhere to the limitations of paper durability. So, why not combine them to get the best of both worlds?

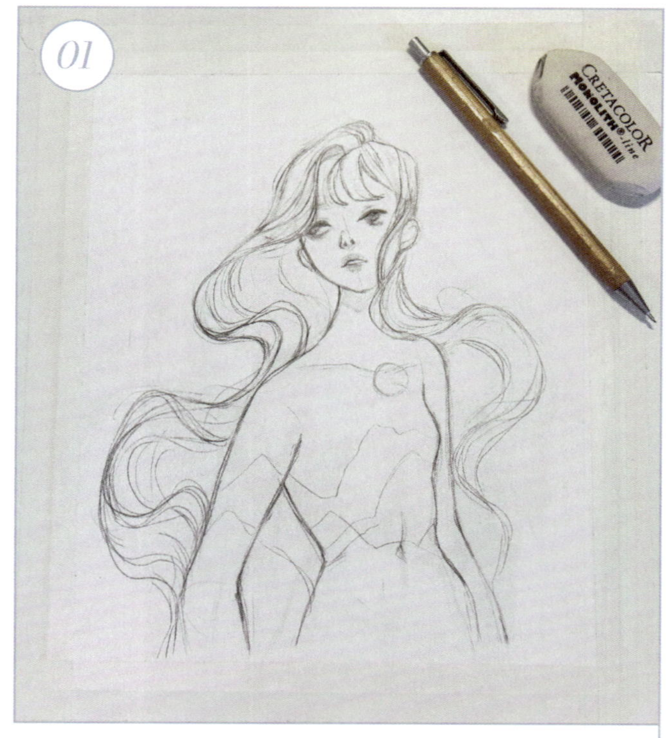

01 Base sketch

I start with a sketch, drawn on watercolor paper. I then tape the sketch down to my desk in order to minimize any warping from the water that is to come.

02 Lightening the sketch

Next, I blot the sketch with a kneadable eraser, picking up excess graphite and making it a little lighter. Since graphite is hard to erase once paint has been applied over it, I like to remove some of it now. This will prevent it from shining through the watercolor later.

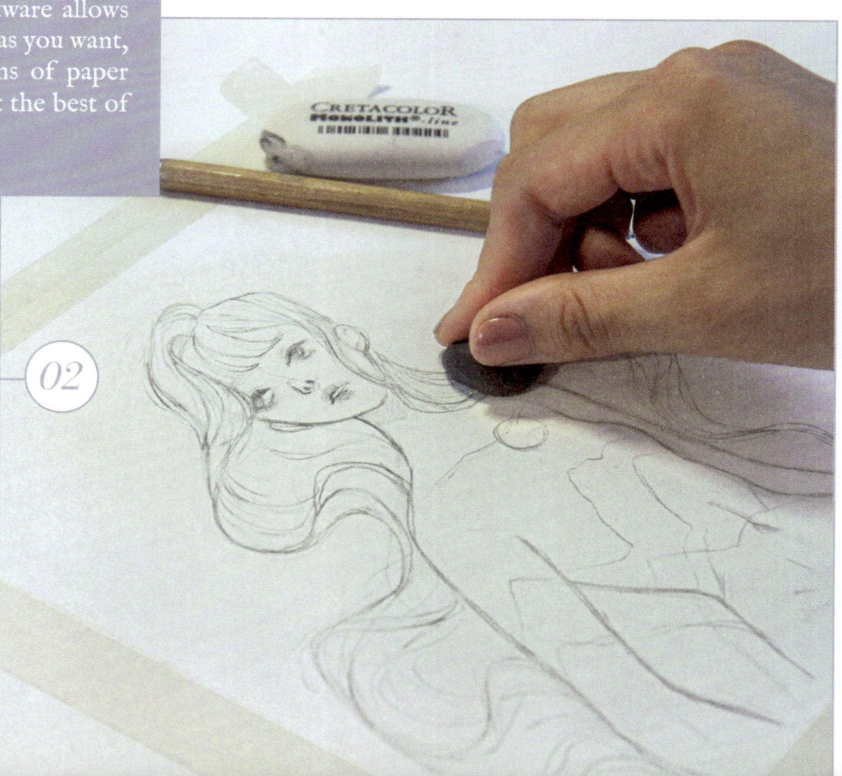

03 Surface preparation

Using a brush, I cover all of the paper with a thin layer of water in order to prepare it for the paint. Painting directly onto dry paper results in the colors being instantly absorbed, which you might want to avoid if you are looking to cover an even surface. By wetting the paper first, the paint can flow more evenly across the surface area – a finish I'm hoping to achieve.

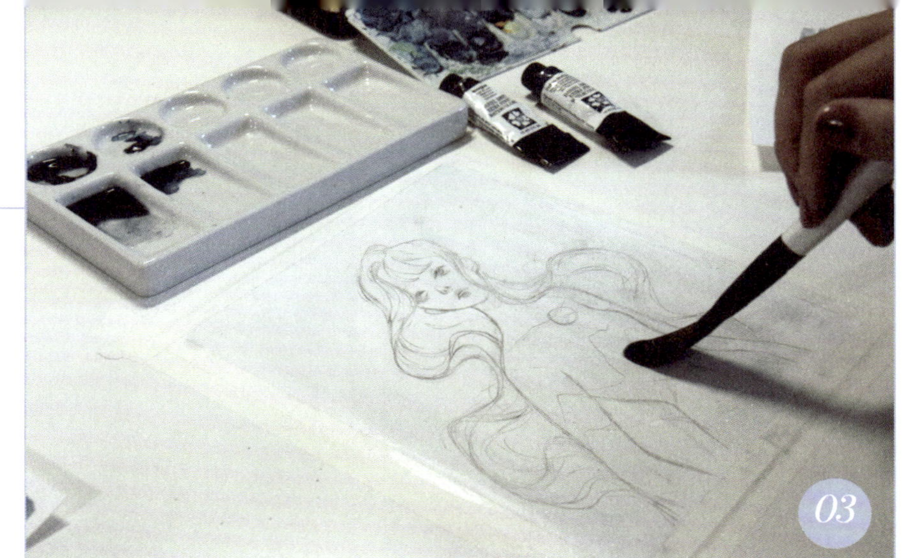

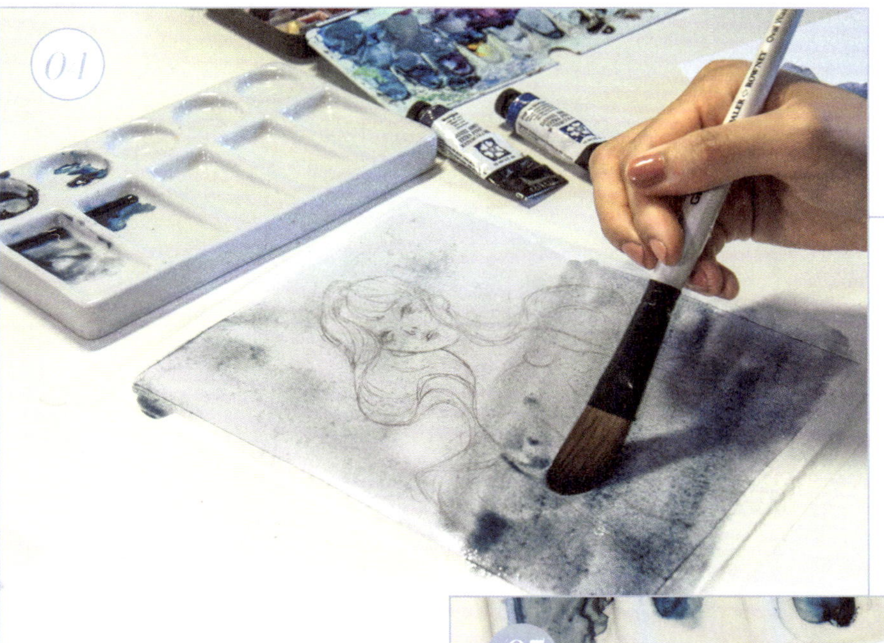

04 Adding base color

Once the surface of the paper is wet, I lay down a coat of watercolor paint and allow it to run freely. Since I'm striving for some shade nuance and texture, I don't have to be super-careful and precise with the application. Instead, I apply it loosely and randomly.

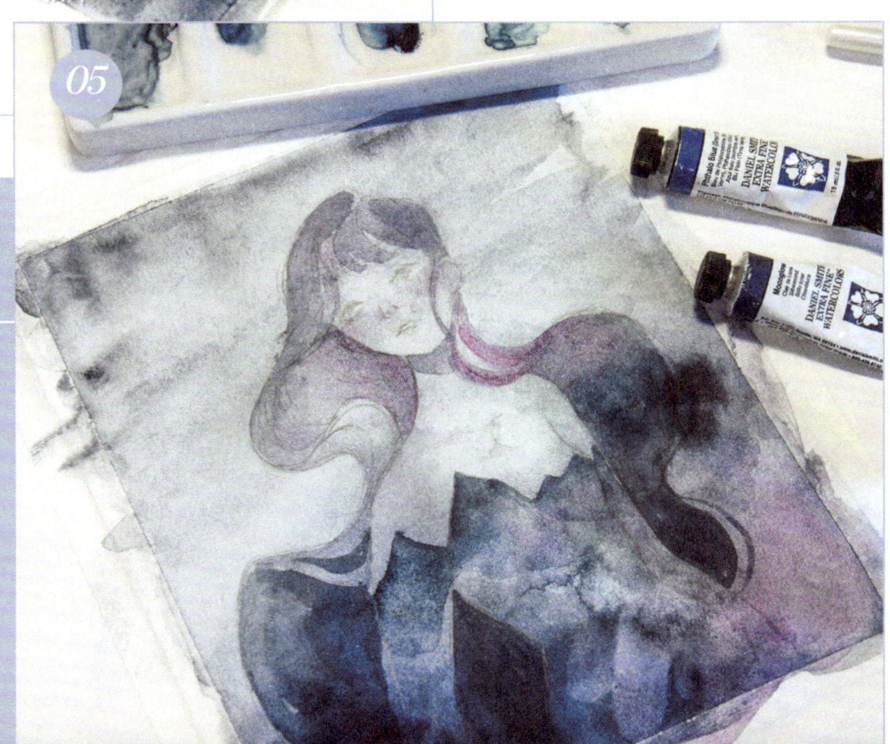

05 Introducing mountain forms

To begin the painting of a mountain range scene, I apply additional hues and paint the top row of mountains first. The idea for this piece was a woman whose silhouette blends with nature, so I paint the mountains directly into her body. At this stage, I also paint in the first layer for her hair.

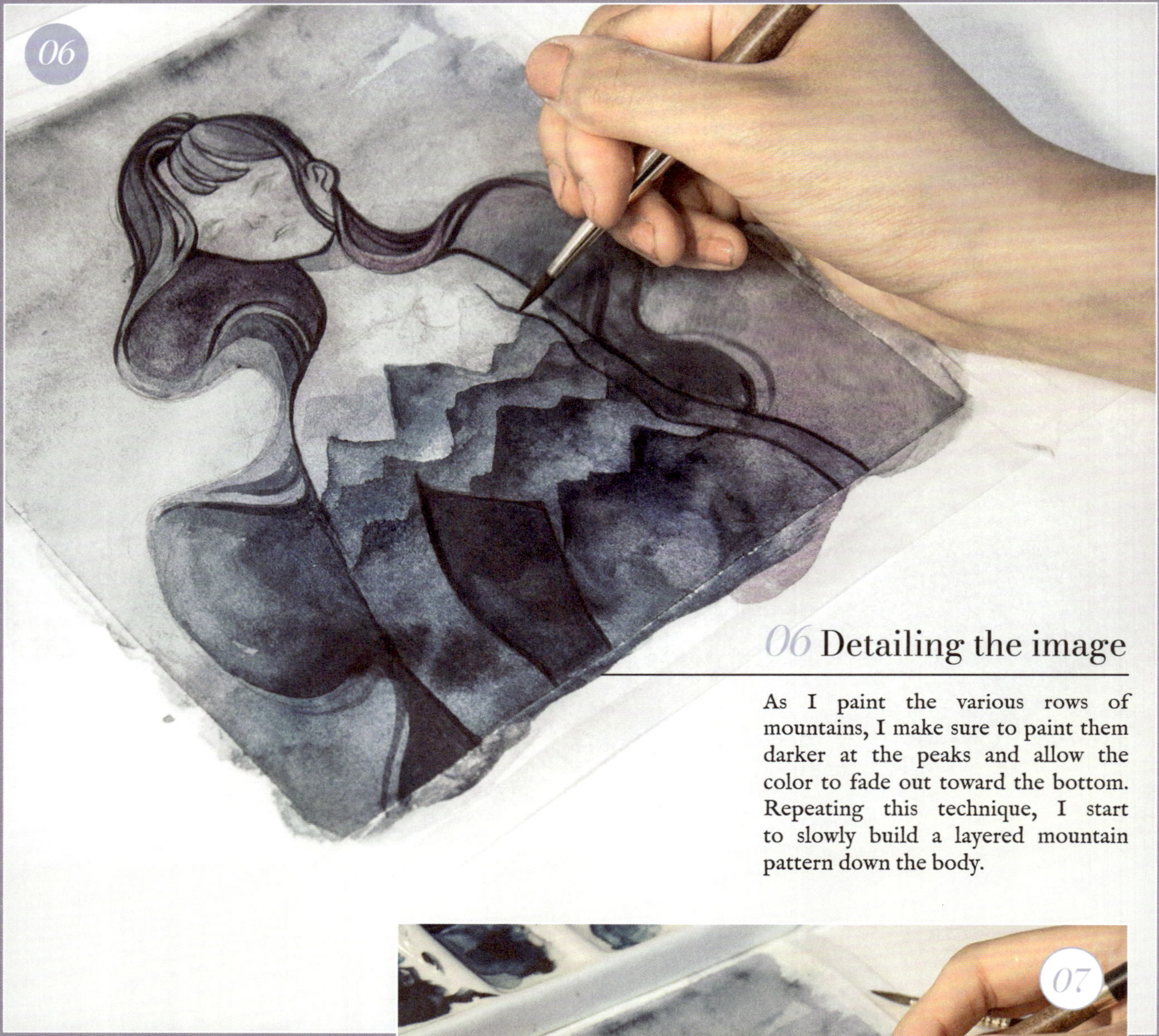

06 Detailing the image

As I paint the various rows of mountains, I make sure to paint them darker at the peaks and allow the color to fade out toward the bottom. Repeating this technique, I start to slowly build a layered mountain pattern down the body.

07 Crisp outlines

I then use a thin paintbrush to outline the painting. I love lining my drawings and I often do it sporadically during the process because I believe it makes everything look more cohesive and defined. Everything can start to look like a jumbled, contour-less blob of paint if I don't add crisp lines every now and then!

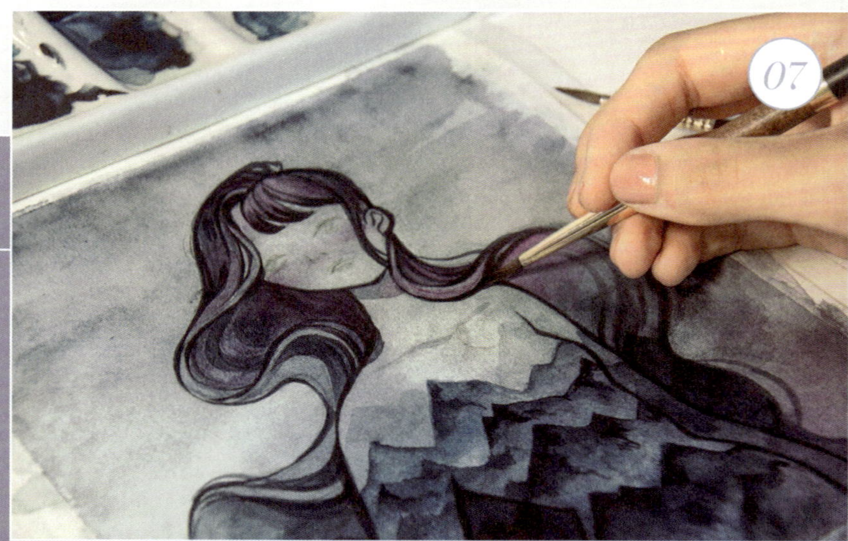

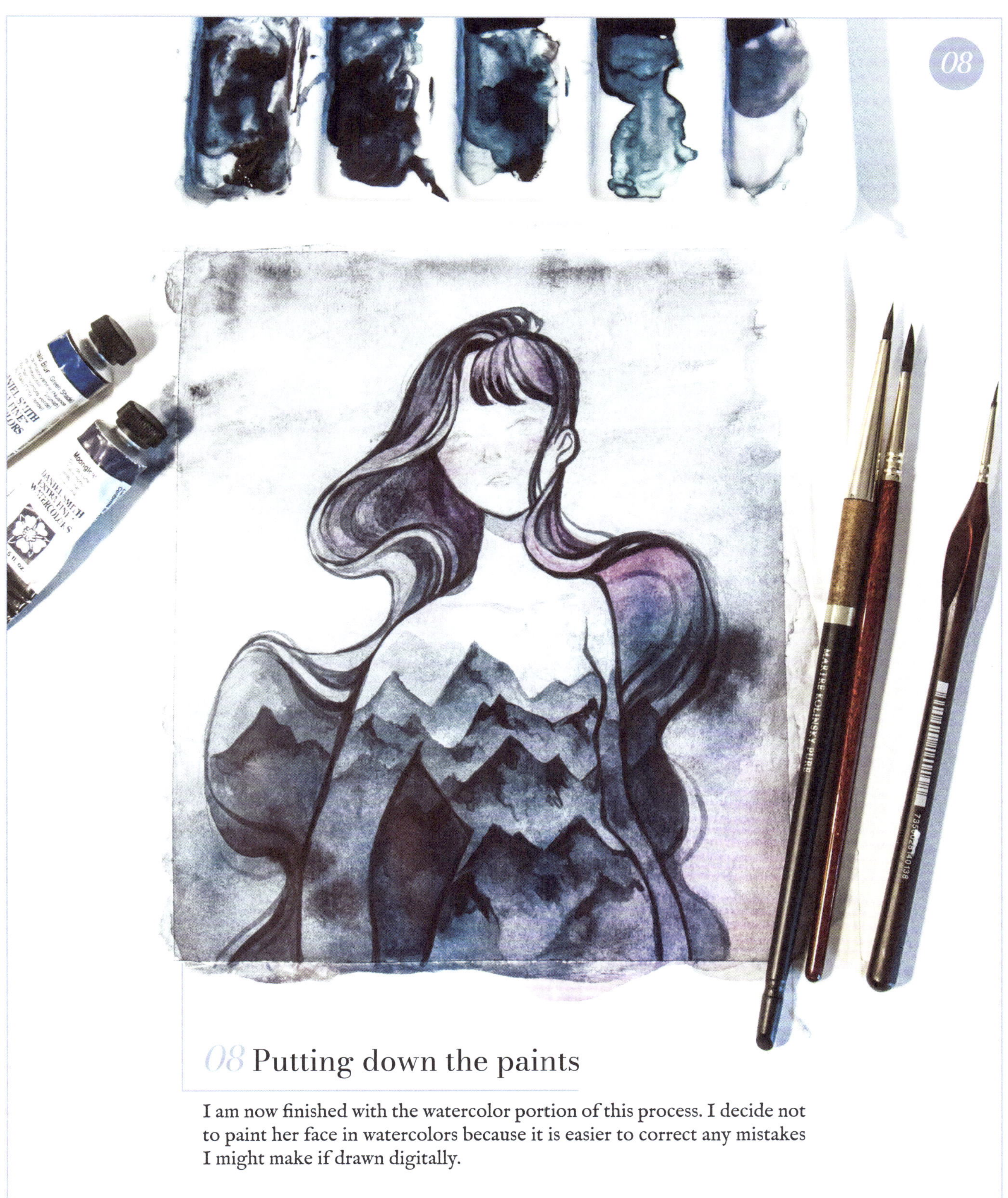

08 Putting down the paints

I am now finished with the watercolor portion of this process. I decide not to paint her face in watercolors because it is easier to correct any mistakes I might make if drawn digitally.

09 Scanning in

Next, to begin the digital painting portion of the tutorial, I scan the painting and open the file in Procreate. I then adjust the contrast slightly to make the colors pop a little more.

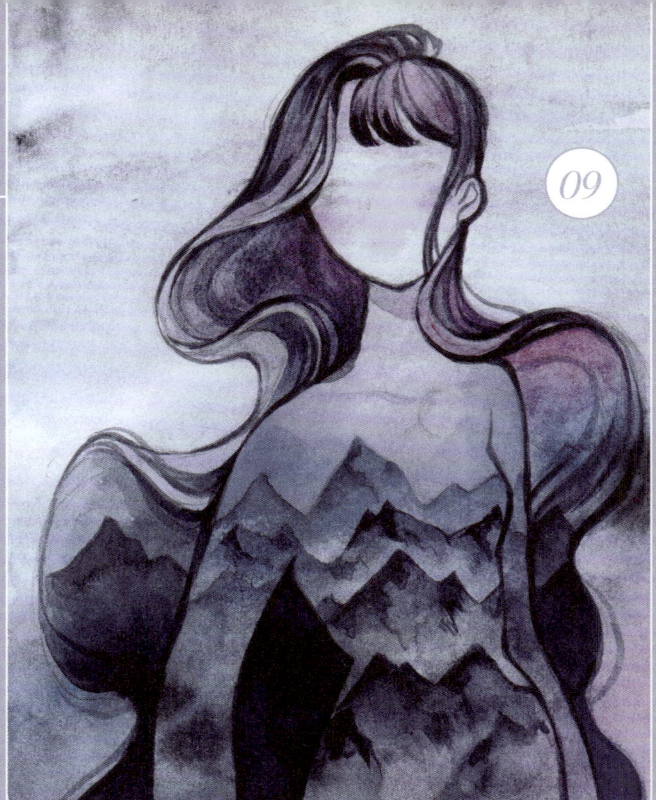

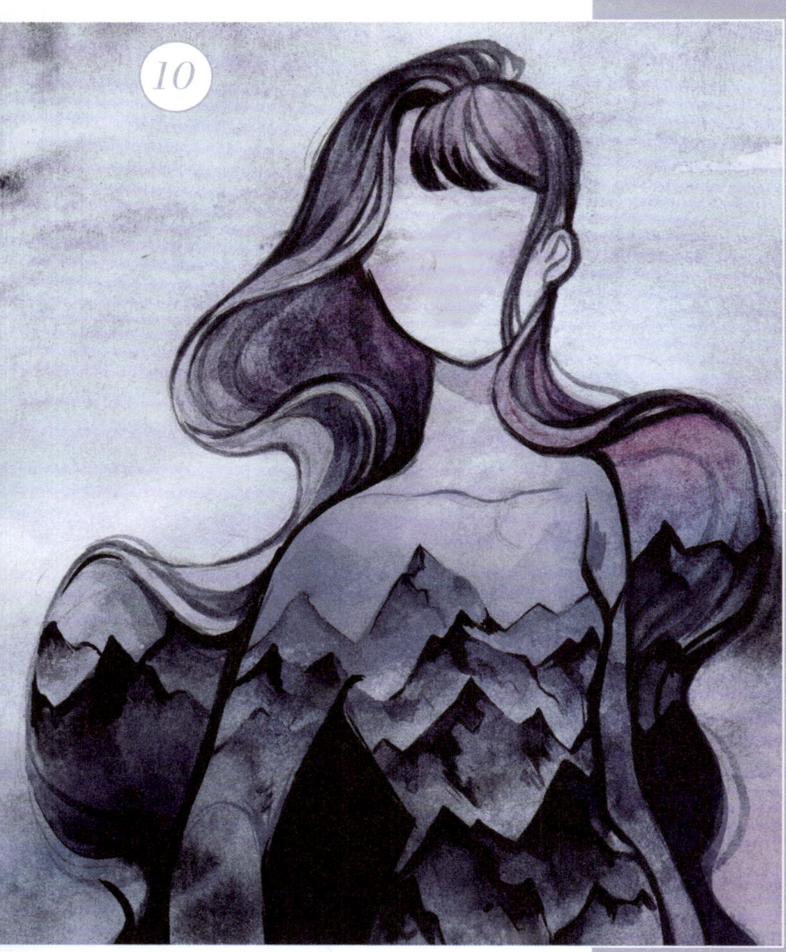

10 Deep blacks

Using black, I thicken and reinforce some of the linework in order to add stronger contrast, and introduce additional details to the mountains to give them greater definition and drama.

11 Soft lights

I then add lighter shades into the image. Since watercolor is a translucent medium that works by staining paper, it can be difficult to paint objects lighter once you've laid down the pigment. And so, it's nice to have the freedom to add light wherever you see fit when working digitally.

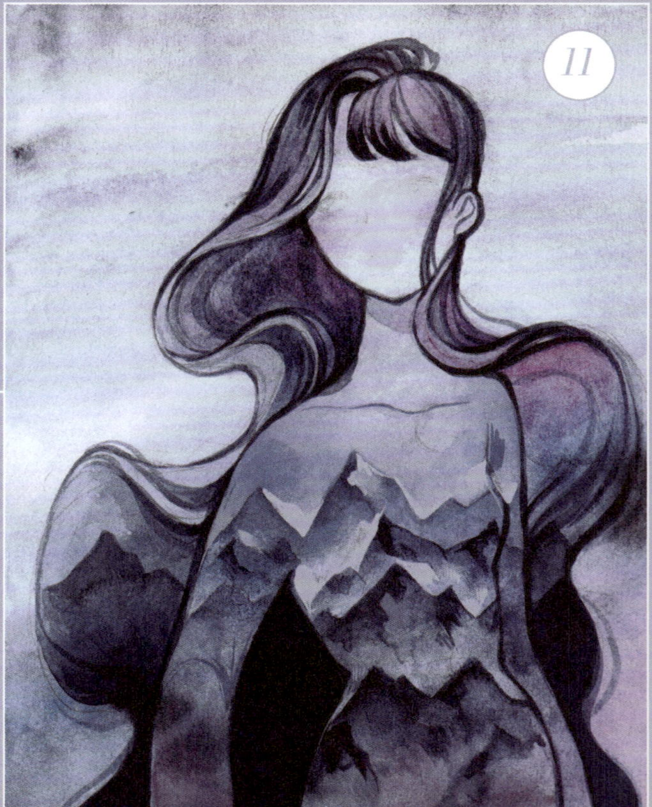

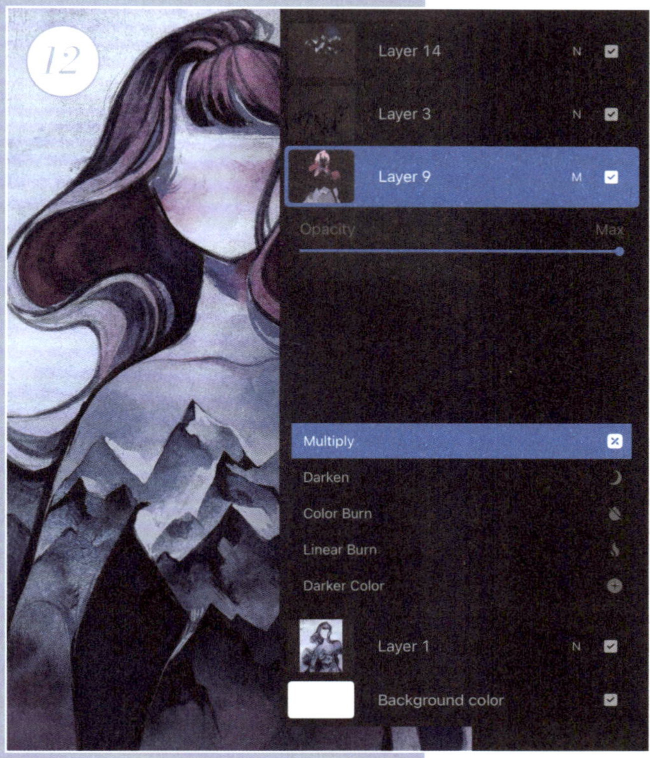

12 Adding a Multiply layer

I want to add more saturated colors to the palette, so I make a new layer and set it to Multiply. This mode makes all white shades disappear, making the colors translucent. It's excellent for layering shadows and maintaining color vibrancy, as the colors blend with the layer underneath rather than laying on top.

13 Painting the face

I decide it's time to paint her face, since you really can't gauge the emotion of the portrait without it! I want the pen strokes to be laid on top and to override the lines I drew on paper, so this layer is not set to Multiply.

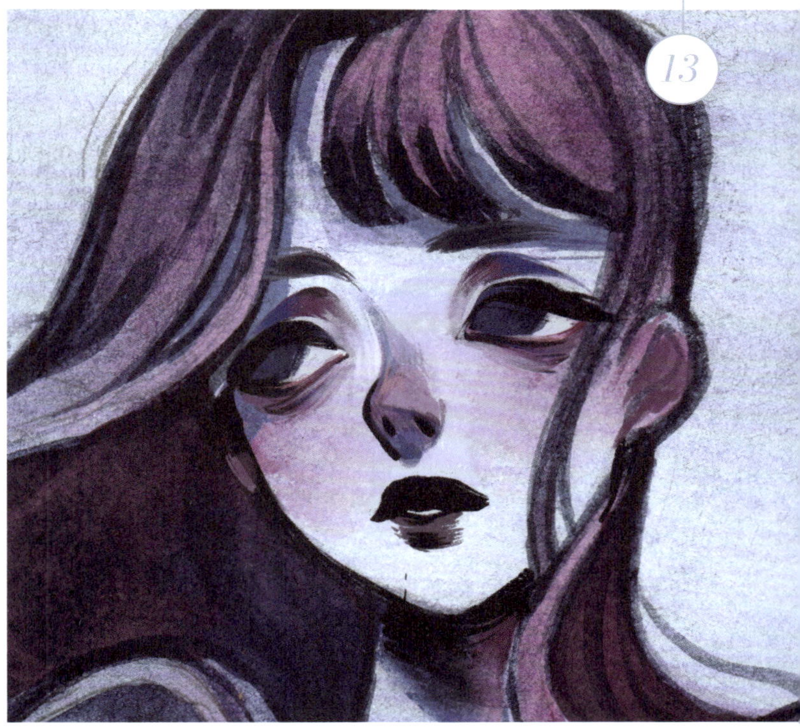

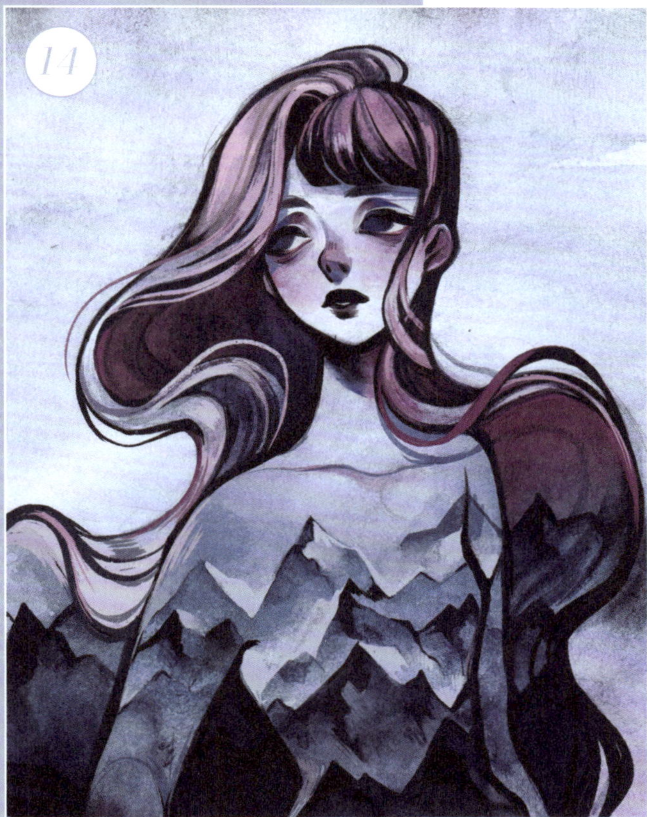

14 Defining the hair

Next, I move on to my favorite part, the hair! I adore drawing long flowing hair and I am often guilty of going overboard with it. I'm unsure whether I gravitate toward long hair in my art because I like how it looks or because I just really, really enjoy drawing its fluid shapes.

15 Imbuing atmosphere

To add graphic elements and some atmosphere, I add a crescent moon and some light specks of stars scattered across her hair. Everything now looks more ethereal, and includes a celestial element, which I always enjoy!

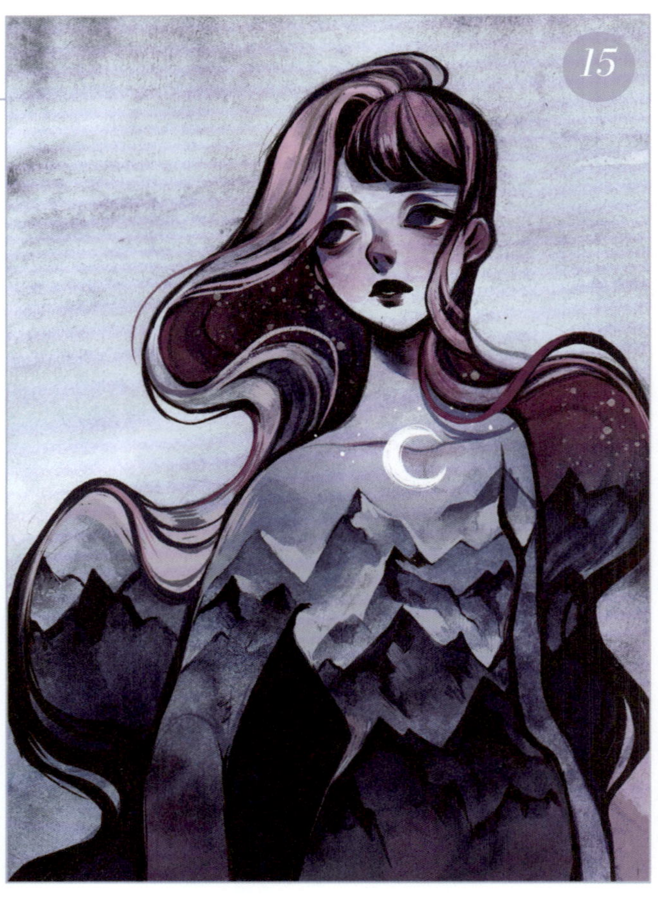

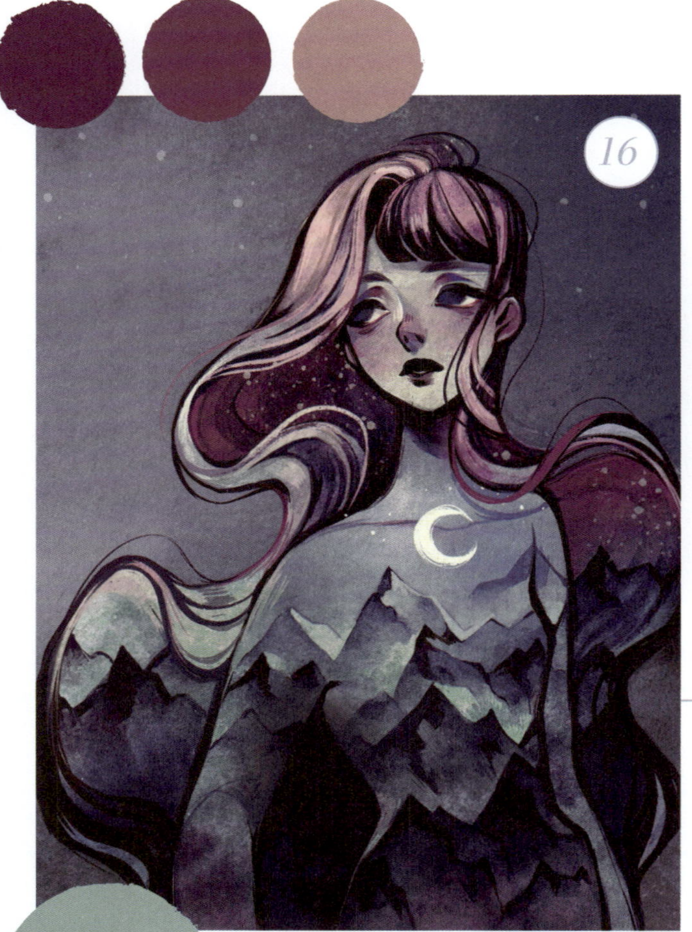

16 Final color adjustments

I adjust some colors and play around with temperature to enhance the nighttime scene. A great quality of working digitally is that almost anything can be adjusted. In order to balance out the cool color palette, I decide to warm up the temperature a little. I also darken the background to complement the scene inside the character.

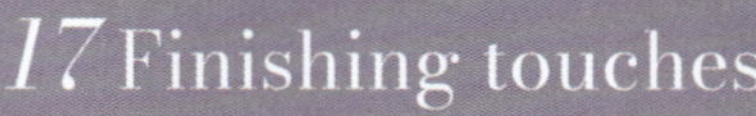

17 Finishing touches

I add a few quick background elements and loose strands to break up the blocky feel of the hair, and the piece is complete! My hybrid watercolor and digital art concoction has lent me the charm of working traditionally, but with the editing magic of digital art. It's a two-for-one deal!

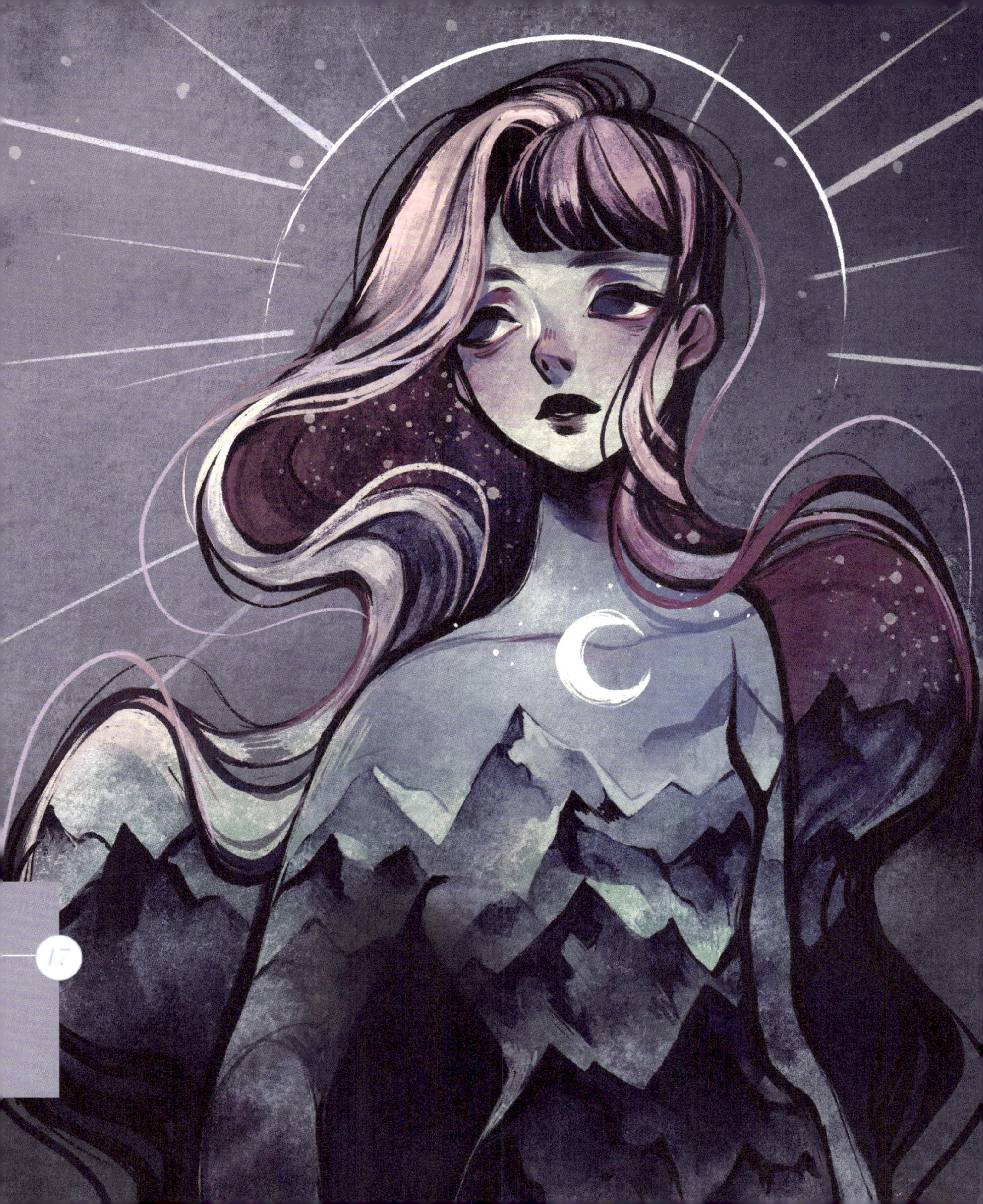

Tutorial: Painting *Apex Predator*

For some reason I have always found it difficult to start a piece digitally. It may be that the endless number of potential corrections prevents me from ever being satisfied, or that I simply prefer the feeling of putting pen to paper. A technique that I love, and one that I use in this tutorial, involves digitally coloring a photograph of a traditional sketch. I struggled to improve my digital drawing skills for years until I discovered this method. I think that the familiarity of the paper sketch makes the digital drawing process feel less daunting somehow, and I really like the way the digital drawing looks when merged with the paper – it's like a faux pencil drawing.

This tutorial demonstrates my process of digitally coloring a sketch made on paper. I used Procreate for this, but the same techniques are applicable to other digital drawing programs such as Photoshop, PaintTool SAI, or GIMP, to name a few. So, if you're trying to become more comfortable drawing digitally but are finding the transition from traditional art challenging, I highly recommend giving this method a go!

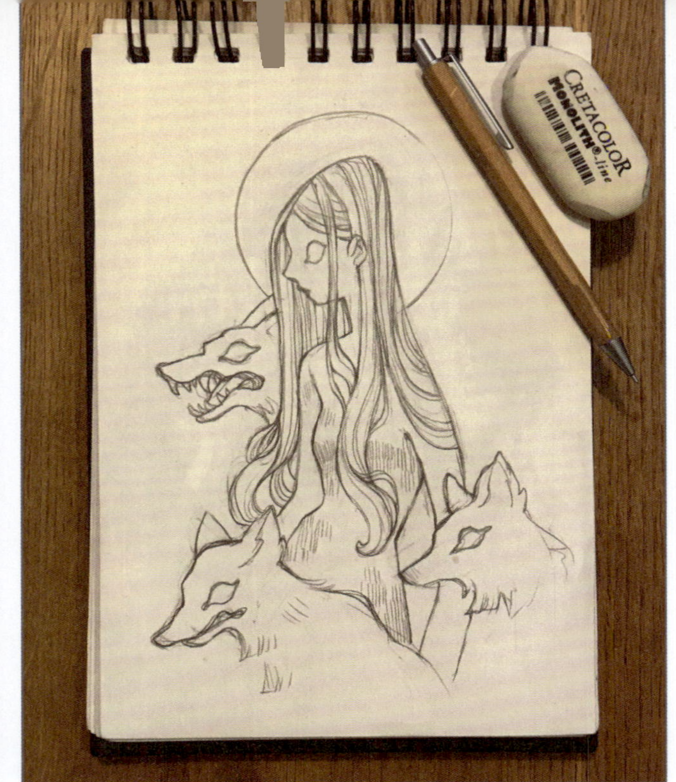

01 Starting with a pencil sketch

I start with an unedited photo of a sketch taken with my iPad Pro. Since I'll be using Procreate (a program specifically made for the iPad), I don't bother scanning the drawing, and am content with a simple photo taken directly with the tablet.

02 Preparing the photo/scan

Next, I open the photograph in Procreate and set the layer to Multiply, making all gradients of white in the image transparent. This means that I can draw freely underneath the sketch without the photo clouding over the brushstrokes.

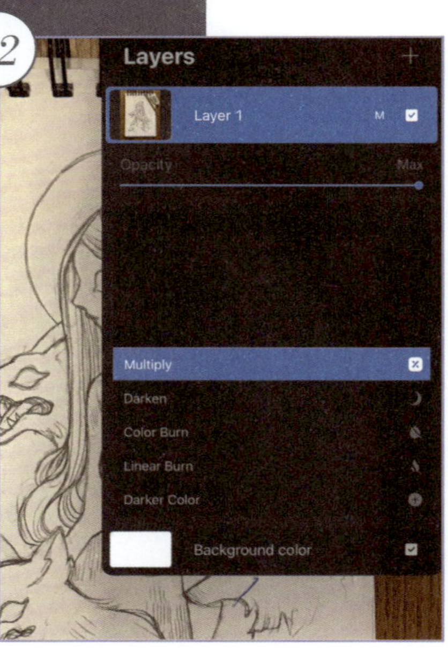

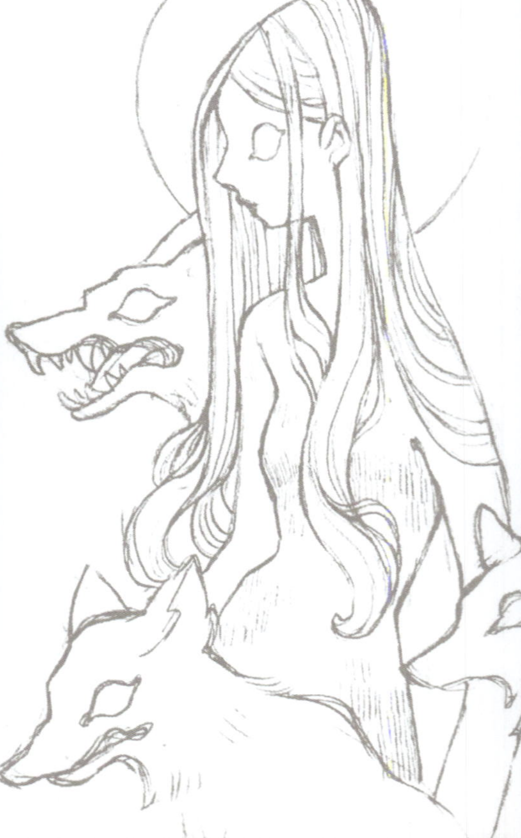

03 Neutralizing the hue

I then edit the photo to minimize all warm shades and increase the contrast. Because I'll be drawing underneath this sketch digitally, I want to neutralize the hue of the paper, as it may affect the colors placed underneath.

03

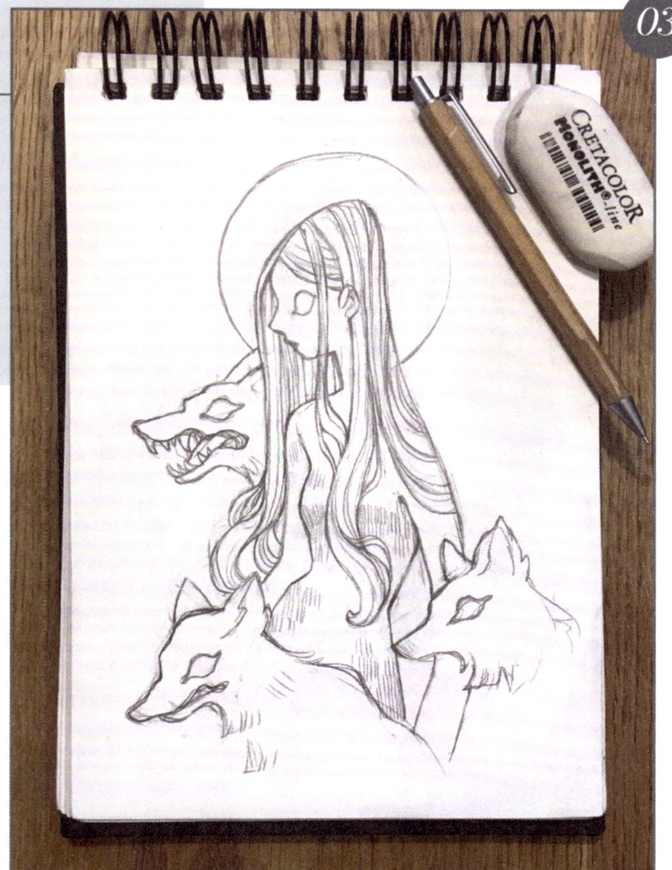

04

04 Blocking in color

Once the color of the image has been effectively corrected, I begin to lay down the base color for the main character. Notice how the pencil drawing on the paper is still visible – pretty nifty!

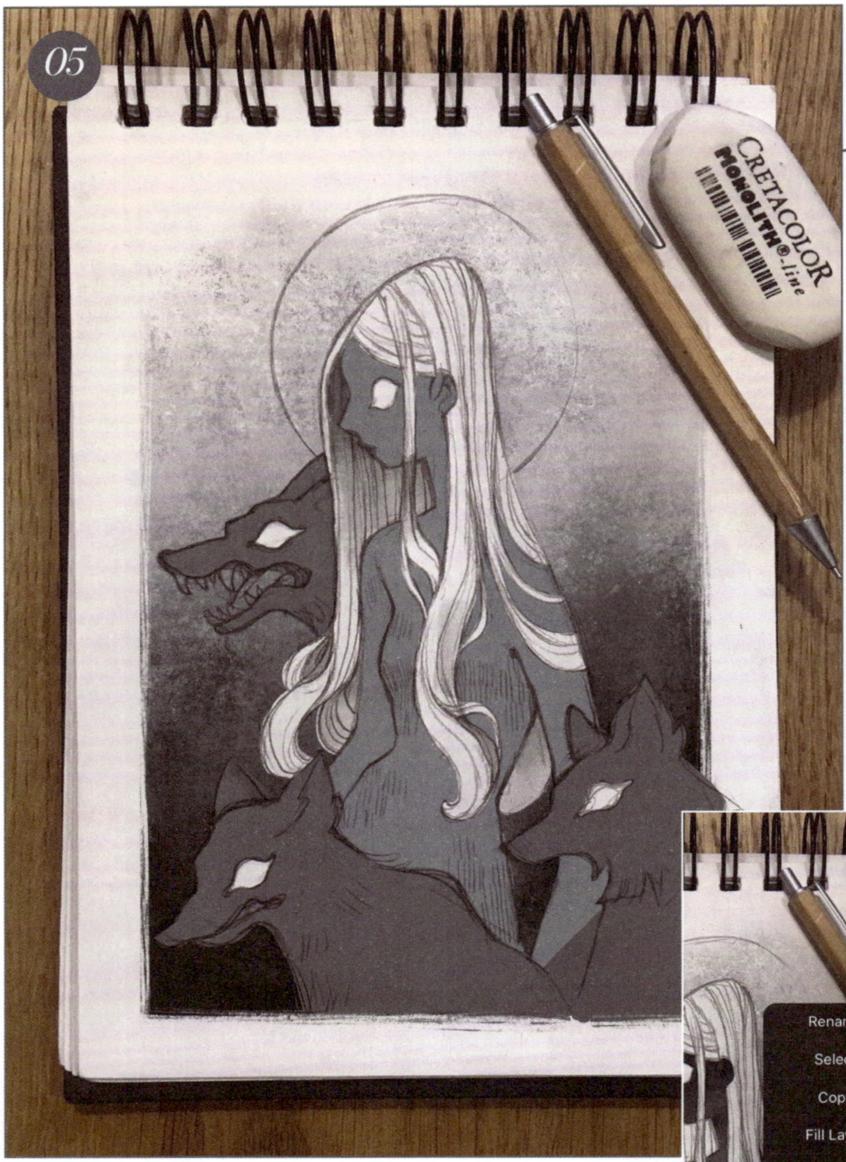

05 Building the palette

I proceed to fill in the colors of the wolves and the background. I paint these new elements on separate layers so that I have the freedom to adjust the colors later. This painting will be monochromatic, so finding the right shades of gray is important.

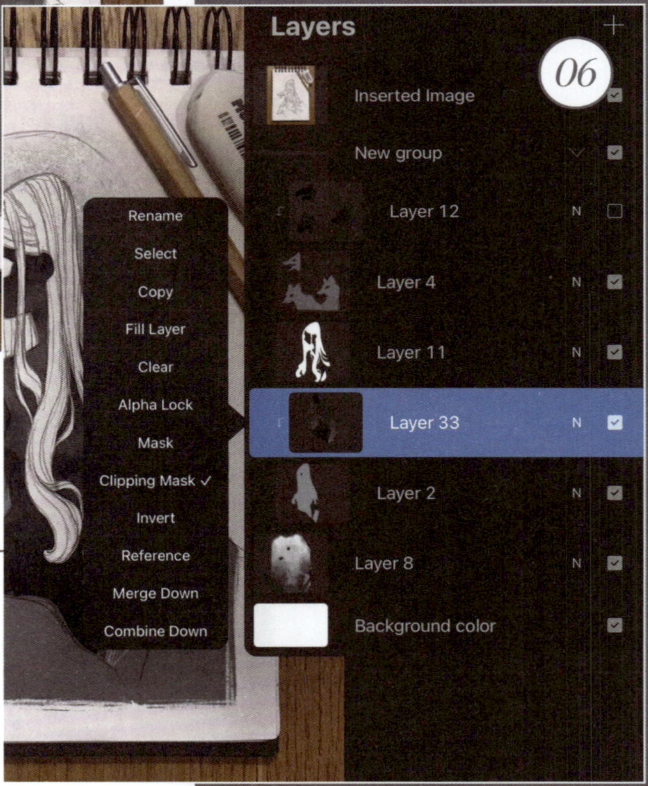

06 Casting a shadow

Next, I add shadow onto the body of the main focal character. To do this, I create an additional layer above the base color layer and set it to Clipping Mask. This limits the surface area of the new layer to whatever has been drawn underneath, so I don't have to worry about staying within the lines. This is a really convenient tool to use when drawing shadows!

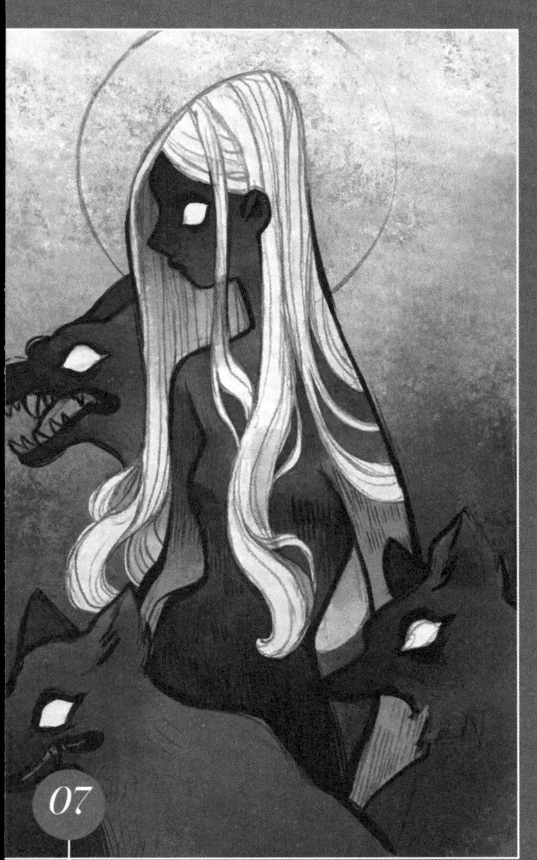

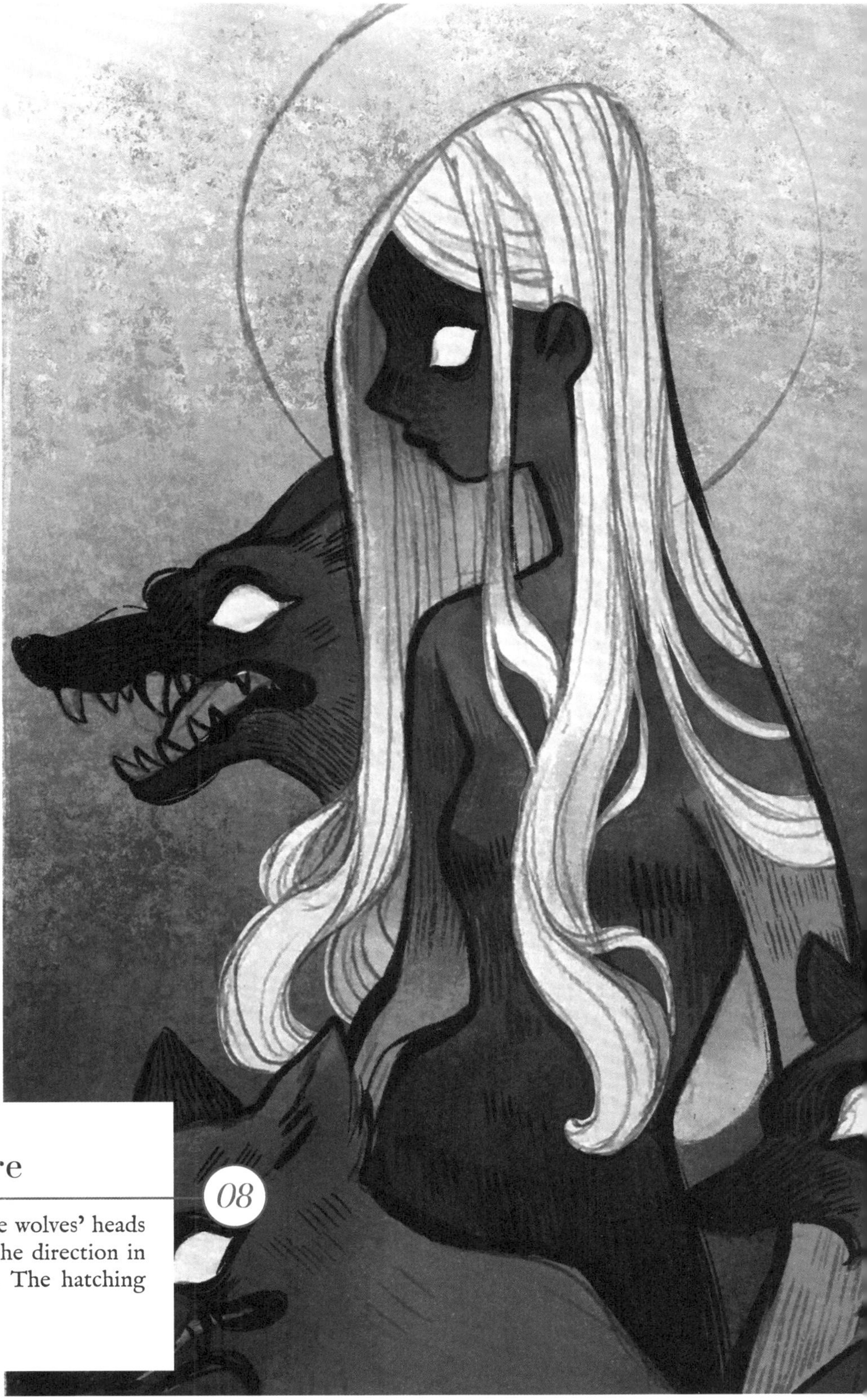

07 Drawing outlines

As the lines of the sketch are quite thin, I decide to reinforce them with additional linework. If your initial drawing already has dark line art, this step might not be necessary. Here, the bold linework strengthens my image.

08 Creating some texture

Next, I paint some light hatching on the wolves' heads for texture, making sure it aligns with the direction in which their fur would naturally follow. The hatching then creates the illusion of fur.

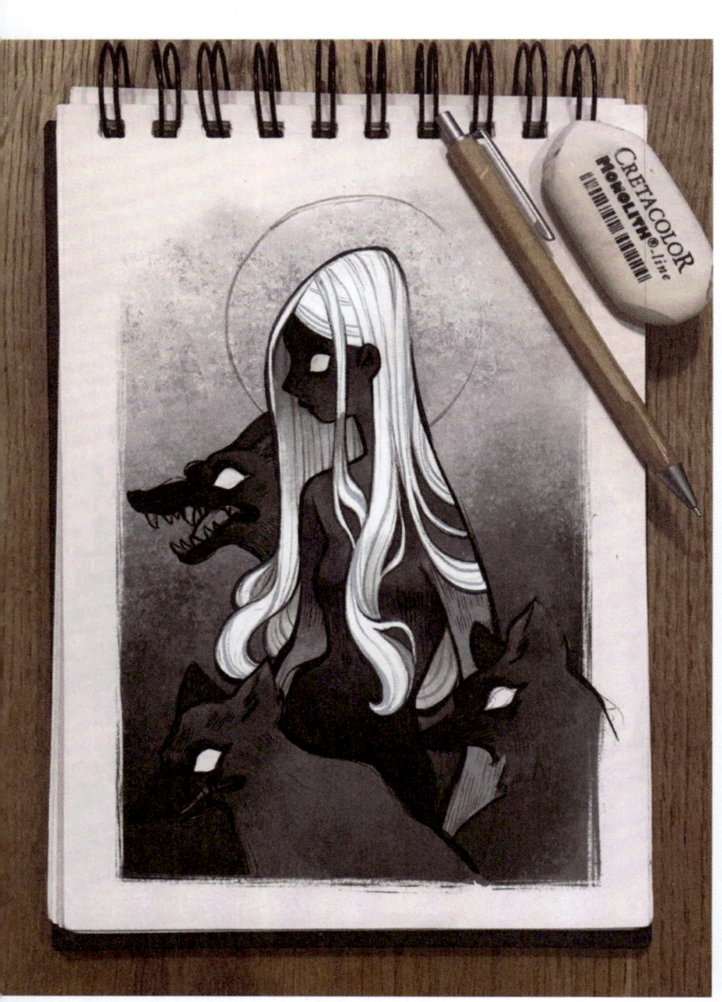

09 Monochromatic contrasts

Because I want the hair to be bright white and in contrast with the darkness of the rest of the piece, when detailing the hair, I opt for a light gray color rather than black. Since I'm limiting myself to a grayscale palette in this illustration, it's extra vital that the different aspects of the piece are in contrast to one another.

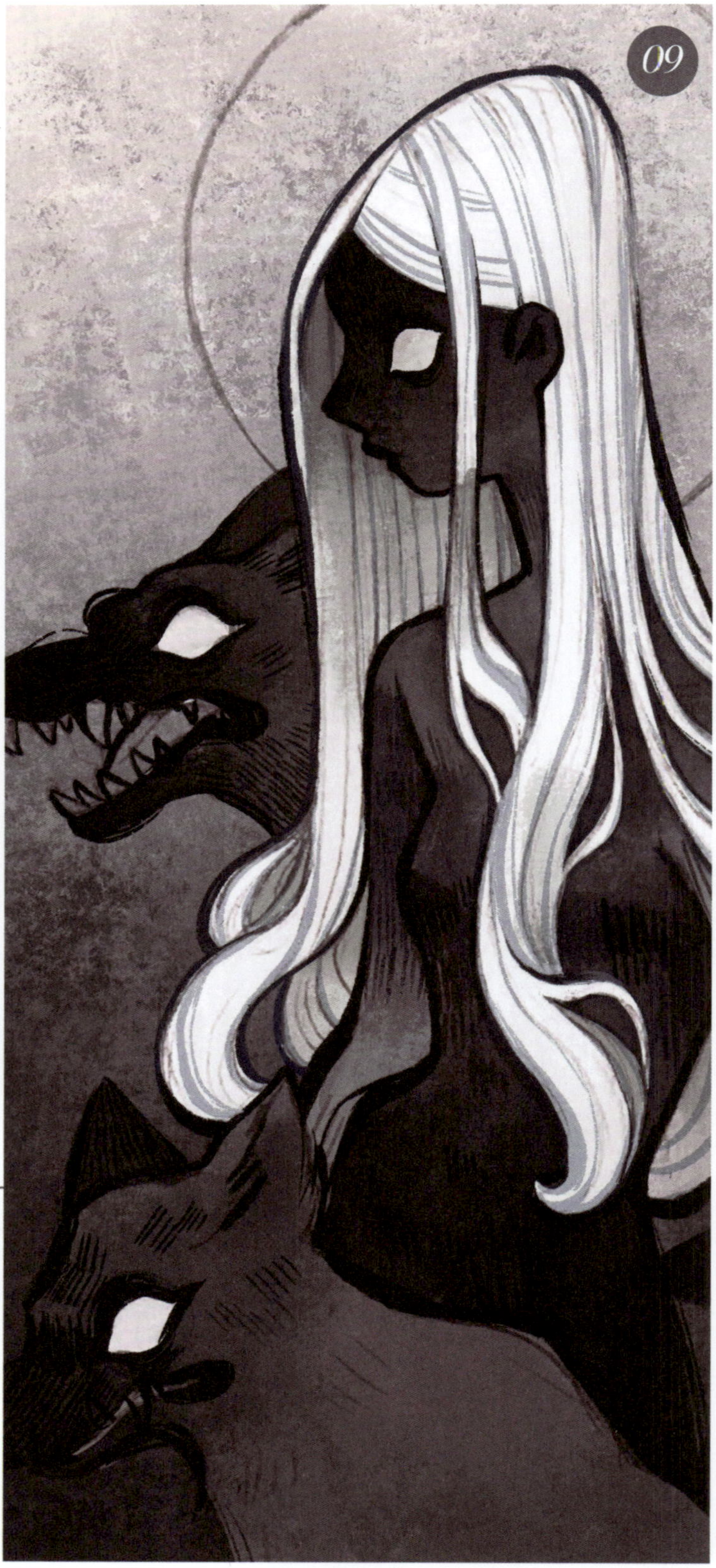

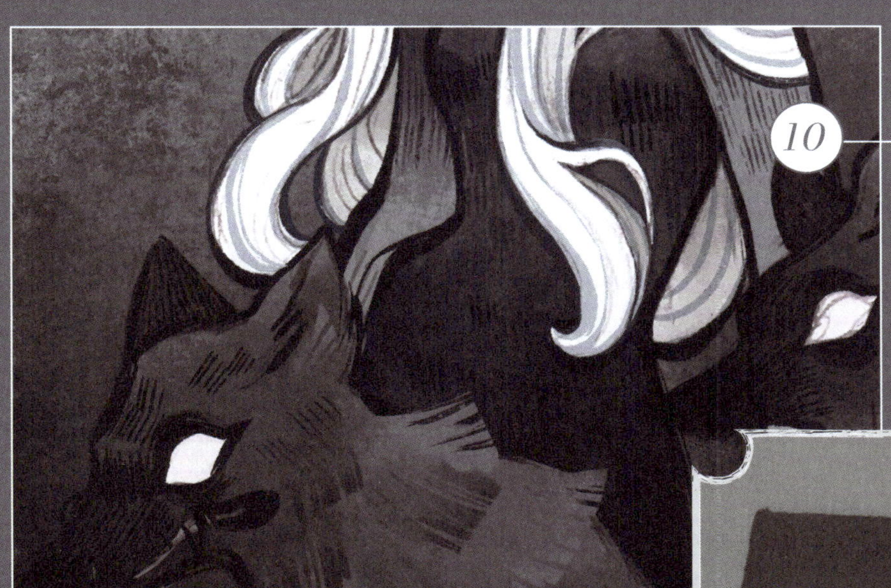

10 Blocks of fur

Next, I paint the fur on the bodies of the wolves. The most common way to paint fur is to draw multiple thin strokes in the direction of the hair, but that's too time-consuming for me! I instead opt to layer fringe-like blocks of hair, which are angular and graphic.

Quick fur technique

To create chunks of fur, I first draw square blocks that I blend into the base color using the Blend tool. I then use the eraser to draw lines where I want the hair strands to separate.

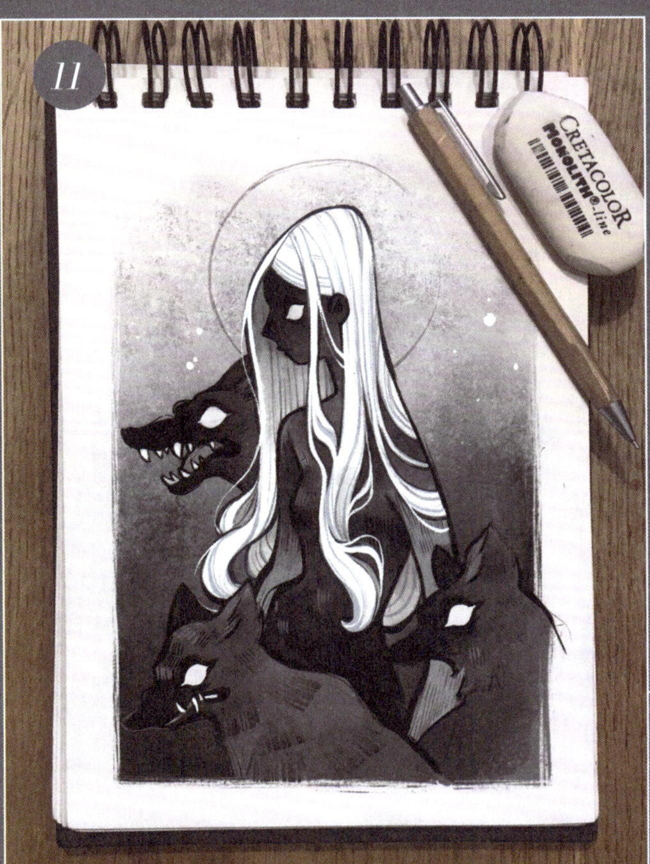

11 Applying highlights

Now I move on to my favorite part, adding highlights! I place a new layer over the initial sketch because I want the colors to sit on top. I then add white strands of hair, fill in the color of the wolves' teeth, and reshape their eyes. As the stark white I'm using is brighter than that of the paper, it stands out in a subtle glowing way.

12 Centering the image

I paint a simple black circle in the background to increase contrast and center the focal point of the drawing. The keyword for this piece is "contrast."

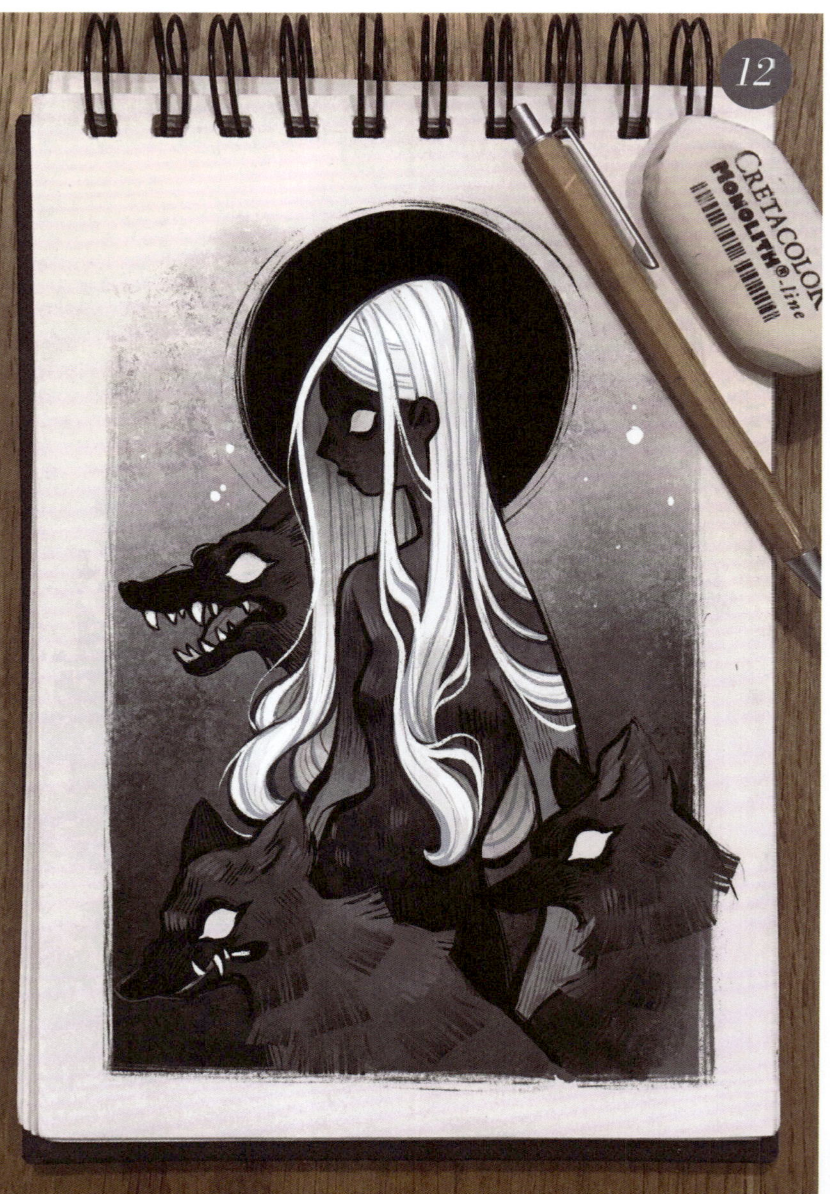

13 Narrowing the gaze

I'm dissatisfied with how her eye looks, so I reshape it into a narrower form. I think she looks more intimidating now and more fit to be the alpha of a wolf pack!

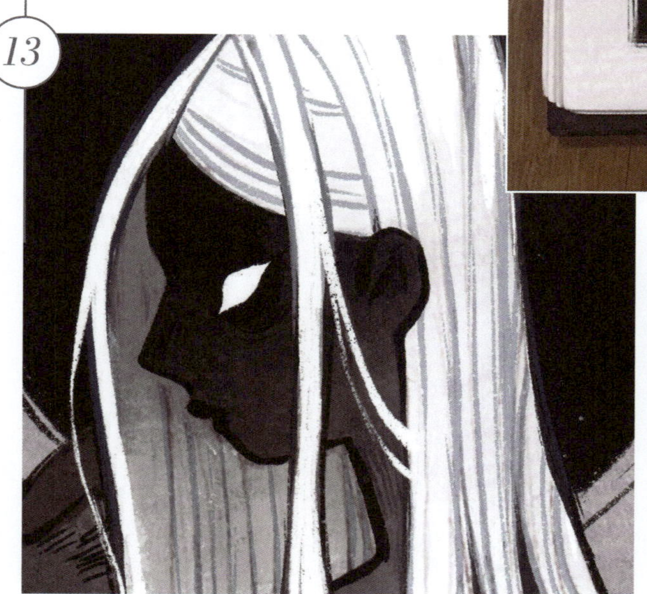

14 Adding final flourishes

I decide to introduce some foliage as an additional background element, because the black circle alone felt a little plain. It's rare for me to have a clear image of what I want to paint from the start, and I often add or subtract elements along the way. The addition of foliage brings a hint of scenery, and depth, to the artwork.

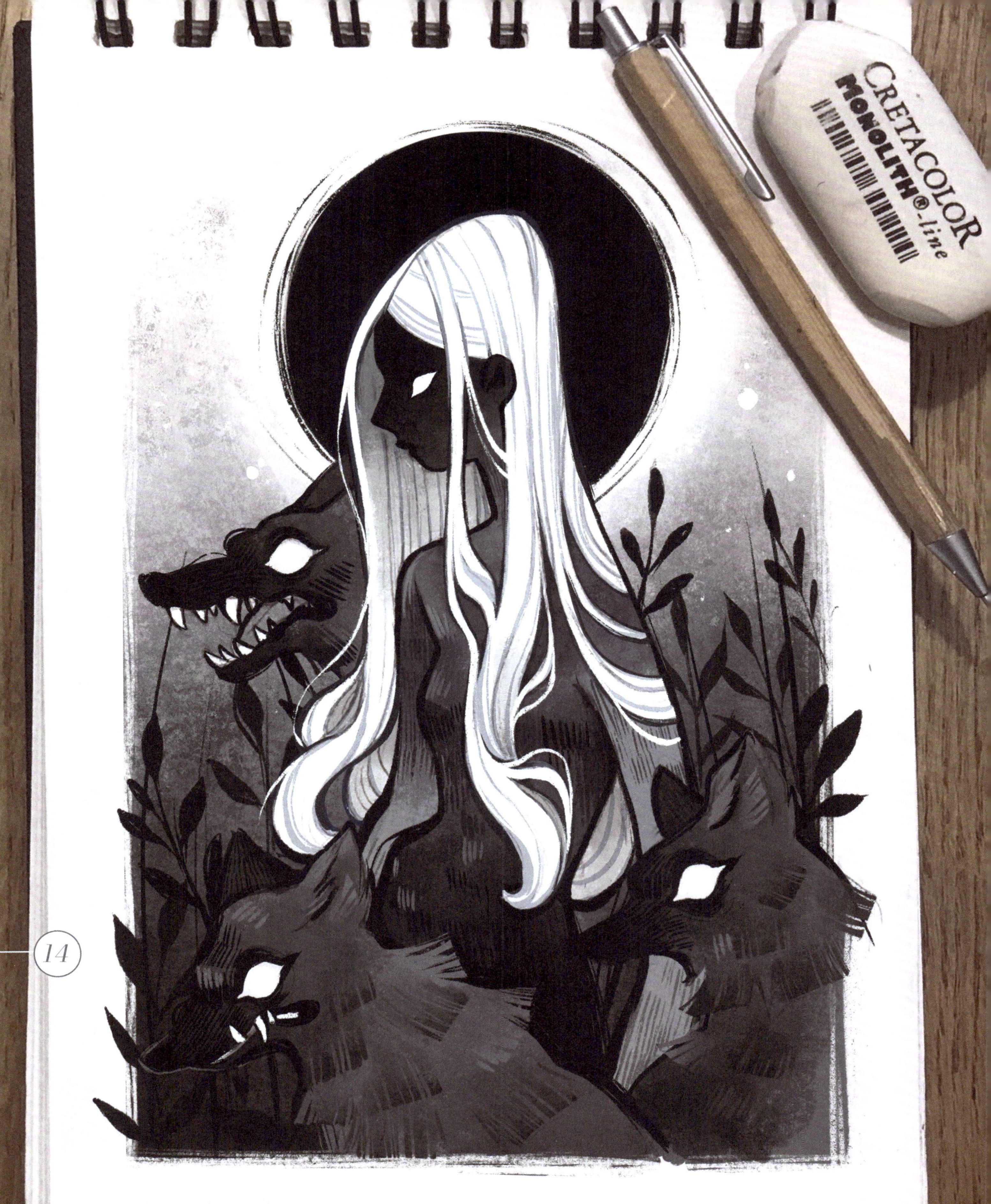
CRETACOLOR
MONOLITH®-line

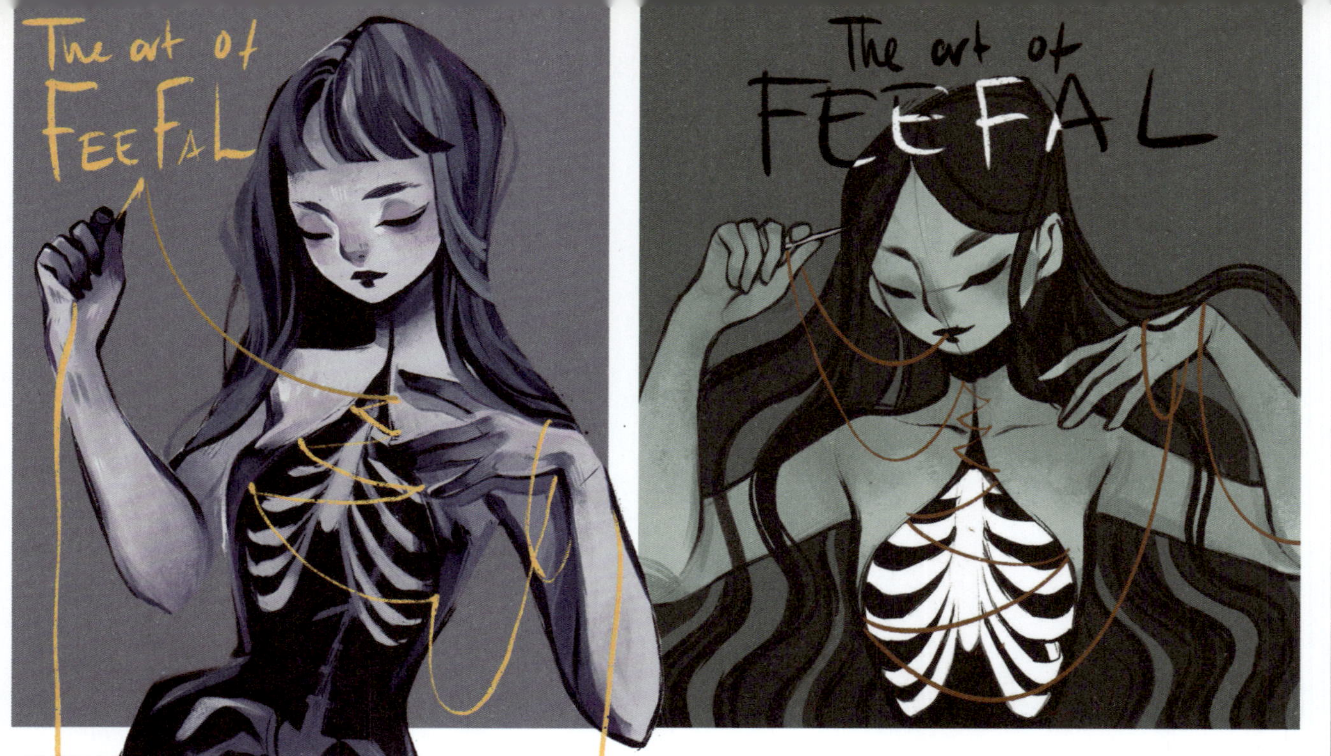

The first and second drafts of the cover design.

Making the cover

Upon starting work on this book, I immediately became struck by panic when I realized I would have to come up with a great image for the book's cover. I wanted it to be the culmination of all that I've learned over the years, and to be the ultimate testament to everything I am as an artist. As it would be the first and most important featured piece of art in this book, I felt that it just had to be mind-bogglingly amazing.

Now, obviously that's way too much pressure to put on one single painting! Not to mention that my drawings have a tendency to turn out really badly when I overwork and overanalyze every detail. After a ton of overthinking and way too much caffeine, I decided to revisit a concept I had drawn back in 2017 that I still really liked. The piece featured a woman stitching herself back together with thread while wearing a gentle expression, and my goal was to convey the message of self-love and the power to rebuild yourself.

I wanted the thread to be in gold because I was inspired by the art of Kintsugi, which is a Japanese art form of piecing together broken pottery pieces with gold. It's built on the idea that in embracing flaws and imperfections, you can create an even stronger, more beautiful piece of art.

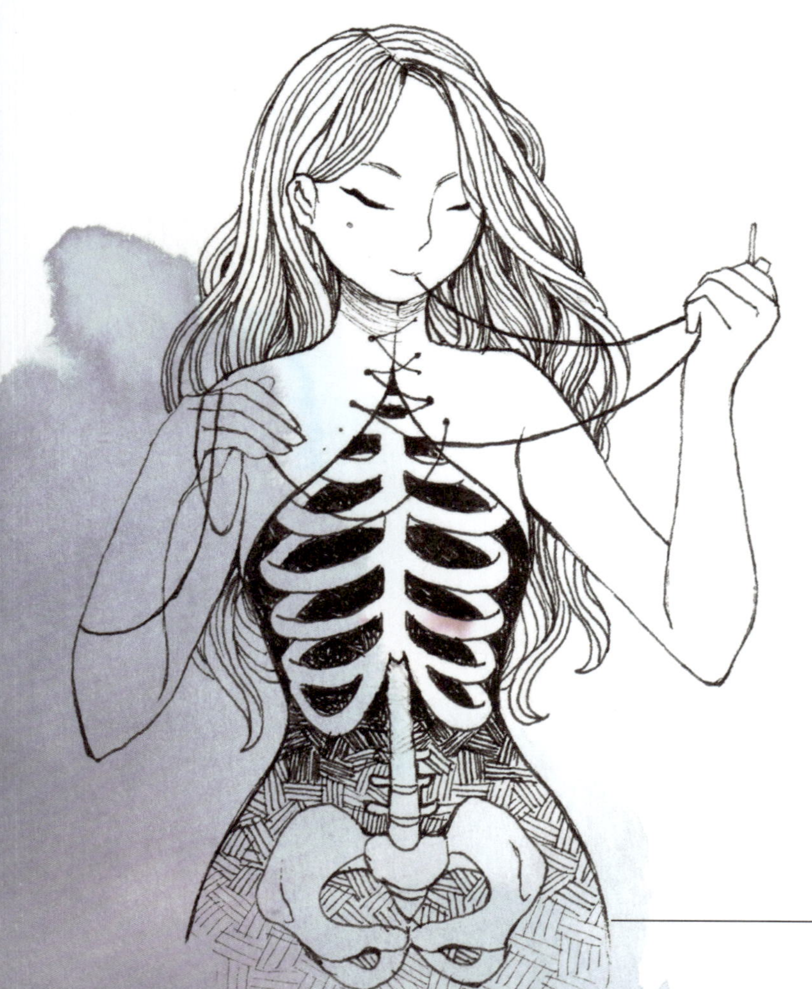

The original drawing from 2017 that inspired the cover art.

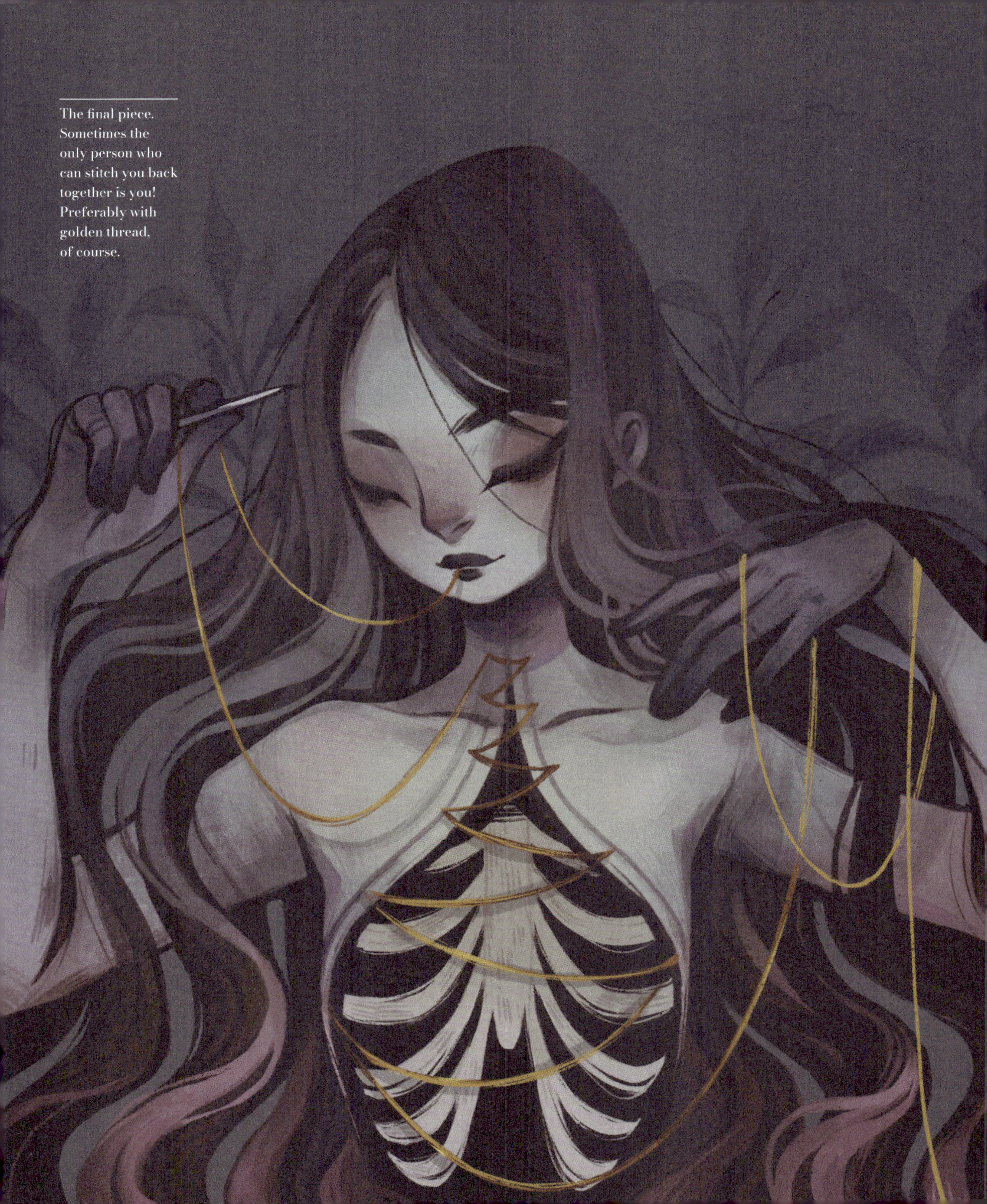

The final piece. Sometimes the only person who can stitch you back together is you! Preferably with golden thread, of course.

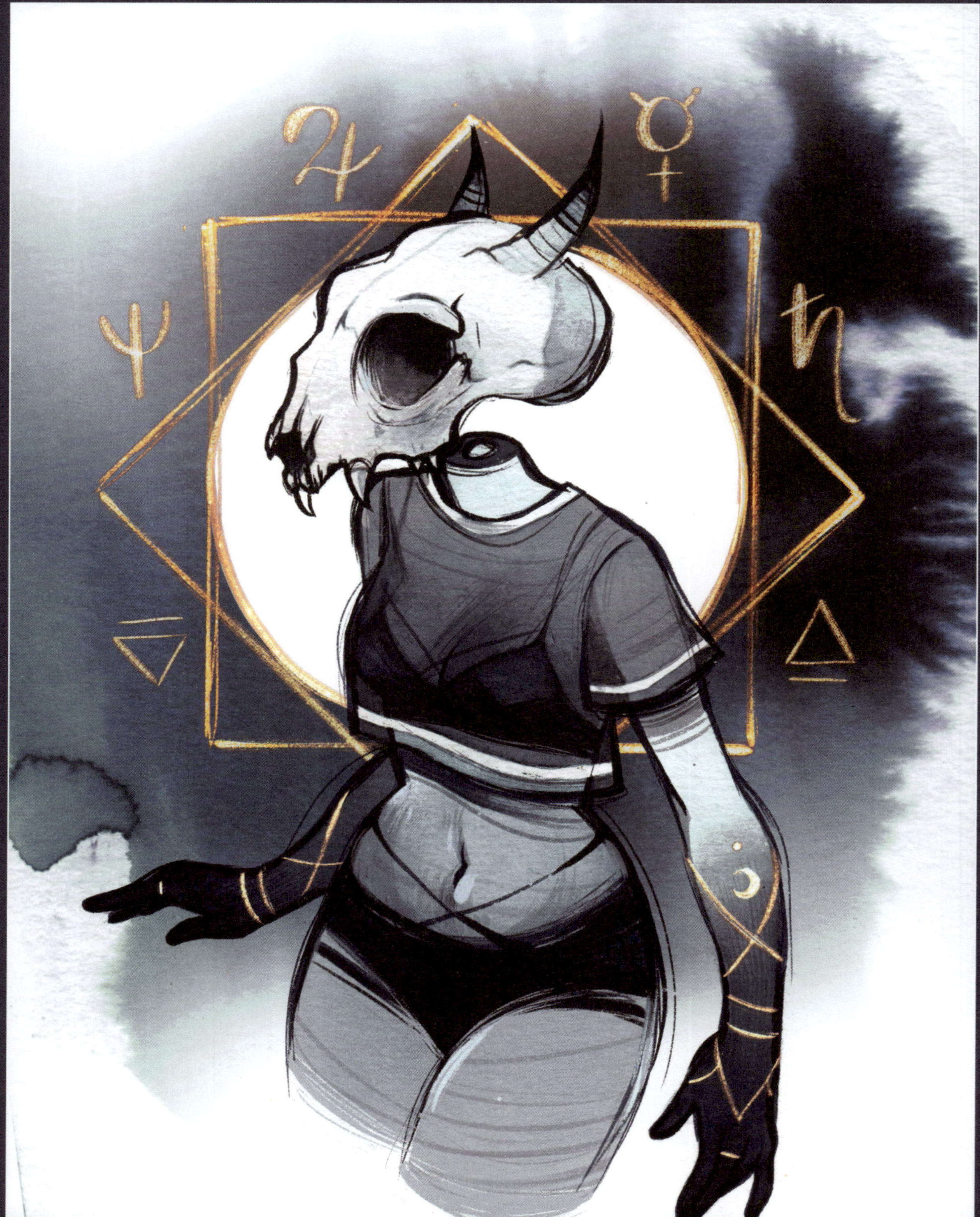

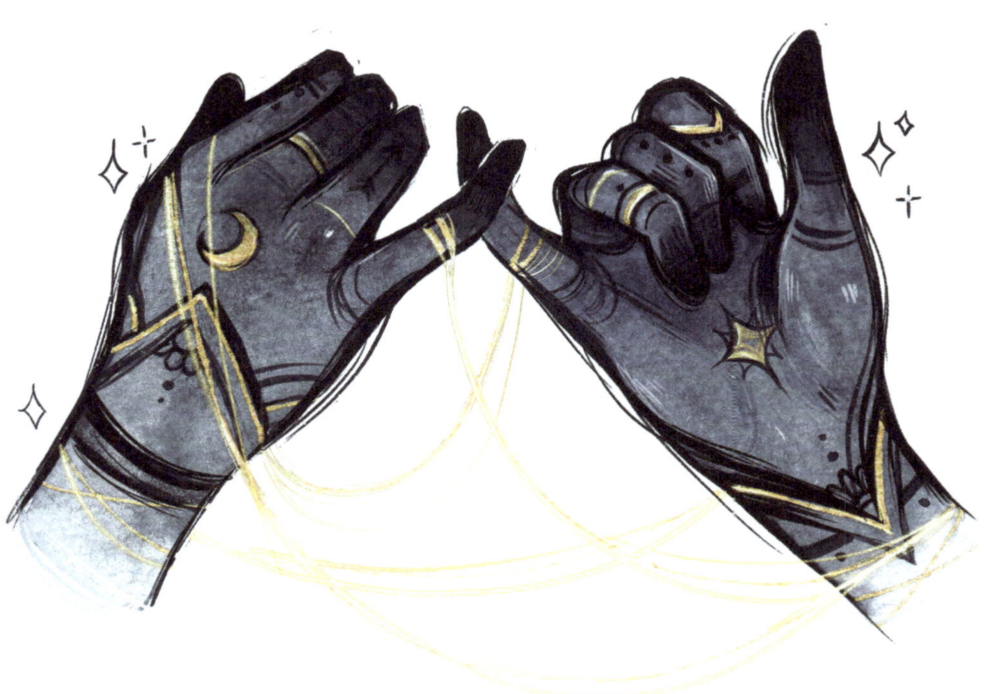

Thank you

A huge and heartfelt thank you to all of you who have supported my artwork throughout my journey and made all of this possible. I'm continually motivated to further explore new and fun ideas and advance my craft because I get to share it with such a loving audience. I don't think I can accurately express in words how much your encouragement means to me. I wish I could hold a party and make a giant pizza for us all to share, but since air travel is so expensive, I guess I'll have to settle with expressing my gratitude via this paragraph.

An enormous thank you to the team at 3dtotal who made all of this happen; creating an art book has been a lifelong dream of mine and it's wild to think that it's now a reality! Thank you, Simon, for reaching out to me and believing in my work enough to want to make a book out of it, to Fiona for making everything look so lovely and refining all the JPEGs I sent, and to my editor Sophie for correcting all of my typos and guiding me through this crazy ride!

Thank you to my mom, family, and friends – ya'll know I love you. A big thank you to my amazing partner Isac for always offering your support, for always being willing to debate art with me, and for pushing me into this career path! There would be no Feefal without you. With that said, I hope we don't break up so I won't have to regret dedicating such a big portion of the thank you speech to you.

Linnea Akemi Kikuchi

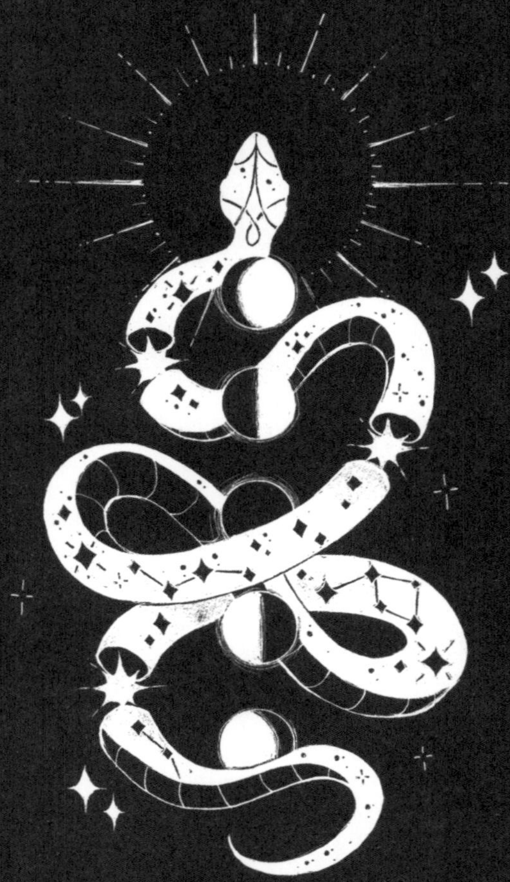

About 3dtotal Publishing

3dtotal Publishing is a trailblazing, creative publisher specializing in inspirational and educational resources for artists.

Our titles feature top industry professionals from around the globe who share their experience in skillfully written step-by-step tutorials and fascinating, detailed guides. Illustrated throughout with stunning artwork, these best-selling publications offer creative insight, expert advice, and essential motivation. Fans of digital art will enjoy our comprehensive volumes covering Adobe Photoshop, Procreate, and Blender, as well as our superb titles based around character design, including *Fundamentals of Character Design* and *Creating Characters for the Entertainment Industry*. The dedicated, high-quality blend of instruction and inspiration also extends to traditional art. Titles covering a range of techniques, genres, and abilities allow your creativity to flourish while building essential skills.

Well-established within the industry, we now offer over 100 titles and counting, many of which have been translated into multiple languages around the world. With something for every artist, we are proud to say that our books offer the 3dtotal package:

LEARN | CREATE | SHARE

Visit us at 3dtotalpublishing.com

3dtotal Publishing is part of 3dtotal.com, a leading website for CG artists founded by Tom Greenway in 1999.